The Rise and Fall of
Jim Crow

"SICH A GETTING UP STAIRS"

A GENOOINE YANKEE AND PARTIKLAR HANDSOME

SONG

Sung by

Mʳ. T. D. RICE.

Ent. Sta. Hall   Price 1-6

London, Jefferys & Cº. 31. Frith Street Soho.

Where may be had the BEST editions

OF JIM CROW, AND "COAL BLACK ROSE."

AND ALSO

THE NEW NIGGER QUADRILLES. 2-6.

The Rise and Fall of Jim Crow

Richard Wormser

St. Martin's Press ❧ New York

Book design by James Sinclair

ISBN 0-312-31324-1

First Edition: February 2003

10   9   8   7   6   5   4   3   2   1

To Annie

Pour le bel aujourd'hui

CONTENTS

ACKNOWLEDGMENTS

I would like to thank Dr. Pat Sullivan for reading and critiquing the manuscript; my editor, Diane Reverand, for her support and belief in the project; my agents, Barbara Lowenstein and Madeleine Morel; my colleagues Bill Jersey and Sam Pollard; Ed Breslin for his editing skills; and WNET/Thirteen for helping make the series possible. I am also grateful to all the scholars without whose help the film series upon which this book is based would not have been possible. And especially those men and women I was privileged to interview and who shared with me their stories of tragedy and triumph in the age of Jim Crow.

INTRODUCTION

First on de heel tap, den on the toe
Every time I wheel about I jump Jim Crow
Wheel about, and turn about en do j's so.
And every time I wheel about, I jump Jim Crow.

In 1828, Jim Crow was born. He began his strange career as a minstrel caricature of a black man created by a white man, Thomas "Daddy" Rice, to amuse white audiences. By the 1880s, Jim Crow had become synonymous with a complex system of racial laws and customs in the South that ensured white social, legal, and political domination of blacks. Blacks were segregated, deprived of their right to vote, and subjected to verbal abuse, discrimination, and violence without redress in the courts or support by the white community.

It was in the North that the first Jim Crow laws were passed. Blacks in the North were prohibited from voting in all but five New England states. Schools and public accommodations were segregated. Illinois and Oregon barred blacks from entering the state. Blacks in every Northern city were restricted to ghettoes in the most unsanitary and run-down areas and forced to take menial jobs that white men rejected. White supremacy was as much a part of the Democratic Party in the North as it was in the South.

Northern racial barriers slowly fell after the Civil War. In 1863, California permitted blacks to testify in criminal cases for the first time. Illinois repealed its laws barring blacks from entering, serving on juries, or testifying in court. New York City, San Francisco, Cleveland, and Cincinnati all desegregated their streetcars during the war. Philadelphia followed two years after the war ended. As Northern states repealed some of the more discriminatory legislation against Jim Crow, socially, if not legally, Jim Crow remained in effect. With a few exceptions, blacks for the most part were not allowed to eat in the same restaurants, sleep in the same hotels, or swim at the same beaches as whites. Schools were usually segregated, as were many public events. Most Northern whites shared with Southern whites the belief in the innate superiority of the white "race" over the black.

As punitive and prejudicial as Jim Crow laws were in the North, they never reached the intensity of oppression and degree of violence and sadism that they did in the South. A black person could not swim in the same pool, sit in the same public park, bowl, play pool or, in some states, checkers, drink from the same water fountain or use the same bathroom, marry, be treated in the same hospital, use the same schoolbooks, play baseball with, ride in the same taxicab, sit in the same section of a bus or train, be admitted to any private or public institution, teach in the same school, read in the same library, attend the same theater, or sit in the same area with a white person. Blacks had to address white people as Mr., Mrs., or "Mizz," "Boss," or "Captain" while they, in turn, were called by their first name, or by terms used to indicate social inferiority—"boy," "aunty," or "uncle." Black people, if allowed in a store patronized by whites, had to wait until all white customers were served first. If they attended a movie, they had to sit in the balcony; if they went to a circus, they had to buy tickets at a separate window and sit in a separate section. They had to give way to whites on a sidewalk, remove their hats as a sign of respect when encountering whites, and enter a white person's house by the back door. Whites, on the other hand, could enter a black person's house without knocking, sit without being asked, keep their hats on, and address people in a disrespectful manner. Whites and blacks never ate together, never went to school together, shook hands, or played sports together (except as children). And while the degree of these restrictions often varied from state to state and county to county, white supremacy was the law of the South, and the slightest transgression could be punished by death.

White violence and oppression, however, were only one part of the story of the era of Jim Crow. The other dimension was the ongoing struggle of African Americans for freedom. This struggle took many forms: direct confrontation, subversion, revolt, institution building, and

This racist postcard, intended to show blacks in a comic stereotypical manner, actually reveals the extent to which segregation had spread over the South by the early twentieth century.

accommodation. This story was a missing piece of history as far as most Americans were concerned, motivating this book and the film series on which it was based.

* * *

The Rise and Fall of Jim Crow was born out of a four-hour television series with the same name for PBS on the African-American struggle for freedom during the era of Jim Crow. We chose to focus on the South, even though racism was endemic in the North, because it was in the South that racism and white supremacy manifested their most virulent form. The South institutionalized segregation and disfranchisement by law, custom, and violence. From the late 1880s until 1930, it was rare for a white person to speak out publicly against segregation and white supremacy, especially in the South. The South's obsession with racial subordination reinforced the same tendencies that existed throughout the nation. By the end of the nineteenth century, white supremacy, once considered a Southern peculiarity, had become a national ideology.

The series took us seven years to plan, research, write, shoot, and edit, two years longer than it took Ken Burns to make his ten-hour documentary on the Civil War. Without our team of some twenty scholars who guided and corrected us along the way, the films would never have been made. One of the difficulties we encountered was finding images and documents to tell our story in the period between 1880 and World War I. There is not an abundance of material on African-American life in this period because Southern whites, who controlled the image-making process, had little interest in documenting or preserving records of black life prior to the 1930s. The most notable exception to this was lynching. White photographers often capitalized on the atrocity by selling images for postcards or souvenirs of the event.

Our research team, however, was able to uncover a sufficient number of photographs buried in dozens of university and state archives. We also found several outstanding collections of pictures by Southern photographers, such as Henry C. Norman of Natchez, Mississippi. We have selected some of these compelling images for this book, ones that convey the dignity, the struggle, and the character of the people whose lives the programs presented.

One of our major disappointments was the discovery that few, if any, issues survived of the many black newspapers published in the South. Relatively few letters and diaries also survived. There was an abundance of the writings of well-known leaders, who published many of their thoughts and experiences. *The Crisis* magazine, published by the NAACP and edited by W.E.B. Du Bois between 1910 and 1934, was an invaluable source. And there were many letters written by Southern blacks to Northern black newspapers such as the *Chicago Defender, New York Age,* and *Washington Bee.*

Images and documents themselves alone do not tell a story. They lie on the surface of history like floating debris from a shipwreck after the vessel itself has long gone down underneath the waves. Scholars had salvaged much of the material before it reached the "trash bin of history," in order to reconstruct a coherent picture of the past. But for filmmakers, who must weave a story out of the remnants, our primary task was to find the appropriate storytellers.

We divided the series into four parts, each part covering a specific time period: 1865–1895,

1896–1917, 1918–1941, and 1941–1945. Since the last film in the series covered a relatively recent time period, we were able to locate a number of people who either made history or witnessed it. This was the first time that many of them told their story, and it was a great privilege for us to be granted access to their lives. Among those with whom we spoke were men and women from Farmville, Virginia, who as teenagers organized a student strike in 1951. The strike became a lawsuit and one of the five cases that the United States Supreme Court reviewed when it ruled that segregation in education was unconstitutional (*Brown* v. *Board of Education*).

We interviewed civil rights leaders Charles Evers and Reverend Hosea Williams, both of whom had served overseas in World War II and returned to the United States determined to challenge Jim Crow. We tracked down, with a great deal of difficulty, Clinton Adams, a white sharecropper's son, who as a ten-year-old child had inadvertently witnessed a vicious murder of two black men and two pregnant women, and Lamar Howard, who as a teenager was severely beaten because he had seen some of the men who committed the murder gathering near the icehouse where he worked. Then there was Gordon Parks of Georgia, a fanatical member of the Ku Klux Klan, who at the age of nine witnessed his first lynching and chillingly told us the horrifying tale of the murder and of his own brutal life as a child.

We interviewed a number of soldiers who had served in a Jim Crow army during World War II, and had suffered a great deal of racial discrimination. Yet what they remembered was the pride they felt at what they had accomplished. They held no bitterness against those who discriminated against them.

For us, recording the personal testimonies was the most rewarding and fulfilling experience of the project. All of us stood in awe of these men and women who had acted with such courage, took such risks, and yet did not see themselves as particularly heroic. Without their struggles, and the risks taken by the men and women in our film, we might still have legalized segregation in the South today.

As far as presenting the earlier years of Jim Crow, our task was to incorporate the written testimonies of those who did leave behind letters, diaries, and other records. We wanted people to speak with their own voices in the film. Some of these records were fragments; others were rich and full texts. We were fortunate to have the oral history of the life of Ned Cobb, an Alabama sharecropper and tenant farmer who was born when the era of Jim Crow began and died as the civil rights movement ended. His moving life story had been recorded by Ted and Dale Rosengarten, then graduate students at Harvard and Radcliffe. Their work enabled us to build a major sequence around Cobb with the help of his daughter and granddaughter.

There was sufficient material to structure major sequences around pivotal figures during the Jim Crow era, such as W.E.B. Du Bois and Booker T. Washington. These two men were diametrically opposed over the best strategy to fight Jim Crow, and we focused on this conflict. For Isaiah Montgomery, Charlotte Hawkins Brown, Ida B. Wells, and Charles Houston, there was far less first-person material. To tell their stories, we had to combine their own words with those of scholars interviewed on camera. We wanted our scholars to bring these men and women to life by conveying their passion and determination to fight against Jim Crow.

We saw all the stories in the program as being connected to one another, as well as to the overall story we were telling, in the same way that streams merge into other streams until finally they become a river. The individual sequences were our streams, and the river that they formed eventually swept away the legal infrastructure of Jim Crow.

These were the elements we had at our disposal. Making them into a coherent piece was a tedious, frustrating, magical, and, if successful, exhilarating experience. It entailed a good deal of trial and error, false starts, and blind alleys. We also needed the help of others. Filmmaking is a community effort, and you have to draw upon the insights and suggestions of your colleagues and crew members as well as your own.

The main issue was how to weave the elements we had gathered into a coherent whole. There were individual stories that we wanted to tell, but at the same time we wanted these stories to be part of a larger story. Our goal was not simply to present a journey down the memory lane of history to show a dark period of American life. We chose this subject because we felt that the past has something to say to the present, that this series of programs could use the Jim Crow era to illuminate present-day race relations. We felt that by understanding this era, we might be able to disentangle ourselves from the coils with which Jim Crow continues to ensnare us today. I believe we accomplished what we set out to do. That's what made every hour and every minute of the seven years we worked on this project so rewarding.

The Rise and Fall of
Jim Crow

Chapter I

The Promise of Freedom, 1865–1877

At 4:30 A.M., on the morning of April 12, 1861, Edward Ruffin, a flinty, irascible old man from Virginia who passionately hated the North and who for twenty years had been haranguing the South to secede from the United States, received a singular honor from the Confederate Army: He fired the first shot of the Civil War. Ruffin lit the fuse that hurled a cannonball blazing across the dark sky like a meteor toward Fort Sumter. "Of course I was highly gratified by the compliment and delighted to perform the service," he later boasted. A Union sergeant on the rampart of the fort remembered watching "the burning fuse which marked the course of the shell . . . mounted among the stars."

The Civil War unleashed a tidal wave of patriotic furor that engulfed both sides. Northerners and Southerners alike clamored for what they believed would be a ninety-day bloodless war in which their side would easily emerge victorious. The bloodless ninety days swelled into four blood-filled years. Almost seven hundred thousand men died before the carnage ended.

Both sides insisted at first that the fight was not about slavery. To Southerners, "states' rights" was the catchword; to Northerners, "preserving the Union." Abraham Lincoln made his position clear in a letter to Horace Greeley, publisher of the *New York Tribune,* when he refused demands by Northern abolitionists to end slavery early in the war: "My paramount object in this struggle is to save the Union, and is not either to save or to destroy slavery. If I could save the Union without freeing any slave, I would do it, and if I could save it by freeing all the slaves, I would do it; and if I could save it by freeing some and leaving others alone, I would also do that."

Lincoln was seen by some as not only the Great Emancipator of blacks but of poor Southern whites as well. He was aware that both of them suffered from the same social and economic problems.

But the battle to preserve the Union inevitably became a battle to end slavery. One month later, after the horrific battle of Antietam forced the Southern armies to withdraw from Maryland, Lincoln formally announced the Emancipation Proclamation: "On the first day of January, in the year of our Lord one thousand eight hundred and sixty-three, all persons held as slaves within any State, or designated part of a State, the people whereof shall then be in rebellion against the United States, shall be then, thenceforward, and forever free." Blacks emancipated themselves even before the proclamation. Whenever Union soldiers appeared near where they were enslaved, they fled their plantations. Tens of thousands of freedmen eventually joined the army, helping transform the Union Army into an army of liberation.

Freedom became official on January 31, 1865, when Congress passed the Thirteenth Amendment. For four million African Americans, the "Day of Jubilee" had arrived—the promised time when God would set his people free. As the Union Army swept through the South, at times led by black soldiers, freedmen and freedwomen marched, danced, worshiped, and gave thanks to the Lord and to "Father Abraham." A woman on a plantation in Yorktown, Virginia, ran to a secluded place so her former owner would not see her express her joy. "I jump up and scream 'Glory, glory, hallelujah to Jesus. I's free. I's free. . . . De soul buyers can nebber take my two chillun's lef' me. Nebber can take 'em from me no mo.'"

People created songs to express their newfound freedom:

> Run to do kitchen and shout in de window
> Mammy don't you cook no mo'
> You's free. You's free!
> Run to de hen house and shout:
> Rooster don't you crow no mo'
> You's free! You's free!
> Ol' hen don't you lay no mo' eggs
> You's free! You's free!

Felix Haywood was herding wild horses on the plains of Texas when the news came. "When we learned of our freedom, everybody went wild. We all felt like horses and nobody made us that way but ourselves. We was free. Just like that we was free." When the wife of a black Union soldier asked her husband if she could name their newborn son James Freeman, he replied, "Take good care of our boy because he is born free—free as the bird, free as the wind and free as the sun and his name is Freeman. That just suits me. Thank God! He shall always be a freeman."

Blacks expressed their freedom by organizing parades. They demanded that whites address them as Mr. and Mrs. Women dressed in brightly colored clothes, carried parasols, rode in carriages, refused to give way to whites on the street, and sat with whites on streetcars. Men carried guns and bought dogs and liquor, all of which had been forbidden under slavery. Restricted in their ability to move about during slavery, freedmen and freedwomen exhibited a passion for travel. They organized train excursions to hold picnics and religious meetings in distant places. Whites could not understand why even those who had been well treated left. When one white woman begged her cook to stay on, even offering to pay her twice as much money as she would make elsewhere, the cook refused. Her baffled former mistress asked why she declined such a generous offer. The cook replied, "If I stay here, I'll never know I'm free." One former slave explained, "They seemed to want to get closer to freedom, so they'd know what it was—like it was a place or city."

Even as they enjoyed their freedom, African Americans struggled to define it. Where would they work? What role would they play in the community? Would Southern whites accept them? Where would they live? Would they be able to own land? Would their children receive an education? What political power would they have? To help answer these questions, Congress authorized the Freedmen's Bureau. Administered by the Union Army, the bureau's task was to organize a system of free labor between freedmen and -women and white planters, settle conflicts and disputes between whites and blacks, administer confiscated land, ensure that blacks received justice in the courts, and organize schools. The bureau was also to provide food, fuel, and clothing to the needy of both races on a very limited basis.

Woefully understaffed, the bureau did receive support from other agencies. Hundreds of black and white ministers, missionaries, and teachers flocked to the South with Bibles and spellers to help "uplift the race." Although blacks welcomed Northern assistance, they recognized that the main responsibility for their future lay with themselves. From the very beginning, African Americans began to build their own communities and institutions. They established churches, built schools, and set up benevolent societies to take care of the sick and the elderly, social organizations, including dramatic societies, debating clubs, fire companies, militia groups, and temperance leagues. There was so much activity that one man commented, "We have progressed a century in a year."

Freedmen and freedwomen attempted to restore families destroyed by slavery. Tens of thousands of children and parents, brothers and sisters had been sold away. Newspapers were filled with advertisements from mothers, fathers, children, brothers, and sisters seeking one another.

Sam'l Dove wishes to know the whereabouts of his mother Areno, his sisters Maria, Neziah and Peggy, and his brother Edmond, sold in Richmond.

$200 reward. For our daughter Polly and our son George Washington, carried away as slaves.

Many husbands and wives, brothers and sisters, and aunts and uncles were lost forever to one another. When Henry Spicer discovered, after remarrying, that his beloved first wife, who had been sold away from him and whom he believed dead, was still alive, he wrote her a heartbreaking letter: "I had rather anything happened to me than to have ever been parted from you and the children. I thinks of you and the children every day of my life. My love to you never have failed. Laura, I have got another wife and I am sorry that I am. You feels to me as much as my dear loving wife as you ever did Laura."

The great passion of the freedman became education. Booker T. Washington, who had been born in slavery and whose climb up the educational ladder would become legendary, observed his people's fervent desire for education: "To get inside a schoolhouse would be about the same as getting into heaven. Few people who were not right in the midst of the scenes can form any exact idea of the intense desire which the people of my race showed for education. It was a whole race trying to go to school. Few were too young, and none too old, to make the attempt to learn."

African Americans had a passionate belief in education and went to great lengths to learn how to read and write.

Sidney Andrews, a Northern white journalist sympathetic to black aspirations, noted the same passion as he traveled through the South after the Civil War: "Many of the Negroes . . . common plantation Negroes and day laborers . . . were supporting schools themselves. I had occasion very frequently to notice that porters in stores and laboring men about cotton warehouses and cart drivers in the streets had spelling books with them and were studying them during the time that they were not occupied with their work. Go into the outskirts of any large town . . . and you will see children, and in many instances grown Negroes, sitting in the sun alongside their cabins studying."

By 1866, an estimated five hundred independent schools had sprung up outside the cities and towns. William Channing Gannett, a white missionary from New England, observed that though blacks welcomed white assistance, they did not want white control: "They have a natural praiseworthy pride in keeping their educational institutions in their own hands. There is a jealousy of the superintendence of the white man in this matter. What they desire is assistance without control."

Many white Southerners resented the "Yankees" who had come South to educate blacks. One Southern white woman tried to convince Elizabeth Boutume, a New England schoolteacher, of the futility of her efforts. "I do assure you," the woman said, "you might as well teach your horse or mule to read as these niggers. They can't learn." Boutume replied, "If they can't read, why are you so afraid of school?"

Boutume knew well her students' desire to learn. She told the story of one cook who had ankle chains shackled to her feet by her master so that she would not run away. The woman had still managed to escape, hobbling and dragging herself day and night until she finally reached the school. Her feet were swollen and bloody from the chains biting into her flesh, and she would never walk normally again. When asked why education was so important to her, she answered that, before she died, she wanted to learn at least one thing to show to God when she met him. When a Union general visited Boutume's school and asked the students what message they had for their friends in the North, a child rose up and answered, "Tell them we are rising."

African Americans were as eager to build their own churches as they were to establish their own schools. Churches were the spiritual, educational, and political centers of community life. W. E. B. Du Bois, one of the great black civil rights leaders of the early twentieth century, wrote of the black church:

> The church was the spiritual and social heart of the black community. Various organizations meet here—the church proper, the Sunday school, insurance societies, women's societies, secret societies, and mass meetings of every kind. Entertainments, suppers and lectures are held here besides the five or six weekly services. Employment is found for the idle; strangers are introduced, news is disseminated and charity distributed. At the same time, this social, economic and intellectual center is a religious center of great power . . . the Church often stands as a real conserver of morals, a strengthener of family life, and the final authority on what is Good and Right.

Under slavery, black congregations had been subject to white ministers and churches. Now they either withdrew from white churches or took control, hiring black ministers to replace white ones. In 1867, the black membership of the Methodist church in the South was 40,000. Six years later it had dropped to 653. In 1858, there were 25,000 black Presbyterians. By 1875, the number fell to 1,614. Along with the church, blacks organized benevolent societies, political clubs, fraternal organizations, women's clubs, and labor unions. They raised money for orphanages and soup kitchens for the poor and the aged. Northern black ministers who came South expected to find their congregations completely degraded by slavery and in need of uplift. They learned instead what Thomas Higgenbotham had already discovered several years earlier about the Southern black troops he had commanded during the Civil War: "We did not know how the religious temperament of the Negroes had checked the demoralization." James Lynch, a Northern black minister, found freedmen and freedwomen a most responsive audience: "They exhibit a desire to hear and learn that I never imagined. Every word you say while preaching, they drink down and respond to with an earnestness that sets your heart all on fire and you feel that it is indeed God's work to minister to them." When Isaac Brinkerhood, a white Baptist minister from the North, tried to teach blacks to abandon their old black preachers who had conducted secret services during the days of slavery, he discovered that he had a lot to learn himself. Listening to one of these ministers preach, Brinkerhood confessed, "He was an unlearned man who could not read . . . telling of the love of Christ, of Christian faith and duty in a way which I have not yet learned."

As African Americans built their own institutions, they organized conventions to debate and define their future. Men, women, and children attended these conventions, participated in the discussion, and voted. At the Convention of the Colored People of South Carolina in

1865, the delegates requested "that we shall be recognized as men; that the same laws which govern white men shall govern black men; that we have the right of trial by jury of our peers; that no impediments be placed in our way of acquiring homesteads; that, in short, we be dealt with as others are—in equity and in justice."

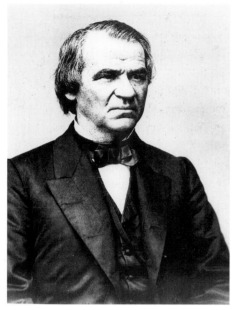

President Andrew Johnson succeeded Lincoln after his assassination. He had promised freedmen he would help them in their freedom, but instead supported those who would restore them to virtual slavery.

For a brief moment, their pleas might have been granted. According to Whitelaw Reid, a Northern reporter touring the South, Southerners seemed to be resigned to the fact that blacks would be major players in a new South. This opportunity was quickly lost. Suddenly and unexpectedly, the South found itself with an ally— the President of the United States, Andrew Johnson.

* * *

Andrew Johnson was described by his contemporaries as quick-tempered, hard-drinking, and mule-headed, a bully whose hatred of slave owners was as intense as his hatred of blacks. Johnson was born and raised in poverty. Through grit and determination he worked his way up in life, becoming governor of Tennessee and a United States senator. Although a slave owner, he favored emancipation. When the South seceded, he remained loyal to the Union. Lincoln rewarded him for his loyalty by choosing him as his vice president in 1864.

During the war, Johnson had taken a hard line regarding the South. "Treason is a crime," he said, "and crime must be punished." Johnson condemned those Southern politicians who had led the South into war. He said that, if he could, "I would arrest them—I would try them—I would convict them—and I would hang them." Many Radical Republicans in Congress—those who supported strong civil and political rights for blacks and harsh punishment of the South—had more hope that Johnson would carry out their policies than they did Lincoln. Some were not at all unhappy that Lincoln had been assassinated. Representative George Julian wrote, "Hostility towards Lincoln's policy of conciliation and contempt for his weakness were undisguised. The universal feeling here among radical men is that his death is a god-send." One senator remarked of Johnson, "I believe that the Almighty continued Mr. Lincoln in office as long as he was useful and then substituted a better man to finish his work."

The Radical Republicans believed that Johnson shared their view of the South. They maintained that the South had forfeited all rights to statehood when it separated itself from the Union. After defeat, it was little better than a conquered nation, barred from representation in Congress and the protection of the Constitution. They wanted to restructure the South to ensure that blacks would receive their rights and whites would be forever loyal to the Union.

Johnson had his own agenda. He did not share the belief that the South had separated itself from the Union. He agreed that the leaders of the South were guilty of treason but, like

Lincoln, Johnson felt that the Union was indissoluble. He wanted to "reconstruct" the South in order to hasten its return to the Union as soon as possible. Moreover, Johnson wanted the South brought back into the Union under white control. While governor of Tennessee, he had promised black people that he would "indeed be your Moses and lead you through the Red Sea of war and bondage to a fairer future of liberty and peace." But Moses became Judas for black people when Johnson became President. For though he had opposed slavery, he did not believe in racial equality. "I believe they [African Americans] have less capacity for governing than any race of people on earth," he said. He opposed extending the vote to blacks and any attempt of the federal government to ensure their civil and political rights.

In May 1865, Johnson issued a proclamation of amnesty and pardon. He generously pardoned all Southerners, except the leaders who supported the Confederacy, as long as they took an oath of loyalty to the Union and accepted emancipation. If Johnson closed the front door to former secessionist leaders, he left the back door wide open. Wealthy white secessionist leaders could be restored to power, and to their property, by individual acts of presidential pardon, which he handed out quite generously.

To ensure that his policies would be carried out, Johnson appointed conservative provisional governors in order to facilitate the return of their states to the Union. These governors had been loyal to the Union until war was declared and then served in the Confederacy. They also echoed Johnson's policies of white supremacy. Governor Benjamin Perry of South Carolina announced, "This is a white man's government and intended for white men only." Governor Benjamin Humphries of Mississippi declared the new order of things: "The Negro is free whether we like it or not. For the purity and progress of both races, they must accept their place in the lower order of things. That place is the cotton fields of the South. Such is the rule of the plantation and the law of God." The *Natchez Courier* editorialized that the two races could not live together as equals: "One must be superior—one must be dominant." If blacks tried to dominate, the *Courier* predicted a race war that would be "a war of extermination."

The South realized that Johnson was their ally. He allowed the states rather than the federal government to determine the future status of blacks. He agreed to the removal of black troops from the South. Contradicting his previous statements to punish traitors, he encouraged the old regime to take political and economic control. In the summer of 1865, whites gathered in political conventions to approve Johnson's demand that they accept the abolishment of slavery, declare secession null and void, and repudiate all state debts incurred during the war. Although all the states eventually did accept his terms, many did so reluctantly and with a great deal of debate. Most representatives the South elected in the fall—even if they had originally been opposed to secession—had supported the Confederacy when war was declared. Having lost the war, the South was determined to win the peace.

★ ★ ★

The burning issue for Southern whites was the future of the freedman. Northern journalist Sidney Andrews found Southern whites obsessed by blacks: "Everybody talks about the Negro, all hours of the day and under all circumstances. What would become of him? How would he survive? Where would he work? What could he do? And would he take revenge?"

Whites complained about the way African Americans exercised their freedom. Enraged at the presence of black soldiers guarding their towns, and infuriated by the independence expressed by men and women they once held in bondage, whites often accused blacks of being "disrespectful," "insolent," "insubordinate," and—the worst charge of all—"ungrateful." One planter commented, "The death of slavery is recognized. . . . But we don't believe that because the nigger is free, he ought to be saucy."

Whites claimed that blacks would not work unless forced to. One black freedman challenged this argument: "They say we will not work. He who makes that assertion makes an untruth. We have been working all our lives, not only supporting ourselves, but we have supported our masters, many of them in idleness. White men," he concluded, "didn't know how to work."

George Trowbridge, a New England journalist bitterly opposed to slavery, discovered that it was black labor that was rebuilding the South. "Negroes drove the teams, made the mortar, carried the hods, excavated the old cellars or built new ones. . . . I could not see but that these people worked just as industriously as the white laborers. And yet . . . I was once more informed by a cynical citizen that the Negro, now that he was free, would rob, steal or starve before he would work." And Sidney Andrews added, "It is both absurd and wicked to charge that Negroes as a class are not at work. Their vitality is at least thirty or forty percent greater than that of the average whites. . . . Of course the whites are forever complaining. They demand that all the labor shall be . . . in the hands of the blacks; and all ease and profit . . . in the hands of themselves."

Whites wanted black labor to plant and harvest their crops under some form of strict control. They wanted to determine what to pay their workers, how long they should work, when they should be paid, and how many members of their family should work. To carry out these goals, white legislators in every Southern state enacted a series of laws known as the black codes. Their goal was to restore slavery in substance, if not in name, with the state taking the place of the former "master." While the codes acknowledged that blacks had some rights, including the right to marry, own property, and make contracts, they severely restricted black freedom, forcing blacks to work the white man's land on the white man's terms. If a black man was found to be unemployed, he could be arrested as a vagrant and fined; if he failed to pay his fine, he was turned over to a planter who paid it and then forced him to work off his debt. Anyone who refused to sign a labor contract was imprisoned and forced to work without pay. Blacks who broke contracts could be shipped, fined, and sold into labor for one year. Orphaned children and even children of families could be taken away from their homes, forced to work as apprentices, and even whipped by their employers. Parents had no legal rights to prevent their children from being seized. To ensure that blacks would remain farmers and servants, some codes prohibited them from seeking any employment other than agricultural labor or domestic work without a special license. They could not lease or rent land, nor were they allowed to buy it. Some states denied African Americans the right to vote, hold office, and work and travel where they wanted to. Black people could not live in cities without a special permit. Tax laws were passed that forced blacks to pay poll taxes and occupation taxes that crippled them economically and often

Whites wanted blacks to return to the cotton fields and work for them as they had done in slavery. Blacks wanted to work their own land and be independent of whites. Without land, they felt there could be no freedom.

allowed the state, as a result of nonpayment, to arrest them and send them into forced labor.

The criminal justice system was as harsh as the codes. Blacks had little chance of winning a case in court against a white man or successfully defending themselves against a white man's charge. Sheriffs, judges, and jury members were all white, and most were former Confederate soldiers. Whites were seldom arrested for criminal offenses against blacks and almost never convicted. If plantation owners could no longer legally whip blacks, the state could and did. The state also began to lease blacks for convict labor gangs. Some Southern states also passed the segregation statutes immediately after the Civil War, later to be known as Jim Crow laws. Blacks were segregated on public transportation in Texas, Florida, and Mississippi, and completely banned from access to public institutions.

The codes enraged blacks and many Northerners. "If you call this freedom, what do you call slavery?" one black veteran bitterly asked. The Freedmen's Bureau, which had legal military powers over the conquered South, nullified most of the codes. Although the bureau was willing to overrule the codes, it was also willing to force blacks to work for whites against their will. Many army officers serving as administrators for the bureau worked hand in hand with Southern whites. They helped round up black workers, many of whom had migrated to the cities, and illegally shipped them to plantations. A delegation of African Americans in Richmond complained about their treatment. "In the city of Richmond, the military and police authorities will not allow us to walk the streets day or night, in the regular pursuit of our business or on our way to church, without passes, and passes do not always protect us from arrest, abuse, violence, and imprisonment." Henry McNeal Turner, then a black chaplain in the army, testified, "I have been told over and over by colored persons that they were

Whites launched murderous assaults on blacks at the end of the Civil War. They blamed them for the war and for their defeat and for wanting to be free.

never treated more cruelly than they were by some of the white Yankees. They were subjected to curfews and passes as they had been under slavery. Unemployed men were arrested as vagrants and sent to work on white plantations."

The army encouraged written labor contracts to be drawn up between planters and black workers, which the bureau would enforce. The contracts heavily favored the planters. Since many workers still could not read, the contracts often contained deceptive clauses that cheated them out of their money. Blacks were required to work for a year, and if they left their jobs before then or were fired, they forfeited their pay. The settlements were usually made at the end of the year. This meant that a planter could fire his workers just before they were supposed to be paid and completely avoid paying them. While some contracts allowed for wages, many were based on shares. The workers would receive a certain share of the cotton crop when it was sold, minus expenses for their food, clothes, and medical care. These items were sold on credit during the working season. Since the workers had no cash, they needed credit to survive. The planters and merchants charged exorbitant rates for merchandise and piled on usurious interest. This system later became the basis of sharecropping. Many planters continued to whip and beat their workers as they had during slavery. Whenever they could, planters treated their former slaves brutally, taking out their revenge on them. One worker who escaped complained, "We seen stars in the day time. They treated us dreadful bad. They beat us and they hung us and they starved us. They . . . told us they were going to shoot us and they did hang two of us; and Mr. Pierce, the overseer, knocked one with a fence rail and he died the next day." In South Carolina, when six field workers escaped a white man's farm on which they had been forced to work, the overseer tracked them down, shot one to death, and hanged the other five.

Whites used terror to ensure black subordination. The defeat of the Confederacy had triggered a tidal wave of racial violence against blacks. A former Confederate soldier expressed his hatred of the freedman: "I hope the day will come when we will . . . kill them like dogs. I was never down on a nigger like I am now." Throughout the South, blacks were whipped, beaten, or driven out of their homes or off their land. In Texas, one woman reported that it was a common sight to see the bodies of freedmen floating down a river. In Pine Bluff, Arkansas, twenty-four men, women, and children from a settlement were found "hanging to trees all around the Cabbins."

White men murdered blacks for any reason, or for no reason at all. One murderer explained that the victim "didn't remove his hat." Another said he "wanted to thin out the niggers a little." A third remarked that "he wanted to see a D——d nigger kick." Bodies were mutilated, ears severed, tongues cut out, eyes gouged. Men were beheaded and skinned, the skin then nailed to the barn. In the countryside, night riders whipped and murdered blacks and their white supporters. Black soldiers or former soldiers were often singled out. Whites cut their throats or shot them in the head. One white man walked with his arm around a black soldier and, as they were talking, secretly drew his pistol and shot the soldier in the back. Whites who committed these murders, many of them known to all, went unpunished. Colonel Samuel Thomas of the Freedmen's Bureau reported, "Wherever I go, I hear people talk in such a way as they are unable to conceive of a Negro as having any rights at all. Men

Most blacks wanted to live simply, to raise their own food and a little cotton for cash. In some areas, they had received land grants from the Union Army, but President Johnson rescinded the grants.

will cheat a Negro without feeling a single twinge of conscience. To kill a Negro they do not deem murder. To take property away from a Negro, they do not consider robbery. The reason for all this is simple and manifest. Whites esteem blacks their property by natural right and they treat the colored people just as their profit, caprice or passion may dictate."

Schools were a major target of white wrath. Seeing their former slaves educated was for many Southerners worse than seeing them free. A Southern senator warned, "Keep the spelling book and the land from the possession of the Negro if you hope to control him." Southern planters were furious when blacks forced them to provide schools as part of their work contract. They depended on their tenants' children working in the fields, which school would prevent them from doing. One planter commented, "If you educate the Negro he won't stay where he belongs. They feel the clutch of the iron hand of the white man's unwritten law in their throats." These planters knew that any educated black man would refuse to accept lowly manual labor if he could obtain a better job.

The black schools became targets of white violence. In Alabama, schoolhouses were burned and teachers terrorized. In Louisiana, the walls of a school in one town were covered with obscene language and pictures, and the teacher threatened. In Tennessee, a white teacher was taken at night from his room by a band of disguised men, choked, beaten, and threatened with death if he did not leave town. Local whites refused to rent rooms to Northern white teachers, who then roomed with black families. They were ostracized and sometimes beaten, and many were forced to leave.

For African Americans, perhaps the worst betrayal was President Andrew Johnson's refusal to keep the federal government's promise of land. Land was the foundation on which African Americans planned to build their mansion of freedom. Land would allow them to escape from white domination and achieve economic independence. "Every colored man will be a slave and feel himself a slave until he can raise his own bale of cotton and put his own mark on it and say, 'This is mine,'" Peter Hall, a freedman, explained.

Blacks living along the Georgia and South Carolina coast had good reason to believe that they would be given the lands of those who had enslaved them. Earlier in the year, Secretary of War Edwin Stanton and General William Tecumseh Sherman had met with a delegation of twenty black men from the Savannah area to discuss their freedom. The group's spokesman was Garrison Frazier, an elder in the Baptist ministry. During the meeting, Frazier told Stanton, "The best way we can take care of ourselves is to have land and turn it over by our own labor. . . . We want to be placed on land until we are able to buy it and make it our own."

Black people in the coastal areas of South Carolina and Georgia had already taken over large tracts of land abandoned by their former masters. Sherman legitimized their actions. Several days after the meeting, he issued Field Order Number 15, setting aside more than four hundred thousand acres of abandoned land for forty thousand blacks living on the Georgia and South Carolina Sea Islands and coastal areas. Blacks were allowed to form their own communities and govern themselves without interference from whites, except for military personnel and the federal government. They also chose to plant corn and potatoes rather than cotton—for cotton "had enriched their masters but not themselves."

President Johnson would not allow this to remain. In October 1865, he sent a troubled Union general, Oliver O. Howard, to Edisto Island off the coast of South Carolina. A deeply religious man who hated slavery, Howard was sent to break the bad news to the islanders. When he arrived, he found two thousand angry people gathered to meet him in the Old Episcopal Church. Howard later described the scene in his autobiography: "The auditorium galleries were filled. The rumor preceded my coming had reached the people that I was obliged by the President to restore the land to the old planters, so that evidence of dissatisfaction and sorrow was manifested in every part of the assembly. No progress was made until a sweet-voiced woman began to sing 'Nobody Knows the Trouble I've Seen.'"

Howard addressed the audience: "I have been sent by the President to tell you that your old masters have been pardoned and their plantations are to be given back to them, and that they would hire blacks to work for them. Lay aside your bitter feelings and be reconciled to them." Voices shouted out in protest. "No!" "No suh!" One man rose and addressed Howard directly: "General Howard, why do you take away our lands! You take them from us who are true, always true to the government. You give them to our all-time enemies. The man who gave me 39 lashes, and who stripped and flogged my mother and sister—who keeps land from me well knowing I would not have anything to do with him if I had land of my own— that man I cannot well forgive." All over the South—with few exceptions—blacks were forced, often at bayonet point, to return lands they had occupied.

The Radical Republicans were the moral forces in the Senate. They had supported abolition before the war, pushed for blacks to join the Union army during the war and after the war, and wanted blacks to have full political and civil rights. Thaddeus Stevens (holding cane) was one of the leaders of the group.

Even with the return of their lands, many whites—perhaps hundreds of thousands—were still ruined. Almost every wealthy family had lost its savings. Many were reduced to poverty and had to sell or abandon their homes and plantations, because they could no longer afford to keep them. The South had lost 260,000 men. Almost four million black men and women—once regarded as property and who had done all of the work—were free. "I never did a day's work in my life," one white planter confessed, "and I don't know how to begin." Many formerly wealthy families suffered the fate of a once-proud Virginia family. "The family, one of the oldest and most respectable, once very wealthy and now reduced . . . to large debts, large pride and large wants . . . are now without servants. The young ladies on Wednesdays and Thursdays milked the cows while their father, the general, held the umbrella over them to keep off the rain." White women were terrified of losing servants, because they had to do the housework themselves. To cook dinner, clean house, wash and iron clothes, and carry out similar chores was too hard for many white women. They bitterly complained and longed for the days when their black servants did all the work. Their anger ran deep. One freedwoman reported that her former mistress "hoped that we'd starve to death and she be glad, 'cause it ruin her to lose us." White women rarely recognized that if the work was too hard for them, it was just as hard for black women. One former slave owner, Kate Stone, gradually realized what life was like for her servants: "Even under the best of owners, it was a hard, hard life; to toil six days out of seven, week after week, month after month, year after year as long as life lasted; to be absolutely under control of someone until the last breath was drawn; to win but the bare necessities of life, no hope of more, no matter how hard the work, how long the toil to know that nothing could change your lot. Obedience, revolt, submission, prayers—all were in vain. Waking sometimes in the night as I grow older, I would grow sick with the misery of it all."

Blacks resisted the efforts of whites to control their lives once again. Whenever they could, they insisted that they work shorter hours than they had under slavery, that they be paid for nonfarming jobs like clearing the land, that they be given land to work for themselves, and that they have schools for their children. They wanted their wives and daughters to remain at home rather than work in the fields. At times, they walked off plantations and refused to sign contracts for another year. When some planters resisted all compromise, occasionally their barns or homes were burned down. On plantations and in the cities, black workers went out on strike for better pay. In New Orleans, black and white workers sometimes joined forces to strike for higher wages or better working conditions.

Gradually Southern whites, aided by the Freedmen's Bureau, began to regain control. As one white planter chillingly predicted, "The nigger is going to be made a serf as sure as you live. It won't need any law for that. . . . They're attached to the soil and to their masters as much as ever. I'll stake my life, this is the way it will work." This attitude, found everywhere, revealed to Sidney Andrews that Southern whites were determined to return African Americans to slavery the first chance they got. "If the nation allows the whites to work out the . . . Negro's future in their own way, the condition in three years will be as bad as it was before the war. The viciousness that could not overturn the nation is now mainly engaged in the effort to retain the substance of slavery. What are names if the thing itself remains?"

One reason the South was so confident it could restore slavery in substance was that most white Northerners had no love for blacks, and wanted the South to be brought back into the Union quickly. Industrialists were eagerly eyeing the fortunes to be made by creating a new, modern South on the ruins of the old. Most Republican politicians and party members were willing to go along with President Johnson's policy to leave the fate of African Americans to the South. Although they were willing to allow whites to control blacks, they refused to tolerate injustice and violence. Nor would they allow Southerners to elect political leaders who were once secessionists. The South appeared arrogant to many Northern Republicans, acting as if it had won the war. Republican leaders first tried to work out a compromise with the President.

The driving force of the Republican-controlled Congress was a small group of senators and congressmen collectively known as the Radicals, because they championed full civil and political rights for blacks. While the Radicals were a minority in their own party, they had tremendous influence in the House and Senate. Every major cause they advocated had triumphed—abolition, emancipation, and the arming of black troops during the Civil War. Now they were about to embark on their greatest struggle—to secure the ballot for the black men (women were still not allowed to vote) and full equality in civil rights for all African Americans. They were aware that most Americans opposed black suffrage. When whites in Washington, D.C., voted in referendum on the issue of black suffrage, only 35 were in favor of blacks voting while 6,951 were against.

In 1866, Congress began to eliminate discrimination on the federal and state levels. It repealed a federal law that barred black people from carrying the mail. It allowed African Americans to testify in federal courts and to sit in the visitors' galleries in Congress. The first black lawyer was accredited to the Supreme Court. The Republicans passed a Civil Rights Act, which held that all native-born Americans were entitled to certain basic rights, including the right to sue, to make contracts, to inherit, purchase, and hold land, and to enjoy "full and equal benefit of all laws." The act's goal was to protect blacks against abuse by the state, but it failed to protect them against discrimination by individuals. The Freedmen's Bureau Bill extended the life of the bureau and granted it the power to intervene wherever blacks were denied civil rights enjoyed by whites.

The Republicans expected Johnson to sign the bills. Instead he vetoed both. Politically Johnson felt that by killing the bills, he would win support from Democrats as well as from Republicans. Johnson believed the issue of federal protection of black civil rights would become the political issue he could use to defeat his Republican opponents in the next congressional election. During a rally, someone in the audience asked Johnson, "What does the veto mean?" Before he could answer, a voice from the crowd boomed out, "It is keeping the nigger down."

Johnson had seriously miscalculated. Black civil rights had become a major issue. Congress overrode Johnson's veto of the Civil Rights Act. To ensure that a future Congress would not undo the act, the Republicans also passed the Fourteenth Amendment, which constitutionally guaranteed due process of law to all persons born in the United States. All states were now required to apply civil rights laws equally to blacks and whites. The amendment also disfranchised from national office those who had served in the Confederacy during the war. Before any Southern state could be readmitted into the Union, that state had to ratify the amendment.

If there had been any doubt that federal intervention was needed in the South, it was dispelled in Memphis, in the spring of 1866. A carriage collision between a black and a white taxi driver led to a race riot in which forty-six blacks and two whites were killed, five black women were raped, and hundreds of black-owned buildings were burned to the ground. Three months later, the mayor of New Orleans incited another race riot in which the police shot and killed at least forty blacks and whites attending a political convention. General Philip Sheridan, who was the military commander of the area at the time, described to President Johnson what happened: "As they came out [of the building] the policemen who had formed the circle nearest the building fired upon them, and they were again fired upon by citizens. Many of those wounded and captured . . . were fired upon by their captors. The wounded were stabbed while lying on the ground, and their heads beaten with brickbats." Sheridan concluded in his report: "It was no riot. It was an absolute massacre by the police which was not excelled in murderous cruelty by that of Fort Pillow." (Confederate soldiers had murdered some two hundred blacks at Fort Pillow during the Civil War after they had surrendered.)

The final showdown between Johnson and the Republicans came in the congressional elections of 1866. Before the elections, the President traveled throughout the country bitterly castigating the Republican Congress. Drunk much of the time, Johnson gave rambling and incoherent speeches that helped his enemies. Southerners aided the Northern Republican cause by rejecting the Fourteenth Amendment and electing staunch supporters of the Confederacy to Congress. The Republican victory was overwhelming. The party controlled more than two-thirds of Congress, with enough votes to override any of Johnson's vetoes. Congress refused to seat newly elected representatives from the South, many of whom had been active in the Confederacy. The only exception was Tennessee, which had complied with Congress's wishes and barred former leaders of the Confederacy from holding public office. Reconstruction was now in the hands of the Radical Republicans, and the terms for readmission for the Southern states would be far harsher than the President's had been.

Chapter 2

Promises Betrayed, 1880–1890

The Radical Republicans seized control of Reconstruction with a burning desire to impose their will on the South. In 1867, Congress passed the Reconstruction Act, allowing the federal government to rule the South until the Southern states were readmitted into the Union. The eleven Confederate states of the South were divided into five military districts. Each general in charge of a district was required to prepare the states in his jurisdiction for readmission to the Union. Every state had to amend its constitution to ensure that African Americans would become full citizens of the United States, with their civil and political rights fully protected. Black delegates elected by their communities were to be represented at all of the conventions. A number of men who had supported the Confederacy were denied the right to vote. To be readmitted to the Union, a state had to approve the new provisions guaranteeing civil and political rights for all citizens and had to ratify the Fourteenth Amendment. Congress made it clear that until the Southern states accepted the conditions for Reconstruction, military rule would remain. Senator Richard Yates proclaimed, "The ballot will finish the Negro question. . . . The ballot is the freedman's Moses."

Blacks celebrated the Reconstruction Act as a second emancipation. Union Clubs, formed right after the Civil War as patriotic organizations, immediately became hives of political activity. The clubs held forums and debates, organized parades and demonstrations, built churches and schools, and provided care for the sick and the elderly. They advised farmworkers how to deal with planters who cheated them out of their wages or tricked them into signing long-term contracts that left them in debt. When Congress legalized black suffrage, the Union Clubs became political organizations, supporting candidates for office and explaining to people their political rights and how to vote. The Bible and the Declaration of Independence were always on display at meetings. Armed men guarded the meetings from interference by hostile whites. Some clubs were integrated and provided a political space in which blacks and whites could meet as equals. Many blacks were in favor of breaking down barriers of discrimination. Some small white farmers, struggling to hold on to their land, recognized that both races were in the same ditch and joined with blacks in common cause.

In the fall of 1867, blacks organized constitutional conventions in almost every Southern

In 1867, Congress empowered African Americans with the vote, enabling them to select their own representatives to state and federal government. This political cartoon shows the joyous response of blacks and the unhappy response of Southern whites.

state. Black voters, fully represented for the first time, campaigned with great enthusiasm. In every city and town, politics became their main preoccupation. Planters complained that they had to shut down their farms, because so many of their black workers took off to attend political rallies and conventions. One planter observed, "You never saw a people more excited on the subject of politics than are the Negroes of the South. They are perfectly wild." Black ministers felt that politics was replacing religion. "Politics got in our midst and our revival or religious work for a while began to wane," one minister complained. To deal with this problem, churches turned to politics and ministers preached the Republican Party and the Gospel.

Although women could not vote, they played an active role in politics. One witness said that women were determined that men should vote the Republican ticket: "Women had sticks; no mens were to go to the polls unless their wives were right alongside them; some had hickory sticks; some had nails—four nails drive in the shape of a cross—and dare their husbands to vote any other than the Republican ticket. My sister went with my brother-in-law to the polls and swear to God if he voted the Democratic ticket, she 'will kill him dead in his sleep.'"

On paper, the new state constitutions promised much. They guaranteed blacks equal civil and political rights with whites, and they established schools, prisons, and asylums for the orphaned and insane of both races. They removed many of the discriminations against blacks and outlawed harsh punishments such as whipping. In most states, African Americans were guaranteed the right to sit on juries and testify in court. In South Carolina, it was forbidden to imprison a man or take away his home for debt. Many of the new state constitutions benefited poor whites as well as blacks. As far as equal treatment in public places and on public transportation was concerned, most constitutions avoided these issues because whites bitterly opposed change. Many blacks were willing to accept such separation temporarily as long as they could control their own schools, churches, and social organizations. Their ultimate hope was that, in time, they could create a truly democratic and fully integrated biracial society.

Whites were enraged at being forced to enfranchise blacks. Governor Perry of South Carolina protested to Congress: "The radical Republican Party forgets that this is a white man's government and created for white men only; and that the Supreme Court of the United States has decided that the Negro is not an American citizen under the Federal Constitution. Each and every state of the Union has the unquestionable right of deciding who shall exercise the right of suffrage."

The *Charleston Mercury* warned the victors, "The constitutions and governments will last just as long as the bayonets which ushered them into being shall keep them in existence and not one day longer."

Benjamin Perry was appointed provisional governor of South Carolina by President Johnson. He had been opposed to secession but supported the Confederacy when war started. He was a white supremacist adamantly opposed to black rights.

Although African Americans were now major players in Southern politics, they still were a minority of the population in most states. The great majority of Southern whites supported the Democratic Party, the party of white supremacy. To gain political power, blacks had to join forces with those whites willing to support the Republican Party and black rights. Many were Northern Republicans who had migrated to the South after the war to make their fortunes. Some were confidence men who became notorious for their corruption. Others were bright and capable men who would prove to be good leaders. White Southerners contemptuously lumped them all together under the term "carpetbaggers," a name inspired from the type of luggage they carried. At the same time, a small number of Southern whites supported the Republican Party. Called "scalawags" by most white Southerners, who considered them traitors to the South, many of them were men of property and influence who had been opposed to secession. They felt that the future of the South—as well as their own futures—lay in identifying with Northern interests. The South lacked sufficient capital to recover from the devastation caused by the war and desperately needed Northern financial support. The scalawags were more interested in convincing Northern capitalists to invest in railroads, mines, cotton mills, and machine shops than they were in racial issues.

Even as congressional Reconstruction was making progress, President Johnson remained intent on undermining it. He removed generals who were sympathetic to blacks or willing to

The Radical Republicans took their revenge on President Andrew Johnson by denying him the nomination for President. Instead, they chose Civil War hero Ulysses S. Grant.

carry out Congress's bidding and replaced them with generals hostile to black rights. He removed Secretary of War Edwin Stanton from office despite a congressional law forbidding him to do so. In retaliation, the Radicals attempted to impeach the President but failed by the narrow margin of one vote.

In the summer of 1868, the anti-Johnson faction of the Republican Party got its revenge by denying Johnson their party's nomination for President. Instead, they chose Ulysses S. Grant, an obvious choice. He was a war hero extremely popular with the American people. He had faithfully carried out the Reconstruction policies of Congress, even though he was not particularly sympathetic to African Americans.

Democrats hoped to play the race card to defeat the Republicans. Those Southern states that had changed their constitutions and were readmitted to the Union (Arkansas, Louisiana, Georgia, Florida, Tennessee, North and South Carolina) rallied around the Democratic Party. They used every means to intimidate black voters in order to prevent them from voting: Democratic merchants cut off credit to black Republicans; landlords evicted tenants who dared to vote. And terrorist organizations arose, the most ruthless of which was the Ku Klux Klan.

The Klan was originally organized in 1865 in Pulaski, Tennessee, as a social club by six Confederate veterans. In the beginning, the Klan was a secret fraternity club rather than a terrorist organization. Ku Klux was derived from the Greek word *kuklos,* meaning a band. Klan has no specific meaning but was used for its alliterative sound. The costume adopted by its members was a mask, white robe, and high, conical, pointed hat. According to the founders of the Klan, there was no malicious intent in the beginning. Yet it quickly grew into a terrorist organization. It attracted such former Confederate generals as Nathan Bedford Forrest, the famed cavalry commander whose soldiers murdered captured black troops at Fort Pillow during the Civil War. The Klan spread beyond Tennessee to every state in the South and included mayors, judges, and sheriffs, as well as convicted criminals.

The Klan systematically murdered black politicians and political leaders throughout the South. Since Johnson had appointed federal officers hostile to Reconstruction, they did nothing to prevent the killings or to arrest the killers. Despite the Klan's efforts, blacks voted in large numbers, carrying the South for Grant. One newspaper reporter observed the determination of African Americans to vote: "In defiance of fatigue, hardship, hunger and threats of employers, blacks had come en masse to the polls. Without shoes, [wearing] patched clothing, they stood on line despite a storm waiting for the chance to vote. The hunger to have the same chances as the white men they feel and comprehend."

Rising above the terror, black votes carried enough Southern states for Grant to be elected. Blacks also elected many local Republicans to office. Despite fears by white Democrats of "black domination," whites won most state and local offices. Whites controlled all legislatures except in South Carolina, where blacks gained control of the lower and upper houses. Many blacks refused to run because they did not want to make the Republican Party a black man's party. They felt that, for the sake of racial harmony, it would be better for whites to control the government as long as they were responsive to black political demands. This would change as Reconstruction progressed, and blacks eventually held some six hundred offices, plus hundreds of positions as sheriffs, clerks, policemen, firemen, and aldermen and councilmen.

In 1869, Congress tried to give additional support to black voters by passing the Fifteenth Amendment. On the surface, the amendment prohibited federal and state governments from depriving any citizen of the vote on racial grounds, something that Frederick Douglass, the great spokesman for the black community, had been urging for years. "The South must be opened to the light of law and liberty. . . . The plain common sense way of doing this . . . is simply to establish in the South one law, one government, one administration of justice, one condition to exercise the elective franchise for all men and all colors alike . . . the right of the Negro is the true solution of our national problems."

The amendment, ratified in 1870, contained many loopholes. It failed to make voting requirements universal and protect the rights of blacks to run for office and to sit on juries. Nor did the amendment prohibit literacy tests, poll taxes, and educational testing as requirements for voting. Republicans were fearful that if the amendment were too strong it would infringe on the rights of a state to regulate its own affairs.

* * *

Despite their victories, Southern Republicans remained an alien presence in a hostile land. Most whites refused to accept the Republican Party as legitimate, considering it to have been forced upon them by Northern bayonets. Blacks and whites fought over issues concerning civil rights, patronage, and elected office. White Republican leaders wanted to win the support of Southern whites by appointing influential Democrats to office. Blacks wanted strong civil rights legislation, public schools, orphanages, asylums for the insane, hospitals for both races, and an end to discrimination on public transportation.

The South still lay in ruins with its state treasuries empty. Republicans proposed to revolutionize the region by transforming it into an industrial economy. They tried to woo Northern capital to the South by offering generous financing and land grants to railroad companies. To win these subsidies and favorable laws, railroads and speculators paid substantial bribes to legislators of both parties and both races. By the early 1870s, the railroad boom had ended, leaving many states deeply in debt with nothing to show for it—except higher taxes to pay the bills for the subsidies to the railroads and increased hostility toward the Republicans.

As Republicans struggled to maintain political control, pass civil rights, education, and social welfare laws, modernize the South, and win white support, the Klan unleashed a murderous rampage. Klansmen were filled with passionate intensity to eliminate, eradicate, or exterminate all Republicans, black and white. They beat, whipped, and murdered thousands, and terrorized tens of thousands to prevent them from voting. Blacks often tried to fight back, but they were outnumbered and outgunned. William Coleman, a black farmer in Mississippi, told a congressional investigating committee on Klan activities in 1868 of his own experience with the Klan:

> I grabbed my ax-handle and commenced fighting and they just took me and cut me with their knives. They surrounded me and some had me by the legs and some by the arms and the neck . . . and they took me out to the big road before my gate and whipped me until I couldn't move or holler, but just lay there like a log, and every lick they hit me I grunted like a mule when he is stalled fast and whipped. They left me there for dead, and what it was done for was because I was a radical and I didn't deny my profession . . . and I never will. I will never vote for that conservative ticket if I die.

Plan of the Contemplated Murder of John Campbell.

The Ku Klux Klan was formed as a social club but quickly became a terrorist organization determined to destroy the gains that blacks had made under Reconstruction. White supporters of blacks were also targeted.

Although the main targets of Klan wrath were the political and social leaders of the black community, blacks could be murdered for almost any reason. Men, women, and children, the aged and the crippled, were victims. A 103-year-old woman was whipped, as was a paralyzed man. In Georgia, Abraham Colby, an organizer and leader in the black community, was whipped for hours in front of his wife and children. His little daughter begged the Klansman, "don't take my daddy away." She never recovered from the experience and died soon after. In Mississippi, Jack Dupree's throat was cut and he was disemboweled in front of his wife, who had just given birth to twins. Klansmen burned churches and schools and lynched teachers and educated blacks. Black landowners were driven off their property or murdered if they refused to leave. Blacks were whipped for refusing to work for whites, for having intimate relations with whites, for arguing with whites, for having jobs whites wanted, for reading a newspaper or having a book in their homes—or simply for being black. Klan violence led one black man to write, "We have very dark days here. The colored people are in despair. The rebels boast that the Negroes shall not have as much liberty now as they had under slavery. If things go on thus, our doom is sealed. God knows it is worse than slavery."

A few state governments fought back. In Tennessee and Arkansas, Republicans organized a police force that arrested, tried, and executed Klansmen. In Texas, Governor Edmund Davis organized a crack state police unit; 40 percent of the officers were black. The police made more than six thousand arrests and stopped the Klan. Sometimes blacks and whites fought back. Blacks lynched three whites in Arkansas who murdered a black lawyer. Armed groups of blacks and whites fought or threatened Klansmen in North and South Carolina. The price paid for resistance could be heavy, and many states were helpless against Klan terror. In Colfax, Louisiana, when blacks tried to defend their town against a white mob, 280 were massacred, 50 of whom had surrendered and were unarmed. President Grant condemned the slaughter in a letter to the Senate: "A butchery of citizens was committed at Colfax, which in blood-thirstiness and barbarity is hardly surpassed by any acts of savage warfare. . . . Insuperable obstructions were thrown in the way of punishing these murderers and the so-called conservative papers of the state not only justified the massacre but denounced as federal tyranny and despotism the attempt of the United States officers to bring them to justice."

State governments pleaded for the federal government to send troops. General William Tecumseh Sherman, who had no love for blacks, agreed: "If that is the only alternative I am willing . . . to again appeal to the power of the nation to crush, as we have done once before, this organized civil war."

Between 1870 and 1871, Congress passed a series of Enforcement Acts—criminal codes that protected citizens in their right to vote, to hold office, to serve on juries, and to receive equal protection under the law. If the states failed to act, these codes allowed the federal government to intervene.

President Grant responded by decreeing that "insurgents were in rebellion against the authority of the United States." Federal troops were sent to restore law and order to many areas where violence was raging. In nine counties of South Carolina, martial law was declared, and Klansmen were tried before predominantly black juries. Much of the credit for prosecuting the Klan belonged to Amos Ackerman, Grant's attorney general, who did his best to make the country aware of the extent of Klan violence. Despite his efforts, only a few Klansmen and their sympathizers were tried and sent to jail. Thousands of others fled or were released with fines or warnings. By the time the terror temporarily ended, thousands of blacks and hundreds of whites had been massacred or driven from their homes. For a moment, it seemed that peace and Republican rule were restored. One newspaper predicted what would inevitably happen to blacks when the federal government no longer came to the rescue: "It is impossible that your present power can endure whether you use it for good or ill. Let not your pride nor yet your pretended friends flatter you in the belief that you ever can or ever will, for any length of time, govern the white man of the South. Your present power must surely and soon pass from you. Nothing that it builds will stand, and nothing will remain of it but the prejudices it may create."

A small but significant number of blacks became quite successful during Reconstruction. John Lynch of Mississippi was elected to Congress between 1873 and 1883. Eventually defeated, he held many posts in the Republican Party and practiced law in Mississippi, Washington, D.C., and Chicago, where he finally lived.

★ ★ ★

As Klan violence diminished, hope for racial progress was reborn. Signs of racial harmony could be found in many Southern cities. In Columbia, South Carolina, one man noted, "The Negroes are freely admitted to the theater in Columbia, and to other exhibitions, lectures, though whites avoid sitting with them. In Columbia, they are served at bars, soda water fountains, and ice cream saloons." In Virginia, an editorial in the *Virginia Dispatch* noted, "Nobody here objects to sitting in political conventions with Negroes. Nobody here objects to serving on juries with Negroes. No lawyer objects to practicing in court with Negro lawyers present. And in both houses [of the legislature] Negroes are allowed to sit as they have a right to sit." The *Raleigh Standard* admitted that in North Carolina "the two races now sit together, eat at the same table, sit together in the same room, work together, visit and hold debating societies together." Some saloons in Mississippi served whites and blacks at the same bar; some restaurants served whites and blacks in the same room if not at the same table. Albert Morgan, a Northerner who crusaded for education and black political rights in Mississippi, reflected years later, "The period from 1869–1875, was one of substantial, and . . . wonderful progress."

By the early 1870s, blacks had won hundreds of political offices. Some politicians were Northern and Southern free blacks; others were former slaves, some of whom had served in the Union Army. Many could read and write. A few black candidates decided to make politics their career and were elected as congressmen, United States senators, lieutenant governors, state treasurers, superintendents of education, and state legislators. These men included black leaders like Robert Smalls in South Carolina, Blanche Bruce and P.B.S. Pinchback in Louisiana, and John Lynch in Mississippi. For the most part, blacks received such low-level positions as justices of the peace, sheriffs, councilmen, judges, alderman, and members of school boards. Blacks were hired as policemen and firemen in some cities, served on integrated juries, and were appointed or elected magistrates or justices of the peace. A biracial democracy was struggling to take root in precarious soil.

Education remained a high priority. Harriet Beecher Stowe, the author of *Uncle Tom's Cabin*, observed that blacks "cried for the spelling book as bread and pleaded for teachers as a necessity of life." By 1870, black voters had ensured that every Southern state had established a public school system paid for by a state fund, although most schools were segregated. Even in the state institutions for the blind, the races were separated, leading one legislator to remark sardonically, "color was distinguished where no color was seen." In New Orleans, after a bitter fight, black and white students did attend integrated schools. The University of South Carolina was integrated. When white students and the faculty withdrew in protest, other whites took their place and got along well with blacks. In Nashville, and in Washington, D.C., Fisk and Howard universities were established to educate blacks for the professions and for leadership.

Many schools offered the same courses that white children received in the North, including reading, writing, spelling, grammar, diction, history, geography, arithmetic, and music. On the college level, pupils studied Greek, Latin, science, philosophy and, occasionally, a modern language. African Americans saw education as the necessary foundation for improving their lives and preparing them to establish a democratic society in which they would fulfill their responsibilities as citizens.

Some Southerners were startled at the progress blacks made. Edward Allford Pollard, a Virginian, admitted that he "always insisted on regarding the Negro as specifically inferior to the white man—a lower order of human being who was indebted for what he had of civilization to the institution of slavery." Yet Pollard confessed that "his former views of the Negro were wrong." Traveling through the South, he found that African Americans were not the "degraded poor, intellectually helpless people" he had thought they were. Instead he found that "this singularly questionable creature has shown a capacity for education that has astonished . . . his former masters; that he has given proofs of good citizenship . . . that his condition has been on the whole that of progress . . . that so far from being a stationary barbarian, the formerly despised black man promises to become a true follower of the highest civilization and . . . exemplary citizen of the South."

Progress came to the North as well. Legislatures repealed laws that prohibited blacks from voting. Schools and public transportation were integrated in some states. But social and economic discrimination remained. Blacks were still forced to live in ghettoes and work at menial jobs, and were denied access to hotels and restaurants.

Northern interest in the Southern "race question" was eroding. Between 1865 and 1873, Americans were prospering from an economic boom. Railroads crisscrossed the country. Wherever the railroads went, towns and farms followed. The West was opened to the large-scale mining of gold and silver, mass production of lumber and cattle, and commercial agriculture. Factories sprang up in cities. The workforce of the country had changed dramatically as unskilled immigrant factory workers and manual laborers replaced skilled artisans. The country was preoccupied with unions and labor conflicts. Big business began to use its power to organize monopolies, dominating economic and political life. In 1873, the nation's economy collapsed. Millions of workers lost their jobs and wandered the country in search of work.

OCTOBER 31, 1874.] HARPER'S WEEKLY. 901

"EVERY THING POINTS TO A DEMOCRATIC VICTORY THIS FALL."—SOUTHERN PAPERS.

By 1873, the Democratic Party, which called itself the Party of White Supremacy, had won back most of the Southern states, often using fraud, violence, and intimidation to do so.

The depression was catastrophic for the South. The price of cotton dropped 50 percent, wiping out many small white farmers. Trapped in the quicksand of the South's credit system, unable to pay their mortgages, they lost their farms to the merchants who had extended them credit. By 1880, one-third of white farmers would be tenants or sharecroppers.

The crash destroyed large planters as well. Louis Manigault, a South Carolina planter, sadly witnessed many of his once wealthy neighbors lose everything they had. "Many families who have managed so far to hold out against immediate distress . . . have finally succumbed . . . and I hear of only poverty and misery among those who were the richest and oldest families prior to the war."

Hundreds of thousands of blacks were worse off than they had ever been in their lives. One federal official in Georgia commented, "I thought I had seen poverty in the city, but I never saw anything to compare with the poverty of those Negroes there." The depression also caused the collapse of the Freedman's Bank in 1874. Chartered in 1865, the bank had actively sought deposits from black men and women, churches, and benevolent societies. Tens of thousands of people had entrusted the bank with their life's savings. The directors, who were white, began to speculate during the boom and made large, unsecured loans to railroads and other companies. Frederick Douglass donated ten thousand dollars from his own pocket to help the bank survive. It was too little, too late. The bank collapsed, taking with it the savings—and the hopes—of its depositors.

In 1874, the country revolted against the Republican Party. Democrats swept to victory in Congress, not only overcoming the one-hundred-man Republican majority in the House of Representatives but also winning an additional sixty seats. Republicans still controlled the Senate, but their majority was dramatically reduced.

With the return of the Democrats to power, Reconstruction was now in the hands of its enemies. Even its former supporters had turned against it. Republicans were unwilling to push Reconstruction further. The old guard of Radical Republicans was dying off, and a new generation was emerging. Business, not civil rights, was the main issue of the day. As a final gesture, Republicans passed a watered-down Civil Rights Act just before the Democrats took office. The act outlawed racial discrimination in schools, churches, and cemeteries, and on juries and public transportation—but it was eventually overturned by the Supreme Court. Former abolitionists suddenly declared black suffrage a failure. Even the strongest supporters of emancipation now argued that the best way to protect black rights was to entrust them to the better class of Southern whites. White Republicans in the South abandoned their black supporters and tried to appeal to white Democrats by supporting discriminatory legislation.

Southern Democrats had little interest in cooperating with the Republicans. By 1873, the Democratic Party had "redeemed" Virginia, Tennessee, Georgia, and Texas. In 1874, the Democrats won Arkansas and captured the Florida legislature. In Alabama, where the black and white voting populations were about equal, Democrats won by murdering blacks at the polls on Election Day. The violence was worse in Louisiana. Democrats formed the White League, an organization dedicated to the restoration of white supremacy. Rumors of a coming race war swept through the countryside. The Shreveport *Evening Standard* announced: "White supremacy first, last and all the time, has always been the motto of the white people of Caddo, and they prove their faith by their works. Let the colored man lay aside all political aspirations and allow the united white men to do what it is utter folly for the Negro to resist. The conflict will continue as long as the colored race aspires to the governing power."

Farmers who planned to vote were threatened. One man reported, "The agent of the place I rented said, 'Jim, we are going to carry this thing our own way. You niggers have had things your own way long enough and we white folks are going to have it our own way or kill all you Republican niggers.'"

Blacks persisted in voting despite the violence. E. A. Lever, a plantation owner, was astonished at their perseverance. "Why is it that niggers keep on tryin to raise above their station in life? Some of them are scared to death of night riders visiting their home. Yet even the most scared of them takes an interest in politics and other matters that don't concern him." The situation in Louisiana became so violent that Grant reluctantly sent federal troops into the state to restore order—an act for which he was severely criticized in the North.

Republicans shakily held on to their power in Louisiana as a tidal wave of white supremacy rolled over the South. Mississippi "redeemed" itself from Republican rule by terror and murder in 1875. This strategy, called the Mississippi Plan, was ruthlessly used with great effectiveness throughout the state. Hundreds of black schoolteachers, church leaders, and local Republican organizers were believed murdered. One man bragged that they were shooting blacks "just the same as birds." Governor Adelbert Ames called on President Grant for help. Southern whites were unconcerned. One official commented, "The . . . North satisfied us that if we succeeded winning control of the government of Mississippi, we would be permitted to enjoy it." His observation was correct.

President Grant refused to send troops to help the victims. He complained, "The whole public are tired out with these autumnal outbreaks in the South . . . and are ready now to condemn any interference on the part of the government."

On Election Day, Mississippi's whites either stuffed ballot boxes or destroyed them and drove black voters away from the polls or murdered them. Eighteen-year-old Ann Hedges's husband, Square, was one of the victims.

> They asked where Square was and I did not tell him. Then he said, "If you do not tell, I will shoot your Goddamned brains out." . . . Then they came into the house and turned back the bed and made him come out and called him a damned son of a bitch. They told him to put his shoes on, and I got them and said, I will put them on; and I could not tie them very well; and someone said "Let the God damned shoes be: he don't need any shoes." I put my brother's coat on him and they carried him before them. I never did find him for a week, until the next Saturday. The buzzards had eat his entrails; but the body down here was as natural as ever. His shoes were tied just as I had tied them.

Despite the fact that tens of thousands of blacks, with a few white supporters, tried valiantly to vote, the Democrats won easily. Mississippi was now controlled by white supremacists. Governor Ames, a Republican, commented, "a revolution has taken place—by force of arms—and a race are disfranchised—they are to be returned to a condition of serfdom—an era of second slavery."

By 1876, Democrats had regained control of every Southern state except Louisiana and North and South Carolina. In the state elections of 1876, they were determined to capture all three states. It was also a presidential election year. Both the Democratic candidate Samuel J. Tilden and the Republican candidate Rutherford B. Hayes made it clear that they were opposed to federal interference in Southern affairs.

While the contests in Louisiana and North Carolina would be close, the election in South

Carolina seemed safe for Republicans. Black voters were in the overwhelming majority. South Carolina also had a popular and honest white Republican governor, John Chamberlain, whom many Democrats were willing to support. Chamberlain reduced the state debt and defied black leaders in his party by removing many blacks from office and replacing them with whites. He blocked some political appointments favored by blacks and rooted out corrupt officials. So pleased were white Southerners with his actions that the *Charleston News and Courier* remarked, "If Governor Chamberlain continues to pursue the course he has done for the past twelve months, I think it would be exceedingly unwise and ungrateful for the Democratic Party to oppose his reelection."

Only in Edgefield County was there determined opposition. Whites, led by Martin W. Gary, set out to destroy the Republican Party in the same way that reactionary white Democrats in Mississippi had—by terror and violence. Gary's plan was simple. "Every Democrat should control the vote of one Negro by intimidation . . . argument has no effect on them. They can only be influenced by their fears."

A confrontation occurred on July 4 that gave Gary his opportunity. A black militia group drilling on a public road blocked the passage of two white farmers. A verbal confrontation took place before the whites were allowed to pass. General Matthew Butler, the most power-ful political figure in the area, ordered the militia to disband. They refused, and forty of the men, led by their commander, retreated to their armory. Butler led an attack against them. The commander was killed and twenty-five of his men were captured. Five black soldiers were taken into the woods in the early morning and executed in cold blood after they had surrendered. When the Northern press called for the guilty to be brought to justice, Ben Tillman, one of the members of the mob, ordered forty white shirts to be made and stained with wild berries to create the effect of blood. The mob then paraded "waving their bloody shirts" in defiance of the North. No one was convicted for the massacre. Tillman's group became known as the Red Shirts, and the organization spread throughout South Carolina and Georgia.

The murders polarized the state. Democrats who had thought of supporting the popular Republican governor could no longer do so. What turned many Democrats against Chamberlain was his criticism of the role of whites in the killings. Instead, Democrats chose Wade Hampton, once the wealthiest planter in the state and a Civil War hero, as their candidate.

In 1876, Rutherford B. Hayes was declared the winner of a controversial presidential campaign which he had lost in all probability. In order to gain Southern support for his claim, Hayes agreed to officially end Reconstruction.

Chamberlain also antagonized whites by refusing to send in troops to put down a strike in the low country rice plantations. Black workers went out on strike for higher wages and payment in cash rather than in company money that could be used only in company stores. The governor, needing every black vote he could get, refused to interfere, and the strikers won.

Democrats, unconcerned that the federal government would interfere in the election, had a free hand in terrorizing Republicans throughout the state. They formed rifle clubs and threatened to kill any blacks who voted.

On Election Day, Gary told his supporters to vote "early and often." Men from Georgia and North Carolina crossed the border and voted Democratic. Some claimed to have voted eighteen to twenty times despite the presence of federal troops. Violence was commonplace. Although blacks had a twenty-thousand-vote majority in the state, the Democrats declared themselves winners in a close race. Chamberlain refused to accept the results and claimed victory for himself. The same thing happened in Louisiana, where both Democrats and Republicans claimed the office of governor. Both turned to the President of the United States to resolve the dispute. The irony was that there was as much confusion in Washington as to who had been elected president.

A bitter presidential election campaign between Hayes and Tilden ended with Tilden the apparent winner. He was one electoral vote short of the number necessary to win. He had also two hundred thousand more popular votes. The final count of four states—Oregon, Louisiana, South Carolina, and Florida—was in dispute. The Democrats had won most local elections in the Southern states, but the Republicans still controlled the electoral boards. They cast their votes for Hayes, thereby giving him the election. Congressional Democrats threatened to block Hayes from taking office by filibustering in the Senate until Tilden was elected. Newspapers predicted that the country was again on the verge of civil war.

In reality, Southern Democrats were unconcerned about who would be President. Their interest was in home rule, the right to control their states—and blacks—as they saw fit. Needing Democratic support in Congress in order to become President, Hayes offered to end all federal interference in the South. One Republican official wrote, "I think the policy of the new administration will be to conciliate the white men of the South. Carpetbaggers to the rear and niggers take care of yourselves."

A bargain was made between Republicans and Southern Democrats, known as the Compromise of 1877. Enough Democrats agreed not to support a threatened filibuster in the Senate by Tilden's supporters that would have blocked Hayes from becoming President. In return the Republicans agreed to officially end Reconstruction. Hayes became President and recognized the Democratic governors of Louisiana and South Carolina over their Republican opponents.

On April 24, 1877, shortly after his inauguration, Hayes withdrew the last federal troops stationed in New Orleans. As they marched to the Mississippi River to board a steamboat and depart the South forever, Louisiana whites were jubilant. "Bells are chiming," reported one newspaper. "Guns, pistols, crackers and cannons are booming." Northerners were also glad that Reconstruction was put to rest. *The Nation* magazine, once a staunch supporter of black rights, editorialized, "The Negro will disappear from the field of national politics. Henceforth, the nation as a nation, will have nothing more to do with him."

Blacks sadly watched the celebrations. Some openly wept. Charles Harris, a black veteran, wrote, "We obey laws: others make them. We support state educational institutions whose doors are virtually closed to us. We support asylums and hospitals, and our sick, deaf, dumb or blind are met at the door by . . . unjust discriminations. From these and many other oppressions . . . we long to be free." Henry Adams, a black organizer for the Republican Party in Louisiana who had once been enslaved, protested, "The whole South had got into the hands of the very men who held us as slaves." Frederick Douglass cried out in rage against the Republican Party's betrayal of his people: "You have emancipated us. I thank you for it. You have enfranchised us. And I thank you for it. But what is your emancipation—what is your enfranchisement if the black man having been made free by the letter of the law, is unable to exercise that freedom? You have turned us loose to the sky, to the storm, to the whirlwind, and worst of all, you have turned us loose to our infuriated masters. What does it all amount to if the black man after having been freed from the slaveholder's lash is to be subject to the slaveholder's shotgun!"

★ ★ ★

In Tennessee, seventy-year-old Benjamin "Pap" Singleton had seen that Reconstruction would fail well before it officially ended. He knew that blacks would not escape the rule of the plantation and the white man's law without their own land. He journeyed to Kansas to see if

One of the main boosters of migration was Benjamin "Pap" Singleton. He organized several groups that migrated to colonies he founded in Kansas, one of which was named after him.

his people could find land there. "We needed land for our children," he later told a congressional committee. "That caused my heart to grieve and sorrow. . . . Pity for my race caused me to work for them. . . . Confidence is perished and faded away. We are going to leave the South." Singleton founded several colonies in Kansas, two of the most successful of which were Dunlap and Singleton's Colony. Another successful black colony, founded by emigrants from Kentucky, was Nicodemus.

To Henry Adams, the Compromise of 1877 signaled the failure of Reconstruction. Adams had risked his life for the Republican Party, successfully recruiting farmers to vote the Republican ticket. After Hayes's betrayal, he organized them to leave the South. He told a congressional committee, "So long as the white men of the South are going to kill us, there was no way that we could better our condition there. We said that the whole South had gotten into the very hands that held us as slaves. We felt we had almost been slaves under these men. Then we said there was no hope for us and we better go."

Adams had hoped to convince blacks to immigrate to Liberia. He did not believe that black people would be accepted in the United States. But Kansas had captured the black imagination. By 1879, Pap Singleton's vision of a mass exodus seemed to be coming true. Kansas had become the Promised Land for tens of thousands of African Americans, a place sacred to them because John Brown struck his first mighty blow against slavery there. God was in Kansas, and black people wanted to go where God was. George Ruby, a black journalist from New Orleans who supported the move, wrote, "The fiat to go forth is irresistible. It is a flight from present sufferings and wrongs to come. The ever present fear which haunts the minds of these our people in the turbulent parishes of the state is that slavery in the horrible form of peonage is approaching." C. P. Hicks in Texas described the anguish of his people in a letter to the governor: "There are no words that can fully express or explain the real condition of my people throughout the South, nor how keenly and deeply they feel the necessity of fleeing from the wrath and long pent-up hatred of their old masters, which they feel assured will ere long burst loose like the pent-up fires of a volcano and crush them if they remain here many years longer."

John Solomon Lewis and his family decided to join the exodus after being threatened by their landlord. "In a fit of madness I one day said to the man, 'It's no use, I works hard and raises big crops and you sells it and keeps the money, and brings me more and more in debt, so I will go somewhere else and try to make headway like white workingmen.' He got very mad and said to me: 'If you try that job, you will get your head shot away.' So I told my wife and she says, 'Let us take to the woods in the night time.' We took to the woods, my wife and four children, and we was three weeks living in the woods."

Although Singleton claimed he was responsible for the movement, in truth there were no leaders. Often people left in small groups, with a minister for spiritual guidance. One migrant said, "Every black man is his own Moses now." Another remarked, "We have found no leader to trust but the God overhead us." The exodusters, as they were called, saw themselves reenacting the exodus of the children of Israel. Whites were considered "Pharoah" and they the "children of Israel." Reaching St. Louis was like crossing over the "Red Sea."

Marching along, yes marching along. To Kansas we are bound.
Surely this must be the Lord that has gone before and opened the way.
Surely this is the time spoken of in history.
Farewell, dear friends, farewell.
Marching along, yes marching along
For Tennessee is a hard slavery state, and we find no friends in that country.
Marching along, yes we are marching along
We want peaceful homes and quiet firesides;
No one to disturb us or turn us out.

Sojourner Truth, who had dedicated her life to fighting slavery, was overjoyed at the exodus. "I have prayed so long that my people would go to Kansas and that God would make straight the way before them. I believe as much in that move as I do in the moving of the children of Egypt going out to Canaan. This colored people is going to be a people. Do you think God has them robbed and scourged all the days of their life for nothing?"

The journey was filled with danger and hardships. Planters, afraid of losing their labor, hunted migrants down and killed many who refused to return. They seized one man who returned to bring out his wife and family, cut off both his hands, and threw them in his wife's lap, saying, "Now go to Kansas and work."

Steamboats passed the exodusters by as they waited patiently along riverbanks for the boats to stop. Their faith that God would ultimately provide for them sustained them. When warned that many might die because they were ill prepared for the journey, one man replied, "In any battle, some soldiers must die."

Those who reached Kansas found that more hardships awaited them. One newspaper reported, "They landed in a cold drizzling rain which soon after turned into a raging storm. Not more than one in fifty had sufficient money to buy medicine with, while the appealing hungry eyes and pinched faces would have turned a heart of stone. Some 245 have died so far. They had expected to be received with open arms and placed immediately in government land, but in place of hospitality, they are met with coldness and distrust."

Although most African Americans supported the exodus, Frederick Douglass was critical: "As a stinging protest against high-handed, greedy and shameless injustice to the defenseless; as a means of opening the blind eye of oppressors to their folly and peril, the Exodus has done invaluable service. As a strategy however, it is a surrender as it would make freedom depend upon migration rather than protection. We cannot but regard the present agitation of an Exodus from the South as ill-timed and hurtful."

The praise for the movement outweighed the criticism. The *New York Times* reported, "It is time to acknowledge that the migration movement among the colored people of the South is one that in its essential spirit and quality must be honored by thoughtful lovers of liberty and progress." In the end, fewer than fifty thousand out of four million blacks living in the South attempted to migrate. And of those who left, many returned. Only a relative few found the promised land in Kansas of which so many dreamed. John Solomon Lewis was one.

"When I landed on the soil, I looked on the ground and I says, this is free ground. Then I looked on the heavens and I said, this is free and beautiful heavens. Then I looked within my heart and I says to myself, I wonder why I was never free before. I asked my wife did she know the grounds we stand on. She said, 'No!' I said it is free ground and she cried like a child for joy."

John Solomon Lewis was one of a fortunate few to gain his own land in Kansas. Most of the four million African Americans who remained in the South would be farmers who worked the white man's land on the white man's terms.

* * *

During Reconstruction, many planters deeply resented the independence shown by black farmers. At first, blacks could often dictate the conditions under which they would work because there was a shortage of workers in many areas, since blacks often migrated to areas where they could make a better living. Republicans passed laws to protect farmworkers from being cheated out of their wages. Planters were required to settle with workers before they could dismiss them. And farm laborers held the first lien on a crop. If a planter defaulted on his debts, his workers would receive the first money before the lenders.

Cotton was still the main crop. Since the South's farm economy was desperately short of money, cotton was the only source of credit. As a result, most farmers were trapped into a one-crop market economy. The self-sufficiency of independent small farmers rapidly disappeared. J. Pope Brown, a cotton farmer, explained, "We were poor, had nothing to go on, had no collateral, and we just had to plant the crop that would bring money right away." As a result, everybody grew cotton, and the overproduction forced the price down.

From this dependency, the sharecropping system evolved. Black (and white) farmers would work the white man's land for a share of the cotton crop. A farmer and his family would contract to grow cotton on a section of land belonging to a landowner. The landowner would supply the sharecropper with a house, animals, tools, and credit at a local store—which he often owned. The sharecropper would use the credit to supply himself and his family during the year with food, clothing, and other necessities. When the crop was sold, the farmer would receive a share of the revenue, from which his debt would be subtracted.

The more a sharecropper could bring to the landlord, the greater his share of the crop. If the farmer offered nothing but his labor, his share would be about a third. If he supplied his own animals or tools, or both, he might receive as much as half to two-thirds.

By the 1870s, variations of sharecropping were the dominant form of labor relations between blacks and whites. The system appeared to be a compromise between black farmers, who wanted to own land, and white planters, who wanted black labor. Black farmers seemed to have gained a certain degree of independence. The family worked their plot of land without daily supervision by their landlord.

But independence was often an illusion, as many sharecroppers became trapped in an endless cycle of debt under the credit system. The landlords and merchants, who were often one and the same, kept the books and charged extremely high prices for their goods. Interest rates could run between 50 and 200 percent. One sharecropper's wife explained, "The furnish man [storekeeper] would put you down in the book for 75 cents for a 50-cent item. Then he would add the interest. Anywhere from 25% to outrageous. So that 50-cent item would end up costing you a dollar or more at least. And that's if the merchant kept an honest book—which of course he didn't."

Some merchants charged sharecroppers for goods they never purchased. After the cotton was sold, many sharecroppers would find that they owed the landlords money for their purchases rather than receive a share of income. As one sharecropper put it, "You'd work all year and come up with five bales of cotton and the landlord would run the books up on you, and you'd come out with nothing." William Holtzclaw of Alabama, a sharecropper's son, remembered how at settlement time their landlord gave them their quarter share of the corn crop. When it came to dividing the five-hundred-pound bales of cotton, then selling at the high price of seventeen cents a pound, every bale went to the landlord. He explained that "they had done ate up their crop that year."

Trouble usually resulted if the tenant or sharecropper challenged the landlord. One farmer reported, "I know we been beat out of money. The landlord said I owe $400 at the beginning of the year. When I said, 'Suh?' he said, 'Don't you dispute my word; the books say so.' When the books say so, you better pay it too, or they will say, 'So, I'm a liar, heh?' You better take to the bushes if you dispute him, for he will string you up for that." One Louisiana farmer reported, "I lived on Joe Williams' place, about two miles southeast of Keachie. I asked Mr. Williams to pay what he owed me on my cotton. He jumped on me and beat me so badly I fear I cannot live. He made me crawl on my knees and call them my God, my master, all because I had asked for a settlement."

When Henry Adams, the Louisiana Republican organizer, tried to get farmers to bring charges against the landlords in court, they were reluctant to do so. "I saw many colored people swindled out of their crops. I led them into the light on how it was done. I told a great many of them to take their contracts to lawyers and get them to force the parties to a settlement, but they told me they were afraid they would get killed. Some few reported to court but were whipped when they went home."

Challenging a landlord could be fatal. Ned Cobb, an Alabama farmer, saw what happened to his neighbor Henry Kirkland and his son Emmet when they dared to question their landlord's accounts. When they presented their set of books to landlord Jasper Clay, "Mr. Clay didn't like that one bit," Cobb recalled. "He flew in a passion—he toted his pistol all the time—over that book business and throwed that pistol on old Uncle Henry and deadened him right there. So he killed the old man on the spot and he throwed his gun on Emmet and shot Emmet through the lung."

William Holtzclaw, son of a black farmer, knew of one black sharecropper who successfully sued. At the trial, the landlord presented his books showing that the sharecropper had received certain items that year. He was confident of victory, because he knew that his sharecropper was illiterate and the jury would be all white. The sharecropper then presented his "books" to the court in the form of a stick that he had bent into the shape of a hexagon. The stick was filled with notches he had cut, organized in such a way that one set represented the purchases that he made and another set the day he purchased it. The jury was so intrigued by his ingenious method that they voted in his favor.

By the end of Reconstruction, blacks were working as sharecroppers on the white man's land, receiving a share of the cotton crop when sold. But most blacks were cheated out of their rightful share and wound up working for nothing.

Since it was dangerous to confront their landlords directly, African Americans protested with humor. In one joke, a black farmer brings in six bales of cotton to a planter and asks for his settlement. The planter examines the books and says, "Well, Josh, looks like you came out dead even again this year." Josh says, "Well, I got two more bales outside still." The landlord angrily throws down his pen. "Damn your ass! Why didn't you say so. Now I got to figure the books all over to make you come out even again." Songs expressed the frustration blacks experienced:

> Our father, who is in heaven
> White man owe me eleven, pay me seven
> Thy kingdom come, thy will be done.
> If I hadn't took that, I woulda had none.

Although it was rare for a black farmer to own land in the rich cotton areas of the South like the Mississippi Delta, thousands of blacks did purchase farms in less desirable areas. Daniel Trotter, a sharecropper in Louisiana, kept an account of how he and his wife saved money penny by penny to buy a farm. His wife would sell dozens of eggs at a time for $5.30 and earn an additional $7.80 from sewing dresses. The family sold four pigs. They earned $70.22 from their share of a cotton crop. He also worked as a repairman, fixing clocks, machinery, and guns. At the end of a year, the family had saved more than $200 and bought a farm. In Texas, Charley and Lucille White purchased a farm for $350. "The house wasn't more than a shack," he later recalled. "Lucille and me always worked hard, both of us. We hadn't ever minded work. But it looks like when we got some land that belonged to us, it just set us on fire. We didn't seem to get half as tired, or if we did we didn't notice it. One day when we was cleaning up the field, Lucille said, 'You know Charley, even the rocks look pretty.'"

The middle ground between sharecropping and owning was tenancy. Blacks would rent farms from year to year, either paying in cash or in bales of cotton. Tenancy was risky, because if the tenant failed to pay his rent, the landlord could take all his possessions. Ned Cobb had seen his father destroyed that way. "They claimed they had a note against him and took all he had. Took his horse and wagon, went into his pen and took his fattened hogs he was raising for his family. They did that because it was out of the knowledge of the colored man exactly how you was subject to the laws. They was a great dark secret to him. Whenever the colored man grew too fast, they'd find a way to cut him down."

Jerry and Addie Holtzclaw began their working lives as sharecroppers. Their son William recalled that their landlord was one of those "gentlemen of the Old South" who had lost most of his wealth during the war, his wealth having consisted mostly of slaves. Since the Holtz-claws had neither tools nor animals, the landlord supplied everything and took three-quarters of the crop. William began working when he was four years old, riding a blind mule while one of his brothers held the plow. He never forgot the "excruciating pain" of hunger he and his brother suffered while his mother worked until midnight as a cook in the landlord's house.

> I remember how at night we would often cry for food until falling here and there on the floor we would sob ourselves to sleep. Late at night, sometimes after midnight, mother would return home with . . . a variety of scraps from the white folks' table; waking us all she would place the pan on the floor, or on her knees, and . . . we would eat to our satisfaction. We used our hands and sometimes, in our haste dived head foremost into the pan, very much as pigs after swill. Sometimes our pet pig would come in. We never made any serious objections to dividing with him and I do not recall that he showed any resentment about dividing with us.

Knowing that they could not gain a foothold in life as sharecroppers, in the early 1880s, Jerry Holtzclaw managed to rent forty acres of land around Roanake County, Alabama. On credit he bought a mule, a horse, and a yoke of oxen. His only obligation was to pay his rent (three bales of cotton, worth about $150) at the end of the year and make payments on his debt. Work that had been drudgery to Holtzclaw on their landlord's farm was now a delight on their own land. "I remember when he announced this plan to us children we were so happy at the prospects of owning a wagon and a pair of mules, and of having only a father for boss, that we shouted and leaped for joy."

Life was still hard for the family, even though they had moved up in the world. Perhaps the largest burden fell on Holtzclaw's mother. She had to watch over the children when they were young, prepare all the meals, fetch water from the well or a stream, help feed the animals, work in the fields, take care of the house, and make and mend clothes. Usually she was up before the rest of the family to prepare breakfast and went to bed after everyone else.

Despite the energy and enthusiasm of the Holtzclaw family, disaster plagued them. As Ned Cobb observed, "all God's dangers aren't white men." One of the oxen broke its neck. A mule got a disease called the hooks and died, forcing young William to replace it. He pulled the plow while his sister held the plow handles.

The second year, conditions seemed to improve. By August, the family's corn crop—the source of their profit—was ready for picking. Everyone toiled from dawn to dark Friday and Saturday to pick the ripe, golden ears and pile them on the field to gather on Sunday, but Addie Holtzclaw forbade them to do so. "Sunday is the Lord's day," she said, "and must be kept holy." The corn could wait until Monday.

While the family was in church on Sunday morning, storm clouds suddenly gathered. Thunder roared, lightning flashed, and sheets of torrential rains drowned the fields. Rushing home after the storm ended, the Holtzclaws arrived in time to watch their corn crop swept down a swollen creek.

As the family held on for two more years, tragedies continued. Everyone was stricken by a slow, lingering, mysterious fever. Unable to afford a doctor, they stumbled about as best they could, receiving some help from neighbors. Lola, Holtzclaw's older sister and "the most beloved member of the family," died. After her death, young Holtzclaw saw his grieving father "pray his first prayer before the family altar."

Although the Holtzclaws eventually lost everything and were forced to return to share-cropping, they were determined that their children should escape their fate by getting an education. Jerry and Addie Holtzclaw had already organized their fellow sharecroppers to build a schoolhouse for their children. Building the school was the easy part; getting there was difficult. William Holtzclaw later described how his mother had outfoxed the landlord. "The landlord wanted us to pick cotton. But mother wanted me to remain in school. So she used to outgeneral him by hiding me behind skillets, ovens and pots. Then she would slip me to school the back way, pushing me through the woods and underbrush, until it was safe for me to travel alone. Whereupon she would return to the plantation and try to make up to the landlord for the work of us in the cotton field."

The children suffered physical hardship to go to school. "The schoolhouse was three miles from my home and we walked every day, my little sister carrying me when my legs gave out," William later wrote. "When there was school in the winter, I went with bare feet and scant clothing. My feet cracked and bled freely."

As the children grew older and their labor was needed in the field, the brothers took turns working and going to school. "One day I plowed and he went to school; the next he plowed and I went to school. What he learned during the day, he taught me at night and I did the same for him."

Rural schools were extremely limited. In Holtzclaw's school, "As soon as a pupil could spell 'abasement' in the old blue-back speller, they were made assistant teachers." Eventually they became teachers, with the best of them having advanced only as far as the fourth grade.

Holtzclaw knew that if he stayed with his family, he would lead the dead-end life of a sharecropper. But he could see that his father was broken in spirit and needed his help.

On Christmas Day, 1889, Holtzclaw's father called William to sit with him by an old oak tree in their front yard to give him the greatest Christmas gift he could—his freedom. "Son, you are nearing manhood," he said, "and you have no education. If you remain with me until you are twenty-one, I will not be able to help you. For these reasons, your mother and I have decided to set you free, provided you make one promise—you will educate yourself."

Holtzclaw promised. He left home to find work until he could go to school. Six months later, he came across a little newspaper published by a school called Tuskegee Normal and Industrial Institute, located in the town of Tuskegee, Alabama. In it was the following invitation: "There is an opportunity for a few able-bodied young men to make their way through school, provided they are willing to work. Applications should be made to Booker T. Washington, principal."

Holtzclaw scribbled a note. "Dear Book, I want an ejurcashun, Can I come?" He addressed the envelope to Booker T. Washington with just his name and no town address. Somehow the letter reached its destination. Washington replied. "Come," he said.

Several months later, Holtzclaw arrived. To a young man who had known only a sharecropper's life in the backcountry of Alabama, Tuskegee Institute seemed like paradise. "When I walked out on campus I was startled at what I saw. There before my eyes was a huge pair of mules drawing a machine plow which to me at that time was a mystery. To the rear was a sawmill turning out thousands of feet of lumber daily. There were girls cultivating flowers and boys erecting huge brick buildings. Some were hitching horses and driving carriages while others were milking cows and making cheese. I found some boys studying drawing and others hammering iron, each with an intense earnestness that I had never seen in young men."

Holtzclaw was soon to encounter the man who would become the best-known black man in America—Booker T. Washington.

Chapter 3

New Roads Taken, 1880–1890

In the early 1870s, sixteen-year-old Booker T. Washington, consumed with a passion for education, was determined to study at the then famous school for black youth—Hampton Normal and Agricultural Institute in Hampton, Virginia. Starting out from Malden, West Virginia, he began his five-hundred-mile journey to Hampton, with only part of the route covered by train. When the train reached the end of the line, Washington rode a stagecoach until his money ran out, then began walking and hitching rides on wagons. By the time he reached Richmond, Virginia, he was broke, filthy, and exhausted and still had a hundred miles to go. After crawling underneath an elevated sidewalk, Washington curled up and went to sleep as pedestrians walked above his head. The next day, he found work as a longshoreman. He bought food but continued to sleep under the sidewalk to save money to finish his journey to Hampton.

Hampton Institute was a model for the educational philosophy that would soon dominate Southern education for blacks. Hampton, established by the Freedmen's Bureau in 1869, was run by General Samuel Chapman Armstrong, a Union general with strong Southern attitudes about African Americans. A handsome man with a commanding presence, Armstrong had been one of the youngest Union generals in the Civil War. His self-imposed mission was to train black students to accommodate to Southern whites economically, politically, and socially, and to regard them as their natural superiors. Hampton was a "normal school," something between an intermediate and high school. Its graduates were trained to teach rural children proper work habits and low-level menial skills.

Hampton's teachers were white, and many were Southerners and ex-slaveholders. Segregation was the rule. One black visitor invited to a concert observed, "The rudest and most ignorant white men and women were politely escorted to the platform; respectable and intelligent colored ladies and gentlemen were shown lower seats where they could neither hear nor see the exercises . . . with any pleasure."

Many black students attended Hampton to learn a trade that they hoped would prepare them for the world as teachers and workers. Instead, they found themselves doing menial, often meaningless work, ten hours a day, six days a week. Male students worked on the farm, in the sawmill, and in the kitchens and pantries. They washed dishes, waited tables, and served as houseboys and painters. Women sewed, washed, ironed, cooked, and mended. The objective of these jobs, Armstrong said, "Is not to teach a trade but to get the work done." He wanted his students to love work for its own sake, no matter how demeaning the task. "If you are the right sort of man, you will engage in any sort of labor and dignify it. A man had better work for nothing than spend his time in idling and loafing . . . plow, hoe, ditch; do anything rather than nothing."

Critics like Bishop Henry Turner, an outstanding black clergymen and leader in Georgia, charged that Armstrong's philosophy would teach black youth to excel in the cornfields rather than in the classrooms. One visitor to Hampton observed, "The prime motive of the white men in the South who urge most strongly industrial education of the Negroes is the conviction in their mind that all the Negro needs to know is how to work . . . that the race is doomed to servitude."

In 1881, Booker T. Washington, then in his twenties, arrived in the town of Tuskegee, Alabama, to found a school for black students—and become a legend.

One argument Armstrong offered in defense of his educational philosophy was that there were few skilled jobs for blacks. In the cities, most blacks held unskilled jobs as hotel workers, drivers, porters, construction laborers, servants, and barbers.

As far as Booker T. Washington was concerned, Hampton was paradise and General Armstrong was God. Armstrong became the dominant figure in his life. "I shall always remember that the first time I went into his presence he made the impression upon me of a perfect man. I was made to feel that there was something about him that was superhuman."

Washington maintained his hero worship of Armstrong and his philosophy throughout his life. "At Hampton, I not only learned that it was not a disgrace to labor, but to learn to love labor, not alone for its financial value, but for labor's own sake, and for the independence and self-reliance which the ability to do something the world wants brings."

By 1879, Washington was teaching at Hampton when General Armstrong called him aside after chapel. He said he had received a letter from some "gentlemen in Alabama" asking him to recommend a white principal for a black school they wanted to open there. The letter came from Tuskegee.

Tuskegee was a town of approximately two thousand people located in Macon County. It consisted of plantation houses owned by wealthy landowners, a number of one- and two-story businesses, and a courthouse around which local people, black and white, gathered in racially separate groups. The town was famous for its marathon domino games that lasted from ten-thirty in the morning until six at night.

By the 1880s, whites were fearful that blacks might leave Macon County and join the exodusters. In 1881, the *Tuskegee News,* a local white paper, reported that Macon had lost more population than any other county in the state.

One way whites decided to keep blacks in the community was by agreeing to start a school for black students. A school could also prove an economic boost to a community that was financially hurting. One of the white leaders of the community wrote to General Armstrong at the Hampton Institute, asking him to recommend a white principal for the school. Armstrong replied: "The only man I can suggest is one Booker T. Washington, a graduate of this institution, a very competent, capable mulatto, clear-headed, modest, sensible, polite and a thorough teacher and superior man. The best man we ever had here."

One week later, a telegram arrived, which Armstrong proudly read to the whole school: "Booker T. Washington will suit us. Send him at once."

The campus of Tuskegee consisted of a rundown building and some sheds. From these humble beginnings, Washington created an educational empire.

* * *

When Booker T. Washington first arrived at Tuskegee, he was favorably impressed by the town but somewhat dismayed by the school itself. "Before going to Tuskegee, I had expected to find there a building and all the necessary apparatus ready for me to begin teaching. I found nothing of the kind. I did find, though, hundreds of hungry, earnest souls who wanted to secure knowledge."

The "buildings" consisted of a shanty that was to be used as a classroom and an assembly room provided by a nearby church. The shanty roof was so leaky that a pupil had to hold an umbrella over Washington's head while he taught. His rooming house was no better. On rainy days, the landlady also held an umbrella over his head while he ate breakfast.

To start a school with only a rundown building, a small amount of land, and limited funding was challenge enough. An even greater challenge was winning the confidence of the local white community. Although they had agreed to permit a black school to exist in their midst, Tuskegee's whites were still wary of blacks being educated. They felt that education might bring trouble between the races. Their greatest fear was that once blacks were educated, they would no longer work as sharecroppers on the white man's farm or as domestics in his house. But Washington had a genius for reassuring whites that his method of education for blacks would "not be out of sympathy with agricultural life." The school would benefit the white community by teaching blacks to be better farmers and better domestics. In time, Tuskegee's whites became its staunchest supporters and, as Washington liked to call them, "friends."

Washington taught his students how to make bricks, and with those bricks, how to build a building. His emphasis was on teaching vocational skills, but Tuskegee also offered basic academic courses.

On July 4, 1881, Washington officially opened Tuskegee with what he described as thirty "anxious and earnest students," many of whom were already public school teachers. Some were forty years old. Washington was the only teacher. As word of the school spread, other teachers and students began to arrive. All were mature men and women; some were quite elderly. His plan was to train most of his students to be teachers. In turn, they would return to their rural communities and teach the people how to "put new energy and new life into farming," as well as uplift the moral, intellectual, and religious life of the people.

With local white support behind him and his growing ability to secure loans and credit, Washington turned to constructing a new building that would enable him to carry out his goals. He borrowed money to acquire land and mobilized his students, with much grumbling on their part, to clear it. Meanwhile, he recruited local people, black and white, to make donations. Whites donated eating utensils; Hampton Institute sent maps, books, and newspapers; and the students made their own blackboards, chairs, and desks. Blacks contributed labor, supplies, funds, and food. One man who had no money contributed a large hog at a fund-raising meeting. He announced, "Any nigger that's got any love for the race, or respect for himself, will bring a hog to the next meeting."

Washington had plans to have the students construct the buildings and, by doing this, learn the required construction skills. He envisioned a school that would teach students everything from sewing, cooking, and housekeeping for girls to farming, carpentry, printing, and brickmaking for boys.

Washington thought that once they had a kiln to fire bricks and the right kind of clay, his students could easily learn how to make them. He discovered how wrong he was. Washington and about a hundred students had to wallow in the muck of a mud pit with water and dirt up to their knees in order to scoop out the clay. Several students quit in disgust. The others molded twenty-five thousand bricks with a mixture of clay and sun-dried soil and then fired them in the kiln. But the bricks were not baked at the proper temperature and dissolved into powder and fragments of clay. Washington started over again. When the second and third kilns failed to work properly, many students and teachers were disillusioned and wanted to quit. Washington refused. He was determined to succeed. As far as he was concerned, far more than bricks was at stake. "I knew that we were trying an experiment—that of testing whether or not it was possible for Negroes to build up and control the affairs of a large educational institution. I knew that if we failed it would injure the whole race. I knew that the presumption was against us . . . I felt that people would be surprised if we succeeded. All this made a burden which pressed down upon us, sometimes it seemed, at the rate of a thousand pounds per inch."

Lacking money for a fourth kiln, Washington pawned his cherished gold watch to raise fifteen dollars. The last attempt succeeded and was seen as a sign that the school would succeed.

For Washington, personal hygiene was as important as any book knowl-

In his early years at Tuskegee, Washington worked alongside his students in order to set an example. His goal was to teach them the dignity of labor.

edge. "In all my teaching, I have watched carefully the influence of the toothbrush and I am convinced that there are few single agencies of civilization that are more far-reaching." He knew that he had to change his students' behavior and personal habits as well as educate them. He had traveled around the countryside visiting the homes and schools of local black people and was shocked by the conditions he found. Many families of twelve or more lived in one-room homes. Their main diet was fatback and beans and they had little or no sense of personal hygiene. Washington quickly came to the conclusion that he would have to model Tuskegee on Hampton.

To take the children of such people I had been among for a month and to give them a few hours of book education, I feel would be almost a waste of time. . . . We wanted to teach the students how to bathe; how to care for their teeth and clothing. We wanted to teach them what to eat and how to eat it properly, and how to care for their rooms. Aside from this we wanted to give them such a practical knowledge of some one industry, together with the spirit of thrift, industry and economy, that they would be sure of knowing how to make a living when they left us. We wanted them to study actual things instead of mere books alone.

Washington preached what he called "the gospel of the toothbrush." One student recalled, "If Booker had what the young fellows now call a bug, it was keeping clean. Next to a liar, he hated a dirty man or woman worse than anything else in the world."

Margaret Clifford, Washington's granddaughter, who was born after Washington had died, understood why cleanliness was so important to her grandfather.

Many of the students who came to Tuskegee from homes in rural areas in Macon County, and the South, and elsewhere, wherever they came from, never had the kind of even hygiene teaching that was emphasized in Tuskegee. One student when he went to Hampton, he did not know what to do with two sheets. There were two sheets on the bed, and the first night he slept on top of them, the next night underneath both of them until he noticed that some people were sleeping between the two. And that's how he learned what the two sheets were for. There were students who came there who'd never seen a toothbrush. These were the kinds of character, hygiene, personal things that a parent would teach a child, and this was the way Booker Washington approached students, as a parent would to help his child learn the necessary things of life so that he could find his place in the world among other people.

Another student, William Gregory, was deeply impressed. "Well, that first class was wonderful. We just knew nothin' worth knowin'. All most of us had was strength and we wanted to learn. Booker just overhauled us. I think of how proud we boys were to have one of us, who had been to college, come back to teach us. How our hearts swelled with the feeling that some day we would do likewise. . . ."

Washington's goal was to have Tuskegee train teachers to work in rural areas, teaching children moral values, personal hygiene, self-discipline, and the virtues of work. "My plan was for them to see not only the utility of labor but its beauty and dignity. They would be taught how to lift labor up from drudgery and toil and would learn to love work for its own sake. We wanted them to return to the plantation districts and show people there how to put new energy and new ideas into farming as well as the intellectual and moral and religious life of the people."

Other teachers strongly believed that education of blacks required more than acquiring good habits of hygiene and work. "What we need are race leaders, not followers," said Lucy Laney, an African-American Georgia educator. Her goal was to develop the minds of students rather than their hands.

Mary McLeod Bethune was an outstanding black teacher who encouraged her students to serve their communities. Women teachers played a major role in helping young people overcome the demoralization suffered under Jim Crow.

In 1887, Lucy Laney opened the Haines School in Augusta, Georgia. Students studied English, mathematics, history, chemistry, physics, psychology, sociology, French, and German. Laney's mission was to turn out a generation of women teachers and community leaders who would be the regenerative force in the African-American community and the source of its salvation. "The educated Negro woman, the woman of character and culture, is needed in the schoolroom, not only in the kindergarten and primary school, but in the high school and the college. Not alone in the classroom but as a public lecturer she may give advice and knowledge that will change a whole community and start its people on the upward way."

During the 1880s, an increasing number of black women graduated from schools built and financed by churches. They were motivated by the desire to enter teaching, the only profession then available to them, to help uplift their people. With ten pupils in an abandoned cotton gin house, Emma J. Wilson, a graduate of Scotia College, opened a school in Mayesville, South Carolina. She accepted eggs, chicken, and produce as tuition. After three years of fund-raising, the school had five hundred pupils—and hundreds of chickens and thousands of eggs.

Local people also constructed schools, contributed food, boarded teachers, and gave money when they could. One elderly black woman wrote, "Deer fesser, plese accept this 18 cents it is all i have. i save it out of my washing this week. god will bless you. Send you more next week." A teacher noted in her diary, "Aunt Hester gave a pound of butter and a dime. Grandma Williams a chicken. Effie McCoy, a cake and five cents; Bessie Harvey a dress."

While many rural black students only received a rudimentary education, some teachers and communities made a major effort to give their children the best education they could afford under the circumstances. In the nineteenth century, few children received more than a fourth-grade education.

Teachers had to be imaginative and resourceful to compensate for the lack of supplies. Young women taught students everything from baking cakes and canning peaches to the Declaration of Independence and the Constitution. To the three Rs of reading, 'riting, and 'rithmetic, they added a fourth—race pride. They used ingenuity to compensate for the lack of books, maps, paper, and pencils. One teacher, denied by the local school board an American flag for her classroom, fashioned her own. "We had students draw the National Flag on the blackboard. These flags were assigned a place of honor on the board and became a permanent picture in the room for years. Pupils were careful not to erase the flag when they erased the blackboard."

Many pupils never forgot their teachers. In Promised Land, South Carolina, an all-black community unique in that many families owned their own land, Lizzie Chiles, a legendary teacher, taught them how to survive in a hostile world. Mary Charles, a former student, remembered, "Mrs. Chiles was the best teacher I had. She was a precious lamb, that woman. When she taught you something, it was right. Lizzie Chiles taught the children history and geography. Most important she taught us mathematics so when we dealt with the white man, we wouldn't be cheated. I still remember the way she taught us. If a man was going to plant an acre of corn, and he could plow twenty-five rows to the acre, and have fifty mounds in each row, with three kernels of corn in each mound, how many kernels of corn did he need to plant an acre of land in corn? 3,750!"

In many communities, churches offered Sabbath schools where children were taught on Sundays to read, write, and spell. They ran children's day programs in which such topics as "Does God Favor Education?" and "Who is the True Man and the True Woman?" were discussed as a means of reinforcing values of self-help, race pride, and community solidarity.

Benjamin Mays, a sharecropper's son who was born in a shack in the town of Ninety-Six, South Carolina, and who would go on to become president of Morehouse College and deeply influence Martin Luther King, Jr., recalled how the community supported his desire to learn. When he was nine, he gave a presentation to the congregation in his church's school. "After my recitation, the house went wild. Old women waved their handkerchiefs, old men stomped their feet, and the people applauded long and loud. It was a terrific experience for a nine-year-old boy. There were predictions I would go places in life. The people in the church did not contribute one dime to help me with my education. But they gave me something far more valuable. They gave me encouragement, the thing I most needed. They expressed such confidence in me that I always felt that I could never betray their trust, never let them down."

To help overcome illiteracy, black colleges throughout the South required their students to teach in rural areas during the summer. One Fisk student taught in a Tennessee school before he left to earn his Ph.D. at Harvard. His name was William Edward Burghardt Du Bois. He later recorded his experiences in his book *The Souls of Black Folk.*

The school house was a log hut. There was an entrance where a door once was. Great chinks between the logs served as windows. Furniture was scarce—rough plank benches without backs and at times without legs. There they sat, nearly thirty of them on rough benches, their faces shading from a pale cream to a dark brown, their eyes full of mischief, and the hands grasping Webster's blue-black spelling book. I loved my school and the fine faith the children had in the wisdom of their teacher was truly marvelous. We read and spelled together, wrote a little, picked flowers, sang and listened to stories of the world beyond. There were some whose appetites were whetted by school and their half-wakened thought and weak wings beat against their barriers—barriers of caste, of youth, of life; at last, in dangerous moments, against everything that opposed even a whim.

Although literacy in the black community steadily increased, by the turn of the century only about one-third of the more than two million black children between the age of five and fourteen in the South attended school. There were no school buildings, teachers, or books for them. In 1890, out of 804,000 black children of high school age, 958 were in public high schools and some 20,000 in private schools. In many black schools, there was only one teacher for every ninety-three schoolchildren; white schools averaged one teacher for every fifty-seven students. The average annual expenditure in Mississippi was $14.94 for each white student and $1.86 for each black student.

Alabama tenant farmer Ned Cobb, who never went to school, saw how whites tried to undermine black education. "Weren't no colored schools here worth no count. The white schools would be all floatin' along, runnin' on schedule, colored schools standin' waiting for a class to open. When the colored did start school, we had to supplement the money the state give us with our own money. Some schools wouldn't run over a month or two months, then they'd send word, 'Close the school down! Close the school down! Money's out! Money's out!'"

For many black people, education became a dead end. "Once I was a great believer in Negro education . . . but now I doubt whether it's good or not. You educate your children— then watcha gonna do? You got jobs for them? You got any businesses for them to go into? What's the use of learning to be a bookkeeper if you got no books to keep? Do you think they're going to be content to come back and live in a lil' one-room house wid no electric lights. No! Education changed their tastes; they got to have better things."

Education was a luxury many black men could not afford. To escape the trap of sharecropping, they wandered in search of work in logging and turpentine camps, levees and railroads.

By the 1880s, thousands of men, despairing of earning a living on the land or gaining a meaningful education, were wandering the countryside seeking jobs in work camps and mines scattered throughout the South. They gathered turpentine in Georgia and Mississippi, mined phosphate off the Florida coast, cut timber and sawed lumber in Texas, and built levees alongside women workers in Arkansas and Louisiana. They dug coal in Alabama, Tennessee, and West Virginia and worked on railroads all over the South. There was a crude democracy in some work camps where black and white men worked together. In some industries, they received equal pay. Even though they socialized separately, occasionally interracial bonds developed. Their hard labor and common exploitation united them even as race divided them. They even united to revolt against their exploitation. In the sugarcane parishes of Louisiana, black and white sugarcane cutters went on strike in 1888 for higher wages. Planters broke the strike by massacring more than one hundred black workers in the town of Thibodaux. Black and white miners struck in Tennessee to protest the use of convict labor to replace them in the mines. Twice the state sent in convict labor and twice the miners freed them until the state backed down.

The wandering workers were "masterless men," not attached to the land, or beholden to landlords. Their presence often terrified whites, who feared any strange black man. One white man noted, "In all communities, there are Negroes of whom none knows the coming, going or real names. The Negroes are restive, the whites apprehensive and both are growing more and more suspicious. Such a status is already half hostile even before an overt act is committed."

Whites minimized their fear by maximizing their control. Police arrested unemployed men without cause, charging them as vagrants or falsely accusing them of crimes. Judges passed down extremely harsh sentences. Blacks received far more severe sentences than whites for the same crime. In some states, whites received two years for stealing a cow, blacks five. Whites were sentenced to five years for burglary, blacks twelve to forty.

Most blacks were sent to convict lease camps, which were organized on a deadly combination of racism and profit. Owners of mines, plantations, railroads, and other industries would contract with the state to lease the labor of men sentenced to jail. The prisoners would then be sent to work camps where they would work six to seven days a week from "can't see" to "can't see"—before dawn until after dark. They cleared snake and alligator swamps, dug coal in gas-filled mines, built railroads, and gathered turpentine in hundred-degree heat. Men were worked fourteen hours a day six to seven days a week in conditions that one convict described as "nine kinds of hell." In some camps, men were chained for days in knee-deep pools of muck, their thirst forcing them to drink the water in which they were compelled to deposit their excrement. The men ate and slept on bare ground, without blankets and mattresses and often without clothes. Beatings never ceased. On one plantation farm, a man was given ten lashes for "slow hoeing," five for "sorry planting." Those who tried to escape and were captured were whipped until the blood ran. One guard chillingly commented, "Kill a nigger . . . get another." Another described the punishment that one man received for an infraction of the rules:

Whipcords were fastened around his thumbs, the loose ends flung over a convenient limb and made taut until his toes swung clear of the ground. The scared convicts watched their comrade as he writhed and yelled expecting every moment that the cords would be unfastened and his agony ended. **B**ut the captain had determined to make an example and he let the negro hang. The poor wretch's agony was a hideous thing to see. They say his muscles knotted into cramps under the strain. **H**is eyes started from his head and sweat ran down from his body in streams. **A**n hour passed—then two. **H**is shrieks had ceased and his struggles grown feeble, so they let him down and he fell like a log—dead.

Sometimes housed in rolling iron cages like those used for circus animals, fed the worst food, denied medical treatment, men died from malaria, scurvy, frostbite, sunstroke, dysentery, snakebite, shackle poisoning, and murder by violent and sadistic guards. At a time when more than a hundred men a year were lynched, thousands died in convict lease camps. Convict leasing, one former government official said, was a death sentence. George Washington Cable, a Southern writer, investigated several camps and found that though many men had sentences longer than ten years, no one survived a camp more than ten years. Death rates in some camps were as high as 45 percent, seldom below 15. In the North, the death rate was about 1 percent.

Many young children as well as adults were sent to work on convict lease gangs for misdemeanors or simply because their labor was needed. Some children were sentenced to as long as twenty years for a relatively minor crime.

In the convict lease camps, the slightest misdemeanor could be punished with great severity.

One prisoner described his condition: "We leave the cells at 3 o'clock AM and return at 8 PM, going the distance of three miles through rain and snow. We go to cell wet, go to bed wet and arise wet the following morning and every guard knocking beating yelling and every day Some one of us were carried to our last resting place, the grave. Day after day we looked death in the face and was afraid to speak."

Inspection reports often described the horror of the camps. The Mississippi Board of

Health reported, "Most of them have their backs cut in great wales, scars and blisters, some of the skin peeling off as a result of the severe beatings. They were lying there dying, so poor and emaciated that their bones almost came through their skin. We actually saw live vermin crawling over their faces."

Children were not exempt. Twelve-year-old Cy Williams was sentenced to twenty years on a convict lease gang for taking a horse he was too small to ride. Eight-year-old Will Evans received two years for stealing change off a store counter. And Mary Gay was sentenced to thirty days for taking a hat. She was six years old.

By the turn of the century, an estimated twenty thousand to thirty thousand African Americans, one quarter of whom were children, were condemned to hard labor in convict lease camps. Convict leasing had become slavery's replacement. To supply the demand for convict labor, sheriffs arrested blacks for misdemeanors and vagrancy.

For some men in the convict camps, a quick death was better than a slow one. They attempted to escape, knowing they would probably be killed. But they also knew that if they escaped the dogs and the guards, they could count on help from the black community. Many black farmers hid, fed, and clothed escaped convicts, breaking and burying their chains. To help a black man to freedom was a victory over their oppressors.

* * *

Oppression and the imposition of segregation laws did not come all at once to the South. In the 1880s, the situation was still fluid in many areas. While the rural South was noted for its increasingly harsh rule, the cities still offered possibilities for a better life for African Americans. T. McCants Stewart, a black journalist who had left South Carolina to live in Boston, returned for a visit to his native state. He was ready to fight anyone who tried to discriminate against him. "I put a chip on my shoulder and dared any man to knock it off." Stewart was astonished to find that he was accepted wherever he went. He sat wherever he wanted on streetcars and trains. "I entered a dining room as bold as a lion. The whites at the table appeared not to have noted my presence. I can go into saloons and get refreshments even as in New York. I can stop in and drink a glass of soda and be more politely waited on than in New England."

Everywhere Stewart went he saw encouraging signs of racial harmony. The two races worked and lived side by side and debated with one another in debating societies. Working-class blacks and whites often socialized in bars, brothels, gambling dens, and sporting events. He even witnessed a black policeman arrest a white man.

What impressed Stewart in South Carolina was that African Americans voted and were still appointed to minor offices. Public schools for children of both races were functioning. African Americans had their own churches, social clubs, and fraternal organizations. These achievements led Stewart to conclude that the ideals of emancipation were being fulfilled. "If you should ask me, 'watchmen what tell of the night,' I would say, 'The morning light is breaking.'"

As an urban South emerged, bursting with economic and cultural energy, tens of thousands of young black and white people began to migrate to the cities, drawn by their energy. Promoters called it the New South to distinguish it from the South of slavery days. A new breed of Southerner had emerged, ambitious, entrepreneurial, enamored of Northern capital and industrial change. Compared to the North, the South was still in the backwaters of the Industrial Revolution. But the railroads were bringing new ideas, new products, new people, and new opportunities.

Seeing a city for the first time was an experience many rural African Americans like young Henry Proctor never forgot. "When we reached the hill that gave us a full view of the city, such a thrill passed over me as I had never felt before. All at once a vision rose before me. Such a bewilderment of houses, steeples, cupolas; such a commotion of people and vehicles—such a labyrinth of streets."

Many families, like that of Walter Pickens, came to build a better life and to see that their children received an education. In the country, the Pickens children could go to school only six weeks a year. In the town, six months.

The Pickens and the Proctor families were entering into a small but rising urban middle class that embraced Victorian family values: patriarchal authority, feminine modesty, moral rectitude, thrift, hard work, and temperance. Some African Americans hoped, often in vain, that shared values between the "better class" of whites and blacks might mitigate racism. Businessmen played an increasingly important leadership role in the life of the community. They provided a variety of services from construction and catering to barbershops and funeral parlors. The *Richmond Planet* boasted, "Once the black man had no lawyers, doctors, theologians, scientists, authors, editors, druggists, inventors, businessmen, legislators, sheriffs. . . . He has them now."

Women formed missionary societies and benevolent associations and cared for the orphaned young, the poor, the widowed, and the elderly. They formed sewing circles, literary groups, and community-reform groups. They created a cultural world of poetry readings, theater, and classical music concerts. Men joined fraternal organizations and formed military companies, baseball teams, and volunteer fire companies.

As separation between the races began to widen in the 1880s, and blacks were increasingly restricted from participating in the social, political, and civil life of the community, they began to stress self-help and economic development. W.E.B. Du Bois, who would become the foremost scholar of black life by the early twentieth century, later observed this trend: "The colored man wakes in his own house built by colored men, rides to work in a part of a car surrounded by colored people. He reads a colored paper, he is insured by a colored insurance company, he patronizes a colored school with colored teachers, and a colored church with a colored preacher; he is buried by a colored undertaker in a colored graveyard."

The church remained central to the life of the black community, offering spiritual and social services. No man was more influential in the African-American community than the minister and none more valued than a minister who served his congregation well. In his four-year tenure in one church, Winfield Henry Mixon recorded that he attended 193 love feasts and prayer meetings, 42 funerals, 21 weddings, saw 116 sick families, baptized 115 adults and 128 children, delivered 1,152 sermons and lectures, and administered the holy sacrament 14,910 times. He preached a gospel of racial improvement despite the difficulties his congregations faced. "We have been carrying the blaze of Christianity," he wrote in his

For most black women, the only job available outside the home was that of domestic worker. These women were often exploited by the whites for whom they worked and against whom they sometimes rebelled in sly and subtle ways.

diary. "We have been watching the dancing rays of wealth. We have been driving the shining steel of education through the head of ignorance. We have been teaching our people to have confidence in each other and help each other in business."

Even whites sat up and took notice of the new black middle class. The *Nashville Republican Banner* praised the middle class in one breath and disparaged the working class in another. "The Negro we come in contact with is the thrifty and cleanly barber or dining room servant, and even sometimes the banker and merchant. He is generally improving his opportunity, but unfortunately he cannot be taken as representative of the indolent and shiftless hundreds of thousands whose highest ambition is a drink and a fiddle and a dance."

Yet most of those streaming into the cities were working-class men and women hoping to find jobs and improve their lot in life. For women, work was relatively easy to find. There was a great demand by whites—even by poor whites—for maids, cooks, washerwomen, nannies, and other domestic servants. Since there were so many black women seeking these jobs, they were easily exploited. White men in the household often took sexual advantage of them. White women determined their wages and hours. Cooks were paid anywhere from $4.00 to $10.00 a month and nurses $1.50 to $5.00, depending on their age. If they did not live in, as many didn't because they had their own families, their day began at four in the morning, when they would feed their own children to be at work by five or six. They would work until after dinner, often returning home after their children were asleep. Most worked six days a week and some seven. One domestic worker wrote an anonymous letter describing her condition: "For more than thirty years, or since I was ten years old, I have been a servant in white families. I frequently work from fourteen to sixteen hours a day. I am allowed to go home to my children only once in two weeks. Even then I am not permitted to stay all night. I not only have to nurse a little white child. I have to wash and act as playmate to three other children. And what do I get for this work. The pitiful sum of $10 a month! With this money I'm expected to pay my house rent which is four dollars a month, and to feed and clothe myself and three children."

Behind the masks, there was sorrow. Dorothy Bolden, a maid in Georgia, was interviewed on her working life.

White folks didn't have no feelin' for you. They pretended they did. They had nannies to give their child comfort. That was my name: "Nanny." They would teach their children they was better than you. You was givin' them all that love and you'd hear them say, "You're not supposed to love nanny. Nanny's a nigger." And they could say it so nasty. Til it would cut your heart out almost and you couldn't say a mumblin' word. A woman knows how to shift the smile when the burden is so heavy. Know how to smile when she want to cry. Smile when sorrow done touched her so deeply. So that's why I feel black women in this field had to pray and had to moan and had to cry. And those prayers were like the waving of an ocean. Like a wave in the ocean you know how it roll over and throw and keep on rolling. Them prayers went a long ways and protected a lot of people. And God wiped away those tears. And the next morning, we had the strength to go on.

Whites often criticized black domestics for being lazy, shiftless, or ignorant when they made mistakes. It didn't occur to them that a cook burning a meal, a washerwoman "accidentally" breaking a button, or a maid leaving without notice was often a deliberate act of rebellion. Behind the smiles, the "yessums," and the masks blacks often wore in the presence of whites was a calculated protest against exploitation. Sometimes this would be expressed in mocking songs:

Missus in de big house
Mammy's in the yard
Missus holdin' her white hands
Mammy working hard . . .

Sometimes the protest was more direct. In 1881, in Atlanta, black washerwomen went on strike. Working outside people's homes gave them independence, but their pay remained low, sometimes as little as fifty cents a day. The work was grueling. A washerwoman had to draw hundreds of pounds of water from a well to wash, boil, and iron clothes. She had to make her own soap from lye and her own starch from wheat bran, and she had to cut beer barrels in half to make tubs.

The washerwomen formed the Washing Society, a union with more than three thousand members. For more than a month, they resisted the combined pressure of their white patrons and a city government that threatened to charge them high fees for licenses. "We can afford to pay these licenses and will do it before we are defeated, and then we will have full control of the city's washing at our own prices, as the city has control over our husbands' work at their prices. Don't forget this. We mean business." The city used its police power to jail and fine the strikers and break the strike.

For men, finding work was harder. Steady work was rare, and the only way that most could survive was to move from job to job. One man described his working life. "I been factory hand, janitor, porter and butler, and wipin' up engines on the railroad. I worked as a helper for carpenter and layin' brick for masons. I been a driver of teams, a pick and shovel man, and drove steel for a section boss. I was a hand on the Mississippi, and workin' in a steel foundry and seem like I did a hundred mo' jobs."

The influx of thousands of new black people to the cities of the South, the rising of an obviously capable black middle class, and the growing militancy of a generation of young people who were born after slavery deeply troubled whites. They complained about the changes that had been taking place since slavery days. One Southern woman, who once owned slaves, lamented, "They don't sing as they used to. You should have known the old days of the plantation. Every year, it seems that they are losing more and more of their own confessed good humor. I sometimes feel I don't know them anymore. They have grown so glum and serious that I'm free to say I'm scared of them." And a white merchant complained, "The colored race are getting more unreliable. Freedom has ruined them in every way. Only the old timey darkies can be trusted. The young ones are sullen and grow more insolent every day." Blacks agreed. One black youth commented, "Younger Negroes, who are ignorant of the so-called instinctive fear of their fathers, are prone to brood in bitterness and suppressed rage over their wrongs and are more sensitive to injustice and quick to resent it."

As the 1880s progressed, the gulf between the races widened. Many whites felt that more laws were needed to control African Americans. The days of flexible race relations and paternalistic attitudes of whites toward blacks were ending. Whites were demanding new, uniform laws as a means of controlling blacks. From this demand, Jim Crow laws would eventually spread across the South like prairie fire in high wind. Into this darkening period came a diminutive young teacher who would challenge the rising tide of white supremacy and become the foremost agitator of her day. Her name was Ida B. Wells.

Chapter 4

"Jim Crow Comes to Town," 1890–1896

In May 1884, Ida B. Wells, a demure, diminutive, well-dressed young black schoolteacher, was quietly reading in a first-class or "ladies'" car in a train in Tennessee. The white conductor ordered her to move to the "colored" car. Blacks were no longer allowed in the ladies' coach. "I refused," Wells later wrote, "saying the forward car was a smoker, and as I was in the ladies car, I proposed to stay. He tried to drag me out of my seat but the moment he caught hold of my arm, I fastened my teeth on the back of his hand."

Nothing was more offensive to African Americans—especially an African-American woman—than to sit in the Jim Crow car where men of both races drank, smoked, cursed, and spat. W.E.B. Du Bois once described his journey in a segregated car: "The 'Jim-Crow' car is caked with dirt, the floor is gummy and the windows dirty. The conductor gruffly asks for your tickets. Lunch rooms either 'don't serve niggers' or serve them at some dirty and ill-attended hole-in-the-wall. Toilet rooms are often filthy."

The conductor dragged a struggling Wells off the train as white passengers cheered. She sued the railroad and won in the lower courts. The judges agreed that she was indeed a lady, having dressed and acted accordingly, had the appropriate ticket, and deserved to sit in the ladies' coach. A higher court reversed the decision on the grounds that Wells rode the train deliberately to create a disturbance—although there was not the slightest evidence that she did so. The reversal devastated her. "I had firmly believed all along that the law was on our side and would give us justice. I feel shorn of that belief and utterly discouraged. If it were possible, I would gather the race in my arms and fly away with them. God, is there no redress, no peace nor justice for us? Teach us what to do, for I am sorely, bitterly disgusted."

That injustice infuriated Ida Wells was no surprise to those who knew her. Her mother and father had been political activists in Holly Springs, Mississippi, during Reconstruction and had organized blacks to vote the Republican ticket. Both parents, Jim and Lizzie Wells, were great believers in education for their children, and Wells went to college to become a teacher. When her parents died during a yellow fever epidemic in 1878, she accepted a teach-

Ida B. Wells was the first civil rights agitator to emerge after Reconstruction. She traveled throughout the United States and England, crusading, speaking, and writing against lynching for most of her adult life.

ing job in Memphis, the following year. Two years later, Tennessee passed its first Jim Crow laws in public transportation.

Wells felt that unless black people resisted discrimination, they would become demoralized and defeated. "Yes, we'll have to fight, but the fight must be with our own people. So long as the majority are not educated in the points of proper self-respect, so long will our condition be hopeless. What steps shall be taken to unite our people into a real unifying force?"

Wells lived the life of a cultured middle-class black woman in the Victorian world of Memphis. She attended social gatherings at which guests recited Shakespeare, read poetry, and sang German songs—in German. She went to plays and musical events. In 1887, on her twenty-fifth birthday, she noted in her diary, "I have suffered more, learned more, lost more than I ever expect to again. In the last decade, I've only begun to live—to know life as a while with its joys and sorrows. . . . May another ten years find me increased in honesty and purity of purpose and motive!"

Wells found teaching difficult because of the poor conditions of the schools. Black schools received crumbs from the educational table of the city. Wells also discovered that some women teachers had to provide sexual favors to white school board members to get their jobs.

By the mid-1880s, Jim Crow laws were spreading. Public parks had been legislated as off-limits to blacks, and theaters were required to segregate them. In 1888, Tennessee's Democrats, using fraud and intimidation, gained control of the state legislature and immediately introduced legislation to disfranchise blacks. When the Tennessee legislature introduced legislation to eliminate the black vote, Wells counterattacked. Since the end of Reconstruction, blacks in Tennessee had held on to their hard-earned political rights. A shaky coalition of blacks and reluctant whites worked together in the Republican Party to elect candidates. Blacks in Tennessee still maintained some seats in city and state legislative bodies. Whites imposed a poll tax, voter registration laws, and a secret ballot that made selection of candidates far more difficult. Both poor blacks and whites were affected by the law.

Wells began to write and edit several newspapers part-time while she taught, expressing her opposition to segregation. Wells attacked the disfranchisement laws as they were being debated in the Tennessee legislature. "The dailies of our city say that whites must rule this country. But this is an expression without a thought. . . . The old southern voice that made the Negroes jump and run to their holes like rats, is told to shut up, for the Negro of today is not the same as Negroes were thirty years ago. . . . So it is no use to be talking now about Negroes ought to be kept at the bottom where God intended them to stay; the Negro is not expected to stay at the bottom." There was little blacks could do but protest. By 1890, Democrats had cut the black vote by half.

In 1889, Wells became editor and part owner of a newspaper, the *Free Speech and Headlight.* In 1891, she went after the Memphis school board for allowing black schools to remain in such poor condition. She also alluded to the issue of the sexual abuse of black women teachers. The board fired Wells from her teaching job. What Wells found most disturbing was the unwillingness of the parents of her students to protest. "I was saddened by the fact that the parents of the children I was fighting for did not seem to show much interest. One said to me, 'Miss Ida. You ought not to have done it. You might have known they would fire you.'"

Wells was now free to channel her energies into full-time journalism. She traveled through the South selling subscriptions to her newspaper while continuing to write. As blacks lost political power in Tennessee, white violence increased. Wells preached a doctrine of armed self-defense. She carried a gun and was determined to die fighting to protect herself from assaults if it became necessary. She encouraged others to do the same. When blacks in Georgetown, Kentucky, burned down part of the town after several lynchings, Wells approved. "So long as we permit ourselves to be trampled on, so long we will have to endure it. Not until the Negro rises in his might and takes a hand in resenting such cold blooded murders, if he has to burn up whole towns, will a halt be called to wholesale lynching. When the white man knows he runs as great a risk as biting the dust every time his Afro-American victim does, he will have a greater respect for Afro-American life."

THE MOB'S WORK

Done With Guns, Not Ropes

The Three Rioters Shot to Death in an Open Field.

They Were Carried a Mile and a Half Before Killed.

The Bodies Left Where They Fell and the Mob Dispersed.

Calvin McDowell's Face and Head Torn to Shreds.

Will Stewart and Tom Moss Nearly as Badly Riddled.

The Lynchers Left No Clew as to Their Identity.

There Were Between Fifty and Seventy-five in the Party.

They Knew the Ways of the Jail and Gained Easy Access.

They Also Knew the Men They Wanted, But Failed to Find One.

Isaiah Johnson, Alias "Shang" Saved by the Jail Porter.

Nothing Developed at the Inquest by Justice Garvin.

A Sensation Caused by a Reported Uprising.

Judge DuBose Locks Up a Gun Merchant for Selling Arms to Negroes--The Sheriff Patrolling the Suburbs--Resolutions Passed Condemning Barrett the

In 1892, three of Ida B. Wells's friends were murdered by a mob when they defended a grocery store against an attack by men hired by a jealous white competitor to destroy it. This incident launched Wells on her anti-lynching campaign.

In March 1892, violence struck close to Wells. Her close friend Tom Moss, along with two of his friends and their supporters, were arrested for defending themselves against an attack on Moss's store. Moss was a highly respected figure in the black community, a postman as well as the owner of a grocery store. A white competitor, enraged that Moss's store had drawn away his black customers, hired some off-duty deputy sheriffs to destroy it. Moss and his friends, not knowing the men were deputies, resisted. A gun battle broke out, and several deputies were wounded. Late one night, masked vigilantes dragged Moss and his two friends from their cells, took them to a deserted railroad yard, and shot them to death.

Enraged by Moss's death, Wells lashed out at the refusal of Memphis police to arrest the well-known killers. She encouraged blacks to protest with boycotts of white-owned stores and public transportation. Whites were furious. One man indignantly remarked, "I don't see what you niggers are riled up about. You got off light. We first intended to kill off every one of those 100 niggers in jail but concluded to let all go but the leaders."

Blacks composed a song in Moss's honor:

> Tom Moss was an innocent man
> He was at home in bed
> Teacher of a class in Sunday School
> Was shot through the head
> Oh me, oh my, Lord have mercy on me.
> Oh me, oh my, Lord have mercy on me.
> They are roaming the streets with guns
> Looking for us to shoot
> All we can do is pray to the Lord
> There is nothing else we can do.

Wells immediately called for a boycott of the streetcars in order to force prominent whites to pressure the police to arrest the killers. The officials of the line asked her why blacks were boycotting the streetcars. Before replying, she asked them their opinion. One of the officials said he heard that colored people were afraid of electricity. "If that's so," Wells replied, "why did they ride the line for six months before the boycott?" Puzzled, the official then asked Wells for the reason. She quietly pointed out that the boycott started after Tom Moss and the others had been lynched. "But we had nothing to do with the lynching," the officials protested. Wells replied that they also had nothing to do with seeing that the murderers were brought to justice. The boycott would remain.

The lynchings were a turning point in Ida Wells's life. She began to investigate and reveal the real motivations that lay behind lynching. Wells, like many middle-class African Americans, had accepted the myth that only poor blacks were lynched for some heinous crime. Wells was now shocked into recognizing that even innocent middle-class black people could be targets. "I had accepted the idea that although lynching was contrary to law and order, unreasoning anger over the terrible crime of rape led to lynching—and that perhaps the mob was justified in taking his life. But then Thomas Moss, Calvin McDowell and Henry Stewart had been lynched in Memphis and they had committed no crime against a white woman. This is what opened my eyes to what lynching really was—an excuse to get rid of Negroes who were acquiring wealth and property and thus keep the race terrorized and 'keep the niggers down.' "

As Wells investigated the reasons for lynching, she discovered that a number of victims were lynched not for rape, but for having sexual relations with consenting white women. "Nobody in this section of the community believes that old threadbare lie that Negro men rape white women. If Southern men are not careful, a conclusion might be reached which will be very damaging to the moral reputation of their women."

The suggestion that white women would willingly have sexual relations with black men enraged white Memphis. Since Ida Wells did not sign her name to her editorials, the white press assumed that a man had written the article. The *Memphis Scimitar* advocated a violent response: "It will be the duty of those whom he has attacked to tie the wretch to a stake, brand him in the forehead with a hot iron and perform upon him a surgical operation with a pair of shears."

A mob destroyed Ida Wells's newspaper while she was out of town and threatened to kill her on sight should she return. Forced to remain in the North, Wells launched a national— and later international—crusade against lynching that would capture the attention of the nation and Europe.

As Tom Moss lay dying in a Memphis train yard, a reporter who witnessed his murder recorded his last words: "Tell my people to go West. There is no justice here." Ida Wells agreed. "There is nothing we can do about the lynchings now as we are outnumbered and without arms. Therefore, there is only one thing left for us to do—save our money and leave a town which will neither protect our lives and property, nor give us a fair trial in the courts, but takes us out and murders us in cold blood when accused by white persons."

By the late 1880s, the belief of many blacks that racial tensions would eventually work themselves out had been revealed as a false hope. For thousands, the only solution was to move to the all-black towns, where they hoped they could live their lives avoiding contact with whites.

In 1887, a train traveling between Memphis, Tennessee, and Vicksburg, Mississippi, came to an unexpected stop at an isolated spot midway between the two cities. Two men stepped down and entered into a swamp wilderness. One was a white surveyor. The other was an imposing black man in the prime of life. His name was Isaiah Montgomery, a successful businessman who grew up in slavery. His dream was to build a utopia for black people in this inaccessible land of unbroken forest. It was a land where ash and elm trees, pecans and water oaks, walnuts and maples, tangled in a chaos of vines, brush, and cane, grew to enormous heights in ankle-deep water. Little sunlight could penetrate the tangled growth and the region remained in almost perpetual shade. Only deer, bear, and Indians ventured into this jungle. It was here that Montgomery envisioned that black farmers would one day own their own land and black merchants their own businesses. He called his proposed colony Mound Bayou after discovering Indian burial mounds on his property. What he hoped would make Mound Bayou particularly appealing to blacks was that it would be a community without whites. "It's a white man's country," he once said. "Let them run it."

Coming to the conclusion that blacks and whites could no longer live together, Isaiah Montgomery founded the all-black town of Mound Bayou. By the beginning of the twentieth century, the town was a social and economic success.

Montgomery was raised on a Mississippi plantation owned by Joseph Davis, the brother of Confederate president Jefferson Davis. Montgomery's father, Benjamin, had managed the Davis plantation before the Civil War and owned and operated it as a successful all-black enterprise during emancipation. The venture failed when cotton prices collapsed in the 1870s, and the Davis family foreclosed.

Isaiah Montgomery's main problem was finding others willing to risk leaving what little security they had to clear a wilderness and start over again. "It was not easy to find settlers in the early days," he said. "The task of clearing a wild country seemed hopeless to men with so few resources and so little experience." The first settlers cut down trees, drained bayous, built up the land, fought off wild animals and snakes, and lived as frontiersmen. Using axes and dynamite, they transformed the wilderness into farmland. Men built crude log cabins and sold timber for cash crops. Women and children worked for whites on nearby plantations. When the colonists, many of whom had been slaves in Mississippi, complained, Montgomery challenged them. "You have for centuries hewed down forests at the request of a master. Could you not do it for yourselves and your children into successive generations that they may worship and develop under your own vine and fig tree?"

Local whites thought the project was doomed to fail. Ben Green, one of the founders of the colony with Montgomery, encountered a white planter who was pessimistic about the project. "A prominent white planter in conversation with me one day remarked, 'Uncle, I can't see what Montgomery brought you up here for, unless to starve.' I replied, 'Our forefathers wrought in the opening up of the United States for settlement; and with a far greater measure of personal interest we are determined to work out the development of Mound Bayou.'"

The wilderness soon became a frontier. The ragged outline of the forest receded in all directions. People built churches, a post office, and schools. Montgomery insisted that all children of Mound Bayou go to school nine months of the year, almost twice as long as most black children attended school in the rural South. "Do you think that our boys and girls can go to and from our schools daily and not realize the benefit that comes from the industry and thrift they see around them? What chance has the Negro boy or girl who lives in the 'nigger quarters' of the city? They learn to despise their race and to think they can never amount to anything no matter how hard they work or how moral they are and that what they do doesn't count. We are teaching here that the Negro counts."

Booker T. Washington saw towns such as Mound Bayou as a vindication of his philosophy of economic progress for blacks, and urged blacks everywhere to follow its example.

Ben Green, who once was a student there, never forgot the impact the town made on him. "For the children of Mound Bayou, the community was a source of pride. Everything here was Negro, from the symbols of law and authority and the man who ran the bank to the fellow who drove the road scraper. That gave us kids a sense of security and pride that colored kids didn't get elsewhere." Another resident recalled, "My grandmother was eighty-seven. She came here from Virginia, during the time that Montgomery and all of them came to this barren area. She always wanted something for black people. She wanted something other than what she had been doing in slavery, doing what other people telling them what to do. She had in her mind that there must be something else, there must be something better than what she was living under." And a third resident added, "Mound Bayou was special to black people because it was governed by black people. Everything from the bank to the post office was directed by black people. That was something that was unbelievable in this race conscious era where there was so few opportunities other than manual labor for black people."

To keep Mound Bayou a haven for blacks, Montgomery was shrewd enough to remain in the good graces of the powerful white planters. As long as the Mound Bayou citizens did not get involved in state politics, their colony was not harmed. In 1890, whites prepared a massive assault on black political rights by amending the state constitution to exclude them and poor whites as well. And Montgomery would be called upon to play a key role.

In Mississippi, the Lords of the Delta, the white planters who ruled the state, also controlled the votes of black labor that worked for them. The planters were deeply concerned that a new force in Mississippi politics—the small, independent white farmer and merchant—would overthrow their rule. They were represented by such demagogues as James Kimble Vardaman, and deeply resented the planters' control of the state. White planters despised the rising class of white farmers and merchants, and feared them as much as blacks. William Alexander Percy, a Mississippi planter, described them in scathing terms: "They were the sort of people that lynch Negroes, that mistake hoodlumism for wit, and cunning for intelligence, that attend revivals and fights and fornicate in the bushes afterward. They were undiluted Anglo-Saxons. They were the sovereign voter. It was so horrible, it seemed unreal."

Mississippi elections had always been violent, and many courageous blacks and whites who opposed Democratic rule had been murdered. To end this violence, a compromise was reached between the planters and their challengers. Blacks would be constitutionally disfranchised, and corruption and violence at the polls would stop. A constitutional convention was called theoretically to legally disfranchise all illiterate voters. Everyone knew the real purpose. Vardaman, then a rising Mississippi politician, unashamedly confessed the actual motive: "There is no use to equivocate or lie about the matter. Mississippi's constitutional convention was held for no other purpose than to eliminate the nigger from politics; not the ignorant—but the nigger."

Whites warned blacks not to interfere in the change. In spite of the warnings, Marsh Cook, an African American, challenged the Democrats in Jasper County for a seat to the Constitutional Convention as a Republican. He was ambushed on a lonely country road. A local newspaper carried the story of his death: "The *Clarion Ledger* regrets the manner of his killing as assassinations cannot be condoned at any time. Yet the people of Jasper are to be congratulated that they will not be further annoyed by Marsh Cook."

Isaiah Montgomery had been invited to the convention by powerful whites to support disfranchisement, as he was considered "safe." The murder of Marsh Cook had reinforced Montgomery's conviction that blacks and whites should remain separate. When he rose to address the assembly, the hall became quiet.

My mission is to offer an olive branch of peace to bridge a chasm that has been developing and widening for a generation that threatens destruction to you and yours while it promises no enduring prosperity to me and mine. I have stood by, consenting and assisting to strike down the liberties of 123,000 free men. It is a fearful sacrifice laid upon the burning altar of liberty. I only ask that the laws be fairly applied, that the race problem be resolved and that issues be discussed on some other basis than the color line. What answer? Is our sacrifice accepted? Shall the great question be settled?

The Mississippi legislators applauded Montgomery. They then amended the constitution so that blacks had to take a literacy test if they tried to vote. The clause read in part that every voter "shall be able to read any section of the Constitution of this state; or shall be able to understand the same when read to him or give a reasonable interpretation thereof." This gave the registrar the power to accept or reject any potential voter. Since all registrars were white and politically appointed, it was highly unlikely they would allow any black voter to pass the test on his own merits. Whites were also required to take the test, but they were seldom questioned.

Blacks were outraged at Montgomery's speech. They called Montgomery a "traitor" and "Judas" for not challenging disfranchisement. Frederick Douglass flayed him. "His address is a positive disaster to the race. He has been taken in by lying whites. No more flippant fool could have inflicted such a wound in our cause as Mr. Montgomery has." Ida Wells, perhaps recalling that Montgomery had helped her newspaper, softened her criticism. "Montgomery never should have acquiesced but it would have been better to have gone down to defeat still voting against this understanding clause."

If Montgomery was willing to sacrifice black voting rights on the altar of white supremacy, other Mississippi blacks were not. I. W. Mannaway, editor of the *Meridian Fair Play,* called for blacks to resist being denied the right to vote by educating themselves in order to pass the literacy test. He urged every black prayer meeting to serve as a night school and every educator and preacher to teach the illiterate to read. "Do away with the midnight dance and the cheap excursion; stop taking Saturday evening vacations and let every man who can stammer the alphabet consider himself appointed by the Lord to teach one another of his race so much as he knows."

The law was appealed to the Supreme Court. In 1898, in *Williams* v. *Mississippi,* the Court sanctioned disfranchisement. The Court's rationale was that since the law did not, on its surface, discriminate by race, then it was constitutional no matter what its intention was.

Montgomery defended himself by claiming he hadn't surrendered anything that wasn't already lost. As far as he was concerned, the new law promised safety for his people from the violence surrounding them. "Mound Bayou," he said, "was the ship. All else was an open, raging, tempestuous sea."

Whether or not Montgomery made an explicit deal with whites to exchange his vote to protect his town, Mound Bayou prospered in the nineteenth and early twentieth centuries. The town eventually grew to four thousand inhabitants with thirty thousand acres of land owned by the community, producing three thousand bales of cotton and two thousand bushels of corn on six thousand acres. It had a town hall, depot, lighted streets, a half dozen churches, more than forty businesses, a train station, sawmill, three cotton gins, a telephone exchange, schools, a library, and a photographer. It was the self-governing and self-sustaining all-black community that Isaiah Montgomery had envisioned. Mound Bayou received national recognition from Booker T. Washington and Theodore Roosevelt, both of whom visited there and praised it. A reporter who visited the community described it in glowing terms. "The negro colonist of Mound Bayou owns his land or rents it from Negroes. He hauls his cotton to the gins of Mound Bayou, stores it in the warehouses and sells it in the markets of Mound Bayou. He buys his fertilizers, his livestock, and building materials in Mound Bayou. He purchases his calico, jeans, and furniture at the Mound Bayou general emporium. He reads his news in the *Demonstrator,* Mound Bayou's paper. He takes his physical from a negro doctor and gets new teeth from the Mound Bayou dentist. Finally he is buried in Mound Bayou by a negro undertaker."

The racial peace that Isaiah Montgomery hoped disfranchisement would bring to Mississippi was not to be. As blacks lost power, violence against them increased. Prosperous blacks throughout the state were targeted and driven from their communities. "Reverend Buchanan was banished from West Point at a mass meeting of some 100 whites who objected to his prospering, to his elegant horse and buggy, his decent house and his piano. Whites thought his mode of living had a bad effect on the cooks and washerwomen who aspired to do likewise and became less disposed to work for whites. He was ordered to sell his business and remove his family under penalty of death." Montgomery reported that Thomas Harvey, a grocery store owner, was ordered to sell his buggy and walk, and Mr. Meachem was ordered to close his business and don overalls for manual labor. Mr. Cook, who had two taxicab vehicles, would be allowed to run only one and had to sell the other.

Years later Montgomery confided in Booker T. Washington, "I am coming to the conclusion that only federal intervention can bring democracy to America. The dominant race is seeking a retrogression of the Negro back to serfdom and slavery."

* * *

As Mound Bayou prospered around the end of the nineteenth century, a great social upheaval taking place in the farmlands of the Midwest and South seemed to hold some promise for blacks. A political revolt was threatening to become a revolution. By the 1890s, that anger took political form in the Populist movement, or "People's Party" as it was sometimes called. In the South, the target of Populist wrath was the Democratic Party. Cotton prices had dropped from eleven cents a pound down to less than five cents. Below seven cents a pound, farmers lost money and had to mortgage their homes—if they could find a bank that would issue a mortgage. The "big mules," the lords of big business, now controlled the Democratic Party. Southern conservatives, who had for more than a decade ruled unchallenged, now found that they had undermined their own credibility. They had also allied themselves with Northern financial interests at the expense of the farmer.

Most Populists were white supremacists and had refused to allow blacks to join their party. Some, like "Cyclone" Davis, were openly hostile to blacks. "The worst sight of social equality to be seen in this land is the sight of a sweet white girl hoeing cotton in one row and a burly negro in the next. Talk of social equality when your industrial system forces a good woman's Anglo-Saxon girl down on a level with a burly negro in a cotton row. Oh my God! And this in a free America!"

When blacks formed their own organization, the Colored Alliance, both races warily started to cooperate. White farmers were troubled by the question of social equality; black farmers had other, more important concerns. At a Populist meeting one black farmer stated clearly the goal of his people: "We don't want to rule the government; we don't want to come into your family; we don't want to enter your schoolhouse. We want equal rights at the ballot box and equal justice before the law; we want better wages for our labor and better prices for our produce; we want to lift the mortgage from the old cow and mule which they have carried until they are sway-backed; we want to school our child and we want a chance to earn our home."

Black organizers risked their lives to help black farmers free themselves from the domination of white planters. In 1889, Oliver Cromwell of the Colored Alliance traveled to Leflore County, Mississippi, to organize a boycott of local white merchants in order to begin a black farmers' cooperative. Cromwell's life was threatened. When blacks rallied around him to give him support, a local posse suppressed the group in a sea of blood. J. C. Engle, a textile merchant from New York, witnessed the reprisal. "Negroes were shot down like dogs. Members of the posse not only killed people in the swamps but invaded homes and murdered men, women and children. A sixteen-year-old white boy beat the brains out of a little colored girl while a bigger brother with a gun kept the little one's parents off."

While white planters wanted to completely suppress the Colored Alliance, white Populists knew that their political futures depended on the black vote. J. P. Rayner, a black organizer in Texas, warned that they would fail without it. "If you want the Negro to vote the straight People's Party ticket, you must put men on the county tickets whom he likes. Kind words and just treatment go further with the Negro than money and promises."

No one had kinder words and promises for black farmers than Tom Watson, a former Democrat turned Populist. Watson recognized that blacks were not simply the straw men claimed by white supremacy, nor the dependent children of liberal Northerners, but an integral part of the South with a valid place in its political and economic life. He made an unprecedented appeal for the black vote in his campaign against Georgia's Democratic Party. He condemned lynchings, spoke on the same platforms with blacks, and recognized that black and white farmers shared the same hopes. "I pledge you my word and honor that if you stand shoulder to shoulder with us in this fight, you shall have fair play and fair treatment as men and as citizens irrespective of color." Watson organized picnics, barbecues, and camp meetings and formed political clubs for blacks. But political cooperation did not mean socializing. Blacks and whites sat separately when together, yet that did not prevent them from cheering wildly when Watson spoke of their common plight. "You are made to hate each other because on that hatred is rested the keystone of the arch of financial despotism which enslaves you both. You are deceived and blinded because you do not see how this race antagonism perpetuates a monetary system that beggars you both. The colored tenant is in the same boat as the white tenant, the colored laborer with the white laborer and that the accident of color can make no difference in the interests of farmers, croppers and laborers."

Watson's actions seemed to match his words. When H. S. Doyle, a black Populist organizer, received death threats from white Democrats, Watson protected him on his property. He sent word to his supporters for help. Throughout the night armed farmers gathered around Watson's house to protect Doyle. Watson claimed that two thousand people arrived to help. Doyle later recounted that many black farmers were deeply impressed with Watson's gesture. "After that, Mr. Watson was held almost as a savior by the Negroes. They were anxious to touch Mr. Watson's hand, and were often a source of inconvenience to him in their anxiety to see him and shake hands with him, and even touch him."

Watson made it clear that he was not endorsing social equality between the races. When Democrats charged that he had entertained Doyle in his house, Watson called it a lie and stated that when he protected Doyle, he put him in his "nigger house," a separate residence on his property. "They say I am an advocate of social equality between the whites and blacks. THAT IS AN ABSOLUTE FALSEHOOD. I have done no such thing and you colored men know it. It is best that your race and my race dwell apart in our private affairs."

Democrats were enraged at the interracial cooperation between black and white farmers. They accused the Populists of "treason to the white race" and rallied against them under the

Lynchings soared in the 1890s to over one hundred victims a year, with blacks being the primary victims. The killings were marked by an intense degree of sadism that often attracted thousands of spectators.

banner of "preserving white civilization." Although they also allied themselves with blacks opposed to Populism, Democrats accused their opponents of supporting "Negro domination." In the rich cotton areas where planters controlled the black vote, they stuffed the ballot box to offset white votes in Populist counties. In Atlanta, the Democratic candidate for governor offered to increase financial support for black education. The black community was divided. Many felt that white farmers were a far greater threat to black rights than the city Democrats. H. H. Style, an African-American supporter of the Democrats, warned other blacks of the dangers involved. "I am afraid the Populists will eventually ruin my people. They remind them of the wrongs done them and promise to correct them. But they do not tell them that they were in the front ranks when that army of oppression came against the Negro." Harry Lincoln Johnson, a prominent black attorney in Atlanta, echoed the refrain. "The intelligent Negroes of Georgia know that there is far more hate and spleen against the Negroes in the populist camp than in the democratic."

On Election Day, black farmers turned out in record numbers. Although Populists legally won a majority of the offices, Democrats used fraud, manipulation of large numbers of black votes, and violence to steal the elections. At least fifteen blacks and several whites were killed. The African-American vote was split almost evenly in Georgia.

Other states also defeated the Populists by violence and terror. Governor William C. Oates of Alabama confessed that the worst tactics were used in his state. "I told them to go to it, boys. We had to do it. I say it was a necessity. We could not help ourselves."

After the defeat of the Populist movements in several states, violence against blacks intensified. Populists resented the way the black vote had been used to help defeat them. Interracial coalitions began to dissolve. Many whites blamed blacks for their defeat. Whites vowed that never again would the black man be a factor in the white man's politics. States imposed literacy tests giving registrars the discretion to accept or reject blacks' qualification to vote. Poll taxes were passed. Lynchings of blacks soared: 113 in 1891, 161 in 1892, 118 in 1893, 134 in 1894. Until 1905, more than one hundred men and women were lynched every year but one.

The lynchings were often marked by an unprecedented level of sadism. The *Greenwood Observer* sent a reporter to the scene of a lynching of a black man allegedly accused of attacking a white woman. "The mob sliced his body with knives, burned his body with red hot irons, hung him by the neck until he almost choked to death, then revived him and continued the torture. Next they dragged him to the home of the victim's parents where several thousand people were waiting. When they stopped in front of the house, a woman came out and plunged a butcher knife into his heart."

Blacks were enraged but had limited power to express their anger. Minister Winfield Henry Mixon of Alabama wrote in his diary, "Every now and then the wicked, ill-gotten, squint eyed, blood suckers hang, lynch, shoot or burn their superiors—the ebony, pure and most God like in their heart Negro. My pen shall never stand, my voice shall never stop, my tongue shall never cease." Richard Wright would later write of the fear of "white death" that intimidated blacks in his autobiography of growing up in Mississippi and Arkansas. "The white death hung over every male black in the South. A dread of white people came to live permanently in my imagination. I had already grown to feel that there existed men against whom I was powerless, men who could violate my life at will. I felt completely helpless in the face of this threat because there did not exist any possible course of action which could have saved me if I had ever been confronted by a white mob."

In 1895, Booker T. Washington, deeply troubled over the racial fury unleashed in the South, searched for a solution. Invited to speak at the Cotton Exposition in Atlanta, a fair that promoted Southern industry, Washington was encouraged by a display of seeming goodwill on the part of whites. One of the highlights of the fair was the Negro Building containing exhibits demonstrating the scientific, cultural, and mechanical achievements of African Americans.

Many blacks boycotted the exposition. They objected to Atlanta's segregating the audiences at public speeches and on streetcars, to the convict labor used to grade the grounds, and to the fact that the only place blacks could buy refreshments was in the Negro Building. When some out-of-state blacks wrote to a local black newspaper asking if they should attend, the editor bitterly replied, "If they wish to feel that they are inferior to other American citizens, if they want to see on all sides signs that say 'For Whites Only,' or 'No Niggers or Dogs' allowed; if they want to be humiliated and have their man and womanhood crushed out, then come."

For Booker T. Washington, the exposition was an opportunity to promote his agenda rather than protest racism. He had been extremely anxious as he made the trip from Alabama to Atlanta, knowing that one false note in his speech could jeopardize everything he had built at Tuskegee. His audience would be mixed: Southerners, Northerners, white people, and black people. What could he say that would appeal to such a diverse group?

On September 25, the exposition opened. As the white speakers stepped up on the platform, the crowd welcomed them with great enthusiasm. James Creelman, a correspondent for the *New York World,* observed the crowd's reaction to Washington: "When among them a colored man appeared, a sudden chill fell on the whole assemblage. One after another asked, 'What's that nigger doing on the stage?'" But when Washington rose to speak and began by criticizing his people for seeking political and economic power during Reconstruction, the crowd suddenly became very attentive. "Our greatest danger," Washington said, "is that in the great leap from slavery to freedom, we may overlook the fact that the masses of us are to live by the productions of our hands and fail to keep in our mind that we shall prosper as we learn to dignify and glorify common labor. It is at the bottom of life we should begin and not the top." Creelman described what followed: "And when he held his dusky hand high above his head, with the fingers stretched apart, and said to the white people of the South on behalf of his race, 'In all things that are purely social we can be as separate as the finger yet one as the hand in all things essential to mutual progress,' a great sound wave resounded from the walls and the whole audience was on its feet in a delirium of applause." Washington continued: "The wisest of my race understand that the agitation of questions of social equality is the extremest folly and that progress in the enjoyment of all the privileges that will come to us must be the result of severe and constant struggle rather than artificial forcing. The opportunity to earn a dollar in a factory just now is worth infinitely more than to spend a dollar in an opera house."

The *Atlanta Constitution* described his triumph in glowing terms: "When the Negro finished, such an ovation followed as I had never seen before and never expect to see again. Tears ran down the face of many blacks in the audience. Governor Bullock rushed across the platform to seize his hand. White Southern women pulled flowers from the bosom of their dresses and rained them upon the black man on stage."

The white press throughout the nation unanimously acclaimed his speech. Former abolitionists, railroad tycoons, political leaders, and President Grover Cleveland wired their congratulations. The young teacher and scholar W.E.B. Du Bois praised the speech. Many blacks and whites felt that a new era had begun. The race question had been settled. Blacks would forgo their civil rights. They would get justice and economic rights. Booker T. Washington never forgot his triumph that day. "As I sat on the platform with the flower and beauty and culture of the South on either side, and these Southern men and beautiful and cultured Southern women wave their hats and handkerchiefs and clap their hands and shout of approval of what I said, I must have been carried away in a vision and it was hard for me to realize as I spoke that it was not all a beautiful dream, but an actual scene: right here in the heart of the South."

The people who showered praise on him were not the ones who would determine the future of blacks in the South. A new breed of politician was emerging, one who pandered to the racial hatreds of the mob. Among them was James Kimble Vardaman, who would soon be governor of Mississippi. He had his own ideas about Washington's philosophy of accommodation. "The man who says the race problem in the South is settled is just about as capable of judging and understanding such matters as the average nigger is about understanding the philosophy of the Decalogue. I am as opposed to it, I am just as opposed to Booker Washington as a voter, with all his Anglo Saxon refinements, as I am to the coconut-headed, chocolate-colored typical little coon, Andy Dotson, who blacks my shoes every evening." Vardaman made it clear that the compromise Washington offered was unacceptable to him and that the prominent whites who applauded him did not speak for him and his followers.

Nor did Booker T. Washington speak for the whole African-American community. Many blacks angrily rejected Washington's accommodating posture. The fiery, militant Bishop Henry Turner of Atlanta harshly criticized him: "The colored man who will stand up and say in one breath that the Negroid race does not want social equality, and in the next predict a great future in face of all the proscription of which the colored man is a victim, is either an ignoramus or is an advocate of the perpetual servility and degradation of his race."

John Hope, soon to be the first black president of Atlanta University, echoed Turner's criticism: "If we are not striving for equality, in heaven's name for what are we living? I regard it as cowardly and dishonest for any of our colored men to tell white people or colored people we are not striving for equality."

Not far from Tuskegee, tenant farmer Ned Cobb had different thoughts as well.

Booker T. Washington was an important man but he didn't feel for and didn't respect his race of people to go rock bottom for them. He never did get to the root of our troubles. The veil was over our people's eyes and Booker T. Washington didn't try to pull the veil away like he should have done. He should have walked out full faced with all the courage in the world and realized, "I was born to die. What's the use of me to hold everything under the cover if I know it? How come I won't tell it in favor of my people?" Wrong-spirited Booker T. Washington was. He was a man got down with his country in the wrong way.

The year after Booker T. Washington spoke at Atlanta, Homère Plessy, a Creole of Color who legally challenged segregation on common carriers in Louisiana, lost his case. The United States Supreme Court, echoing Booker T. Washington's compromise speech, sanctioned segregation under the fiction of "separate but equal."

Washington's speech earned him a great deal of goodwill but did nothing to help his cause. As racial hatred continued to increase, rumors of impending race war engulfed the South. White voices were heard demanding not only total segregation and disfranchisement but also exclusion and extermination. A Georgia congressman said, "The ultimate extermination of a race is inexpressibly sad, yet if its existence endangers the welfare of mankind, it is fitting that it should be swept away." Black workers in Montgomery, Alabama, prepared to fight back. "We have made up our minds to go down for the race. We expect to carry a goodly number of whites with us. Revenge we will have one way or another. Fires will burn and this town can be sent down to ashes."

As the nineteenth century came to a close, the message sent to African Americans was clear: There was no place for them in white America. Their great hope of emancipation—to earn their livelihoods by their own freely chosen labor, educate their children, enjoy their communities, participate in government, receive justice under law, and become American citizens—had been either denied them or severely restricted. For thirty years, African Americans tried a variety of strategies to deal with the crisis: confrontation, accommodation, resignation, rebellion, separation, and emigration. They met with varying degrees of success. Abandoned by the North, without allies in the South, they would continue their struggle alone, relying on their families, churches, schools, culture, and organizations to sustain them during the virulent onslaught unleashed on them as the twentieth century dawned. Drawing on the great reservoir of faith that lay within the heart of their community, their leaders never let them forget that the promise of emancipation was ordained and would eventually be redeemed.

Chapter 5

Victories and Defeats, 1897–1900

As wave after wave of racial fury inundated the South, a flicker of hope appeared. America declared war on Spain in 1898 and invaded Spain's colonies of Cuba and the Philippines. Black soldiers were needed to fight for their country. Of America's twenty-five-thousand-man standing army, two thousand five hundred were experienced black veterans. They had been fighting America's Indian wars on the deserts and plains of the West for more than twenty years. The Cheyenne called them "Buffalo Soldiers" for their courage in battle and their rough, shaggy appearance.

Black soldiers welcomed the Spanish-American War. Chaplain George Prioleau saw the war as an opportunity for the soldiers to prove themselves. "The men are anxious to go. The country will then hear and know of their bravery. The American Negro is always ready and willing to take up arms to fight and lay down his life in defense of his country's honor." Another soldier viewed the war as a chance to strike a blow against Jim Crow. "We left our homes, wives, mothers, sisters and friends to break down that infernal race prejudice and to have a page in history ascribed to us."

The black press was divided. Not all papers supported the war. The *Washington Bee* editorialized, "The Negro has no reason to fight for Cuba's independence. He is as much in need of independence as Cuba is. His own brothers, fathers, mothers, indeed his children, are shot down as if they were dogs or cattle."

As the soldiers traveled from the North to Florida, intermingled crowds of blacks and whites gathered at stations to welcome them. Chaplain Prioleau never forgot the reception they received. "All the way from Northwest Nebraska this regiment was greeted with cheers. While the Ninth Calvary band played, the people would raise their hats, the heavens resound with cheers. The white hand shaking the black hand. The hearty 'goodbye and God Bless you.'" When the train crossed into the Jim Crow South, the cheering stopped. Reaching Lakeland, Florida, John Lewis of the Tenth Cavalry remarked, "Lakeland is a beautiful little town, . . . but, with all its beauty, it is a hell for the colored people who live here, and they live in dread at all times." Lewis and his fellow soldiers confronted whites when a local druggist refused to sell them a bottle of soda. Abe Collins, a local barber, warned them, "You damn niggers better get out of here," and went to get his pistols. The soldiers stood their ground. Lewis remarked, "I suppose that he was of the opinion that all blacks looked alike to him; but that class of men soon found out they had a different class of colored people to deal with." Collins came out with his pistols and was shot dead.

The soldiers were immediately rushed to the battlefields of Cuba where several soldiers won medals of honor and the regiments were recognized for their bravery and fighting ability. Black troops played a major role in Colonel Theodore Roosevelt's victory at the battle of San Juan Hill. Although Roosevelt acknowledged their contribution at the time, later he would disparage their conduct. Lieutenant John Pershing, who during World War I would command the American army in Europe, was one of many whites who had praise for black soldiers. "White regiments and black regiments representing the young manhood of the North and South fought shoulder to shoulder. It was glorious. For a moment, every thought was forgotten but victory. We officers could have taken our black heroes in our arms."

The era of good feeling passed quickly. White Americans brought Jim Crow to Cuba and the Philippines. They called the people of color of the islands "niggers," and officials denied them their civil and political rights on the grounds that they were racially inferior. John Galloway, a black soldier with the Twenty-Fourth U.S. Infantry, wrote home, "The whites have begun to establish their diabolical race hatred in all its home rancor in Manila, even endeavoring to propagate the phobia among the Spanish and Filipinos." A Filipino boy challenged William Sims, another black soldier: "Why does the American Negro come to fight us when we are a friend to him and have not done anything to him? He is all the same as me—and me is all the same as him. Why don't you fight those people in America who burn Negroes, who make a beast of you?"

A few soldiers did desert to the Filipino cause. Most, Chaplain Prioleau observed, lived bitterly with the contradiction. "Yes, the Negro is loyal to his country's flag. Forgetting that he is ostracized, his race considered dumb as driven cattle, yet, as loyal and true men, he answers his country's call with tears in his eyes and sobs as he goes forth; he sings 'My country tis of thee, Sweet Land of Liberty,' and though the word liberty chokes him, he swallows it and finishes the stanza."

Even as black men fought for their country overseas, 101 were lynched in the South. At the Chicago Exposition of 1898, the usually circumspect Booker T. Washington delivered a sharp speech to an audience that included President William McKinley: "I make no empty statement when I say that we shall have, especially in the Southern part of the country, a cancer growing at the heart of our country, that shall one day prove as dangerous as an attack from an army within or without."

Although Washington almost immediately backed down from his strong words, the cancer he warned about was spreading. In 1898, it reached Wilmington, North Carolina, a city many black residents considered immune from the virulent racial turmoil surrounding them. David Fulton, an African American, found race relations there harmonious. "The best feeling among the races prevailed in Wilmington. The Negro and his white brother walked their beats on the police force; white and black committeemen sat down together in the same

Alex Manly, whose father was a plantation owner, was the African-American editor of the only black daily newspaper in North Carolina, the *Wilmington Daily Record.*

There were many small business owners in North Carolina and other Southern cities. Many of them had originally catered to a white clientele. But by the 1890s, most of their customers were black.

council; white and black teachers taught in the same school. We boast of Wilmington as being ahead of all other Southern cities in the recognition of citizenship among her inhabitants, unstained by such acts of violence that have disgraced other cities." The good feeling that Fulton found in Wilmington seemed to prevail throughout the eastern part of North Carolina. As long as the Democrats ruled, white paternalism gave everything a patina of racial harmony. When a coalition of predominately white Populists and black Republicans defeated the Democrats in 1896 and won political control of the state, Democrats vowed revenge. For many Democrats, black political power, no matter how limited, was intolerable. Julian Carr, one of the most powerful men in Durham, warned that white paternalism had its limits. "If we can wean the Negro from believing that politics is his calling by nature and turn the bent of his mind into the development of manufacturing industries, what will the end be? It is unlimited. But if the Negro is to continue making politics his chief aim, there can be but one ending."

Alex Manly, the fiery black publisher and editor of the *Wilmington Daily Record,* disagreed. Politics was exactly what African Americans needed. "How can the Negro," he asked, "expect to assert his manhood if he denies himself what is his constitutional right to vote and hold office?"

Located in the eastern part of the state, where the Cape Fear River enters into the Atlantic

In 1898, the Democratic Party in North Carolina, determined to drive all blacks out of political office despite the fact that they were a small minority, launched an openly racist campaign based on white supremacy. Blacks were shown in vitriolic cartoons as a threat, especially to white women.

Ocean, Wilmington was a prosperous port town in 1898. Almost two-thirds of its population was black, with a very small but influential middle class. They were teachers, clergymen, lawyers, doctors, businessmen, and journalists, many of whom had attended college. Some had acquired pianos, servants, lace curtains, and expensive carpets. Black businessmen dominated the restaurant and barbershop trade, owned tailor shops and drugstores. Black people held jobs as firemen, policemen, and civil servants. The county had the highest black literacy rate in the state, with more than half the voters able to read and write. Most members of the black community were workingmen and -women, primarily laborers and domestic servants. Wilmington's workers had a reputation for militancy. In the 1890s, the city's whites were shocked when both men and women went out on strike for higher wages.

Alex Manly was one of the leaders of the black community. His father had been a slave owner and former governor of the state, and Manly could easily have passed for white had he wished. He had married into the most prominent and prosperous black family in the city and had started the only black-owned daily newspaper in the state. Though he had a good rapport with whites, many of whom advertised in his newspaper, he believed that the goal of black people was full equality. Throughout the state blacks took pride in their accomplishments and their adoption of white middle-class Victorian values. They felt that by doing so they could establish a bond with whites based on class while separating themselves from the "lower classes." Reverend William C. Smith noted, "Our conduct should teach white people that we are not to be judged as a people by the vulgar rough set that loafs around the street in fifth and idleness." Smith failed to realize that it was not unsuccessful blacks that concerned whites. It was the successful ones.

In 1898, the Democratic Party resolved to take back the state by launching a virulent campaign based on white supremacy. Daniel Schenck, a party leader, warned, "It will be the meanest, vilest, dirtiest campaign since 1876. The slogan of the Democratic Party from the mountains to the sea will be but one word . . . Nigger!" Schenck had also been quoted as saying, "Nothing prevents the white people of the South from annihilating the Negro race, but the military power of the United States government."

The Democrats argued that only they could save the state from what they called "black rule," which, in reality, never existed anywhere. Furnifold Simmons, a Democratic leader, proclaimed, "North Carolina is a WHITE MAN'S STATE and WHITE MEN will rule it, and they will crush the party of Negro domination beneath a majority so overwhelming that no other party will ever dare to attempt to establish Negro rule here."

White terrorist groups like the "Red Shirts"—so-called because they wore red shirts as a symbol that they had killed a black man—mobilized to stop blacks from voting in North Carolina on election day.

The Democrats launched their campaign by appealing to whites' deepest fear—that white women were in danger from black males. Political cartoons exploited that racial myth by showing images of black men or mythical black creatures threatening white women. White women appeared in parades in white dresses holding up signs that said, "Protect Us!" The white newspaper in Wilmington published an inflammatory speech given by Rebecca Felton, a Georgia feminist, a year earlier: "If it requires lynching to protect woman's dearest possession from ravening, drunken human beasts, then I say lynch a thousand negroes a week . . . if it is necessary."

After the election, a white mob in Wilmington began to rampage. They burned down Alex Manly's newspaper offices and opened fire on blacks. A race riot erupted.

The article infuriated Manly. He responded with an editorial sarcastically noting that many of these so-called lynchings for rape were cover-ups for voluntary interracial sexual relations. He pointed out that interracial sex was a two-way street. "Every Negro lynched is called a big burly brute when many had white men as fathers and are not only not black, but are sufficiently attractive to white girls of culture and refinement to fall in love with them. Don't ever think your women will remain pure while you are debauching ours. You sow the seed. The harvest will come in due time."

Manly's editorial fueled raging fires. One white citizen claimed, "This article had made Wilmington seethe with uncontrollable indignation, bitterness and rage. It directly started the overthrow of negro domination and rule in the community." Alfred Waddell, a leader of Wilmington's white militants, declared, "We will not live under these intolerable conditions. We intend to change it if we have to choke the current of Cape Fear River with Negro carcasses." South Carolina's Governor Ben Tillman encouraged members of the Red Shirts, a white terrorist organization whose members wore red shirts to symbolize the blood of black men they had murdered, to take a hand.

Occasionally, a white voice tried to calm the storm. Jane Croly, a local citizen, criticized the Democrats: "The Negroes here are an excellent race and under all the abuse that has been vented on them for months, they have gone quietly on and been polite as if to ward off the persecution they have felt in the air."

Most white women supported Rebecca Cameron, who urged her cousin, Alfred Waddell, to defend white women as violently as necessary. "It has reached the point where blood letting is needed for the health of the commonwealth, and when the depletion occurs, let it be thorough. Solomon says, 'There is a time to kill.' That time seems to have come so get to work. . . . It is time that the shotgun play a part, and an active one, in the current election. We applaud your determination that our old heroic river be choked with bodies of our enemies white and black."

Waddell urged his followers to kill any blacks who tried to vote. "Go to the polls tomorrow," he instructed, "and if you find the Negro out voting, tell him to leave and if he refuses, kill him; shoot him down in his tracks. We shall win tomorrow if we have to do it with guns."

A black women's organization published an advertisement pressuring black men to vote. "Every Negro who refuses to register this next Tuesday in order that he may vote, we shall make it our business to deal with him in a way that shall not be pleasant. He shall be branded as a white-livered coward who would sell his liberty."

Black voters turned out in large numbers, but the Democrats stuffed the ballot boxes and swept to victory. The Republican/Populist coalition was completely routed. Julian Carr telegraphed President McKinley that whites reigned triumphant. "Men with white skins, who drafted the original Magna Carta of American Independence, will rule North Carolina ever hereafter; no need of troops now, praise God!"

In Wilmington, the political victory did not soften white fury. A mob set Manly's newspaper offices on fire and a riot erupted. Whites began to gun down blacks on the streets. Reverend Allen Kirk, a black minister, watched the terror unfold. "Firing began and it seemed like a mighty battle in war time. They went on firing it seemed at every living Negro, poured volleys into fleeing men like sportsmen firing at rabbits in an open field; . . . the shrieks and screams of children, of mothers and wives, caused the blood of the most inhuman person to creep; men lay on the street dead and dying while members of their race walked by unable to do them any good."

Harry Hayden, one of the rioters, stated that many of the mob were not rabble but respectable citizens. "The men who took down their shotguns and cleared the Negroes out of office yesterday were not a mob of plug uglies. They were men of property, intelligence, culture . . . clergyman, lawyers, bankers, merchants. They are not a mob. They are revolutionists asserting a sacred privilege and a right."

Some whites protected blacks. When the mob reached the Sprunt Factory, intending to shoot down the eight hundred workers gathered inside, James Sprunt, the owner, barricaded the doors and pointed guns on the mob from his yacht docked nearby. The mob retreated.

Many blacks took to the woods and swamps to hide. They were followed by Charles Bourke, a journalist from *Collier's* magazine. "In the woods and swamps innocent hundreds of terrified men and women wander about fearful of the vengeance of whites, fearful of death. Without money or food, insufficiently clothed, they fled from civilization and sought refuge in the wilderness. In the night I hear children crying and a voice crooning a mournful song. 'When the battle's over we kin wear a crown in the New Jerusalem.'"

By the next day, the killing ended. Officially, twenty-five blacks had died, but many more may have been killed, their bodies dumped into the river. Hundreds of others were driven out of town, among them Alex Manly, who narrowly escaped a lynch mob. His fair complexion enabled him to pass safely through a white patrol that mistook him for white. One of the mob members even gave him a gun, instructing him, "If you see that nigger Manly, shoot him!" Manly solemnly agreed.

Since a few black and white Republicans still remained in office, Waddell staged a coup

Charlotte Hawkins Brown (right) came to North Carolina to teach as a teenager. By the time she was in her early twenties, she had started her own school with a staff of teachers.

d'état by leading a delegation of Democrats to city hall and the courthouse, and forced the officeholders to resign. Jason Dudley, a local black resident, observed in a letter to Booker T. Washington how well-to-do blacks were targeted: "I met about a thousand soldiers who were drumming four negroes from the city. They were not indolent paupers or drones; they represented between thirty and fifty thousand dollars worth of property ... It was not the insignificant Negroes that were disturbed, it was the well-to-do and prosperous ones."

Della Johnson, a Wilmington resident, appealed to President McKinley for help. "I, a Negro woman of this city, appeal to you from the depths of my heart to do something in the Negro's behalf. I call upon you as head of the American Nation to help these humble subjects. Are we to die like rats in a trap? Can we call on any other Nation to help? Why do you forsake the Negro? Is this the land of the free and home of the brave? There seems to be no help for us." McKinley did not reply.

As the violence finally ended, David Merrick, a successful black businessman in Durham, stated that Wilmington's blacks had brought the riot upon themselves. "The Negroes have had lots of offices in this state and they have benefited themselves but very little. Nothing compared with what they could have done along business and industrial lines had they given the same time and talent. What difference does it make to us who is elected? Had the Negroes of Wilmington owned half the city, there wouldn't anything happen compared with what did."

George White, the only black congressman from North Carolina, and soon to lose his seat, had another explanation. "This crisis has been brought about by the fact that despite all the oppression that has fallen on our shoulders, we have been rising, steadily rising. This tendency of some of us to rise and assert our manhood is what has brought about this changed condition."

The victory of the Democratic Party led to the disfranchisement of blacks. The black middle class was astounded that they should be included in the new discriminatory legislation. They felt that they had earned the right to be an exception. Reverend L. S. Flag of Asheville wrote, "Surely the men who have befriended us in the past will not, because of the conduct of irresponsible persons, enact a law that will have a tendency to crush the self-respect of those among us who are endeavoring to rise to genteel manhood and true womanhood." The plea fell on deaf ears. The haven that North Carolina had once been for African Americans now became a desert of white supremacy like the rest of the South.

The disastrous election of 1898 did not deter one woman from launching her own fight against Jim Crow in North Carolina. Her name was Charlotte Hawkins Brown, and by the time she was seventeen, she was filled, as she wrote, "with a burning desire to return to the state of my birth and help my people."

Charlotte Hawkins was born in North Carolina but moved with her family to Cambridge, Massachusetts, when she was six. Her parents had named her Lottie Hawkins, but just before graduation from high school, she decided to change her name to Charlotte Eugenia Hawkins. A chance meeting with Alice Freeman Palmer, the wife of a Harvard professor and the first female president of Wellesley College, opened up doors to her that would otherwise have remained closed. Palmer happened to see Hawkins pushing a baby carriage while reading a book of Latin poetry. Palmer took an interest in Hawkins and helped pay her tuition to college. Hawkins had completed one year when she was offered a teaching position at Bethany Institute in rural Sedalia, North Carolina, by the American Missionary Association (AMA). Although only eighteen years old, Hawkins immediately accepted.

In 1901, as Hawkins traveled through North Carolina, the train in which she was riding suddenly stopped in the middle of the woods. The conductor told her that she had arrived at her destination. She warily descended from the train with her suitcases and found herself alone in the forest. She set out and eventually found someone to take her to the school in a horse and wagon. She was shocked at what she saw. "It was unpainted and much weatherbeaten. Large, gaping holes showed forth where window panes had once been. The yard was unkempt and grown with stubble. No one seemed to be expecting me. I felt as though I wanted to go back home. I did not then know, as I know do, that God knew what was best for me. I wanted to enter His service but had not thought of entering such a barren field. I said, This is God's way. I must be satisfied."

Hawkins's greatest assets were her own inner strength and fifty pupils eager to learn. Some walked as much as fifteen miles a day to attend school. Most could attend school only during the winter, the harshest time of the year, because their labor was needed on the farm the rest

Religion was central to the life of the black community. It sustained African Americans through the whole era of Jim Crow. Whites would often attend black religious services.

of the year. Organizing her students and their parents, Hawkins cleaned up the school and several adjacent buildings, which she converted into dormitories for girls so they could live there during the school year. Just as the school began to succeed, the AMA withdrew its funding. They offered her another teaching position elsewhere, but the parents of her students begged Hawkins to remain. She agreed. She traveled back to New England on a fund-raising tour, determined to raise enough money to keep the school going for the next year. She visited resorts where wealthy whites gathered. Some hotels allowed her to make a little presentation of music and poetry, give a ten-minute talk about the school, and take up a collection. Her goal was to raise one hundred dollars, which was enough to get her through the first year. She met her goal and became the first black woman to open up a normal school in North Carolina.

Hawkins knew that she had to find patrons in order for her school to survive. Alice Freeman Palmer had indicated that she would give some support, but she died during a trip to Europe. Hawkins named her school the Alice Freeman Palmer Memorial Institute in honor of her friend and set about to raise more funds to keep it going.

During the early years, Hawkins, along with her staff and students, wrote dozens of letters every evening to potential funders.

Dear Mrs. Worth:
I have worried your patience no doubt but I have delivered the message of my soul to you. It is not the message of an individual but the cry of a struggling race.

Please make all checks payable to the treasurer.

Whenever an envelope arrived that contained money, the students and teachers would cheer. When they received a large donation, they would sometimes cry. Whatever the amount, they gave a prayer of thanks. Sometimes the letters they received were patronizing, if not hostile. One woman wrote, "I am sending you ten dollars for your school which I hope will be put to good use. I advise you to instruct your girls to be virtuous, for moral looseness is an unfortunate quality of many young women of your race."

While struggling to keep her school afloat, Hawkins married for a short time and changed her name to Charlotte Hawkins Brown. She continued her campaign to raise money for the school, often using subterfuge. Most white donors would make contributions as long as the school was modeled on the industrial program of Tuskegee Institute. Since Palmer grew its own vegetables and raised livestock, she emphasized these in her fund-raising appeals. As one teacher recalled, "You would pretend to have a vocational school on the outside, and then you'd go in your classroom and teach them French, or Latin and all the things you knew." At one point, Booker T. Washington sent a representative to visit her school. He was critical of the academic program. "All your literary and industrial teaching needs to be made more practical, and especially does the literary teaching need to be correlated with the industrial teaching."

Brown modeled her curriculum based on her own education in Massachusetts. In the

The founders and builders of North Carolina Mutual Life—John Merrick, C. C. Spaulding, and Dr. Aaron Moore—started with a $250 investment and turned it into a multimillion-dollar enterprise.

lower grades, teachers taught spelling, reading, writing, hygiene, and arithmetic; in the upper grades, literature, grammar, geography, history, and agriculture. Foreign languages and civil government were offered to students going to college. Students read books like *Black Beauty, Robinson Crusoe, Silas Marner,* and *Ivanhoe.* They memorized poems and writings of Longfellow, Whittier, Tennyson, and Emerson. Ruth Totton, a former teacher at the school, recalled, "People said she had high falutin' ideas and high aims for her students and she was teaching them the three R's but she was also intent on teaching them leadership qualities."

Brown successfully juggled financial support from the North while cultivating the support and friendship of powerful local whites in nearby Greensboro. Even though racial tensions had cooled in North Carolina after 1898, Jim Crow laws were intensifying. Blacks had been disfranchised in 1900, and Jim Crow signs were proliferating. Brown refused to accept Jim Crow, even though, at times, she had to conform to it. Whenever she had an appointment with her doctor or lawyer, she would phone ahead so that when she arrived, she would be ushered directly into the office rather than wait in the Jim Crow waiting room or into a

Jazz musicians gathered for a picture in New Orleans at the boys' home where Louis Armstrong (seated, front row center) first learned to play music in a band.

vestibule past both the colored and white rooms. She sat in the "ladies' section" of the train. If a conductor forced her to sit in the Jim Crow section, she would sue the railroad. When her students went to town for a concert or movie, she would reserve the theater for them, so they would not be forced to sit in the balcony. Her life was a balancing act between appeasing powerful whites whose support and protection she needed while finding ways to undermine Jim Crow without endangering her school. She tried to instill in her students a refusal to internalize Jim Crow, to go around and above it, to be smart enough and resourceful enough and duplicitous enough not to antagonize white people, and yet to get what they wanted. Elizabeth Meade, one of her early students, recalled, "She taught us that we could do anything that anyone else could do if we wanted to, if we tried to. She always taught us that we could be as good as anybody else regardless of what our color was. And we appreciated that. Cause you go around thinking you can't do this or you will never be nothing or something like that. She told us it wasn't true. We could be anything we wanted to be."

Brown saw herself as part of an ongoing African-American freedom struggle. Later on, she would be one of the leaders in the fight for black woman suffrage. She devoted much of her energies to interracial work with white women's organizations, trying subtly to recruit support for her agenda. She was a member of the National Association of Colored Women, an umbrella organization for state and local women's clubs dedicated to improving the quality of life for African Americans. The NACW was founded in 1896 by the leading African-American women in America, including Ida B. Wells; Mary Church Terrell, its first president; the great abolitionist Harriet Tubman; and May Murray Washington, Booker T. Washington's wife.

Brown's life as a leader in the NACW and as a builder of a school with a reputation for educational excellence often took its toll on her. "Recognizing the need of a cultural approach to life, I have devoted my life to establishing for Negro youth something superior to Jim Crowism. Sometimes the prejudice is so great I feel that I can't stand it a day longer . . . but then I look in the delicate faces of the children and determine to stick it out no matter what the cost."

Many African-American women, like Charlotte Hawkins Brown, dedicated their lives and energies to education. Others, such as Virginia Broughton, focused on church work, using it as a vehicle to improve the lives of women living in poverty. Broughton was a preacher in the Baptist church, who traveled to the deeply rural, semiwild areas of Arkansas and Missouri bringing the word of God. On one journey, she crossed the Mississippi River in a skiff, bailing out water as they crossed from Tennessee to Arkansas, continued her journey in an open-air ox wagon with a stove in the cart to keep warm, and then took a trip on horseback to Cooter, Missouri, a place, she later wrote, referring to herself in the third person, "where few Negro men dared to go to preach and a woman missionary of no race had ever gone." Much of the road was underwater and she was guided on her journey by a minister. "The preacher would ride on ahead and bid Virginia follow him, which she did with much fear and trembling, the water often coming up to her saddle skirts." She not only preached the word of God to men and women but also helped women become literate by reading the Bible.

Some male members of the church adamantly objected to her preaching. One man remarked, "I would rather take a rail and flail the life out of a woman than to hear her speak in church." One minister went to hear her speak in order to verbally destroy her in front of the audience. When she had finished her sermon, the minister rose and addressed the gathering. He confessed his original purpose, adding that after hearing the eloquence of Virginia Broughton's preaching, "I have been washed, rinsed, starched, hung up, dried, sprinkled and ironed, and am now ready to do service; not to destroy but to do all in my power to forward this branch of God's work as zealously as I had determined to oppose it."

* * *

As black men were eliminated from the political life of the community, in some racially moderate communities they were able to gain an economic foothold. In Durham, North Carolina, three black men launched a business enterprise that would become a major force in the life of the city's black community. They were John Merrick; Dr. Aaron Moore, the first black physician in Durham; and C. C. Spaulding.

John Merrick, like Booker T. Washington, had been born in slavery and had worked his way up the economic ladder as a hod carrier, bricklayer, and barber. By 1890, Merrick owned six barbershops and extensive real estate. He cultivated the support of Durham's most powerful whites, including Washington Duke, the tobacco king, and Julian Shakespeare Carr, mill owner and financier. Carr exemplified the disassociated thinking that characterized many paternalistic Southerners. He was genuinely concerned for the well-being of blacks and supported their economic progress. He was also a rabid white supremacist who approved the killing of blacks who stepped out of "their place" by entering politics.

Merrick recognized that as blacks moved into the cities, they had an increasing need for some kind of protection in case of sickness or death of the main family wage earner. In 1898, Merrick formed an insurance company, eventually known as the North Carolina Mutual Life Insurance Company, in partnership with five other local black businessmen. The company's total capital assets were $250 and business prospects seemed so dismal at first that three of his partners dropped out.

While Merrick was the man with economic vision, C. C. Spaulding, his manager and later president of the company, was a dynamic workaholic whose energy and dedication were the driving force behind much of the company's success. Spaulding developed the markets and trained the workforce that would make the company a success. An employee described him as a man who "came to work early in the morning, rolled up his sleeves and did janitor's work, then rolled down his sleeves and worked as an agent. And a little later in the day, he put on his coat and became the general manager."

Spaulding had a number of serious obstacles to overcome. There was a great deal of competition from white insurance companies, many agents of which continually slandered black companies. They charged that black insurance companies were "of little concern and no account and soon bust. They call and call and collect very promptly when you are well but when you are sick, they never come near your house." Spaulding countered these charges with advertisements in the company newspaper stating when, to whom, and how much benefits had been paid.

One problem that infuriated Spaulding was the tendency of black people to buy from whites rather than blacks. He complained that blacks did not support their own people, even when it was cheaper for them to do so. As one of his agents noted, "It is past our understanding why there are colored people who still think that 50 cents in benefits from a white company is as much as $1.00 from a black one."

Spaulding and Merrick's strategy for success was threefold. The company published its own newspaper, the *North Carolina Mutual,* and launched an aggressive advertising campaign that favored the hard sell. One of its ads read, "Death is pursuing you this moment. Don't let your departing words be, 'Good-bye darling. I bequeath you my troubles and my debts.'"

Spaulding also kept premiums low and affordable. Rates started as low as five cents a week. But his strongest asset was well-trained agents. He taught them that the best way to sell policies was to treat customers with respect. "White agents walk into a Negro home without even knocking or taking off their hats. It is up to us to put an end to such discourtesy, and the best way we can do it is to convince them to patronize a colored insurance company of standing. Tell them that every time a Negro takes a policy, its protects him and it employs another Negro."

The company drew well-educated salespeople and office personal. One major attraction of the office was the aristocratic-mannered Susan Gilles, a college graduate who was hired as executive secretary. In an age when very few black women were white-collar workers, Gilles provided a role model for Durham's youth. Impeccably dressed in black skirts, white puffed-sleeved blouses, and whalebone collars, speaking perfect English, and educated with a classical background, Gilles taught stenographic and typing skills to young people. Children visited her office just to see her type. They called her "the girl with the flying fingers who types without even looking at the keys."

Dr. Aaron Moore, the third partner, helped North Carolina Mutual become the driving force of the social and cultural life of the black community. Moore helped establish Lincoln Hospital for blacks as well as a library. He encouraged the company to support a literary society that sponsored reading programs, offered lectures, and held debates, and the Schubert-Shakespeare Club, which offered classical music, plays, and lectures on "social betterment" of the race.

By the early twentieth century, North Carolina Mutual was on its way to becoming a multimillion-dollar corporation. It created hundreds of jobs in the black community and inspired a number of smaller businesses. One of the original agents described its success in a way that would have pleased Booker T. Washington: "The North Carolina Mutual is one of God's ways through which he is reaching our people. His message to us is: 'Lower your buckets where you are.'"

For most black men and women, the comfortable world of the middle class still seemed as remote as the most distant star. The cotton fields and the mule were to be their likely destiny—as it would be their children's and their grandchildren's destiny. Tens of thousands of African Americans rejected farming and headed for the work camps of the South. Wandering black men built levees and laid railroad tracks, dug coal, and gathered turpentine. They were "masterless men" who were not attached to the land or beholden to landlords. The work was hard, the life was brutish, violence was common, and men were exploited. Men sang as they worked. They sang about everything and anything. "Trains, steamboats, steam whistles, sledge hammers, fast women, mean bosses, stubborn mules—all became subjects for their songs," J. C. Handy, the great popularizer of the blues, noted. Singing allowed the workers to blend their physical movements and provided a means of expression and communication. Some were work songs that often poked fun at their white bosses.

> Captain oh Captain you must be cross
> It was six o'clock and you won't knock off.
>
> Captain oh Captain, you must be blind.
> You keep hollerin hurry an I'm darn near flyin.
>
> Cap'n did you heah about all you men going to leave you
> Jes because you make yo' day so long.

In addition to the work songs, a new music was being heard around the turn of the century. The blues had just begun to emerge out of the Delta, and the rich musical tradition of church music, spirituals, work songs, calls and shouts, and African rhythms combined to become a distinct art form. The blues grew out of the hard lives of poor black workers and sharecroppers. Handy pointed out, "the blues did not come from books. Suffering and hard luck were the midwives that birthed these songs. The blues were conceived in aching hearts."

> The first time I met the blues mamma, they come walking through the wood.
> The first time I met the blues baby, they came walking through the woods.
> They stopped at my house first mamma, and done me all the harm they could.
> Now the blues got at me Lord and run me from tree to tree.
> Now the blues got at me Lord and run me from tree to tree.
> You should have heard me begging, Mr. Blues, don't murder me.

One of the early well-known blues singers was Charley Patton. He wandered from town to town, playing in improvised clubs called "juke joints," fighting, drinking, loving women, and free from the control of whites. Patton rambled through western Tennessee, eastern Arkansas, and northeastern Louisiana, entertaining workingmen and -women wherever he went. He was a Saturday night entertainer who sang about troubles with the law:

> When you get into trouble, it's no use screamin and cryin
> When you get into trouble, it's no use screamin and cryin
> Tom Rushend will take you back to the prison house flyin

and about women:

> Baby got a heart like a piece of railroad steel . . .

and about life's sorrows:

> Hard luck is at your front door, blues are in your room
> Hard luck is at your front door, blues are in your room
> Calling at your back door, what is to become of you.

People sang the blues in the fields where they worked, in homes, in prisons, and in clubs. Sidney Bechet, who would become one of the greatest of all the jazz musicians, first heard it in a jailhouse sung by a prisoner protesting his unjust arrest.

> Got me accused of murder, I never harmed a man.
> Got me accused of forgery, can't even write my name.
> Bad luck, bad luck is killin' me
> I just can't stand no more of this third degree.

Bechet noted, "The way he sang it was more than just a man. He was like every man that's been done wrong. Inside of him he's got the memory of all the wrong that's been done to all my people. When the blues is good that kind of memory grow up inside it. The blues, like spirituals, were prayers. One was praying to God and the other was praying to man. They were both the same thing in a way; they were both my people's way of praying to be them-selves, praying to be let alone so they could be human."

The blues was carried by drifting men and women into the cities of the South, like New Orleans, where often it blended with other sounds to help create new and vibrant musical forms. At the turn of the century, New Orleans was a lively, exciting world of brass bands and string orchestras, French and Italian opera, Neapolitan music, African drumming, Haitian rhythm, Cuban melody, American spirituals and blues, ragtime and popular music. People sang British folk songs, danced Spanish dances, played French dance and ballet music, and marched to the strains of brass bands based on the Prussian or French models.

New Orleans had two distinct black communities. The oldest was the Creoles of Color, with roots in the French, Spanish, and Caribbean cultures that existed before Louisiana was purchased by America. Creoles of Color were French-speaking Catholics who specialized in

KILLING THE PRISONER.
Angered Citizens Wreak Vengeance on Jackson.

In 1900, Robert Charles, harassed by police, became involved in a shootout with tragic consequences. This drawing from a newspaper article shows the arrest of a friend of Charles, who was not involved but was shot by an enraged white man while in police custody.

such crafts as plastering, carpentry, and tinsmithing. A small number were quite wealthy and educated their children in France. They enjoyed a rich musical tradition, and many were formally trained and could play a variety of music from ragtime to classical. The other black community was English speaking and Protestant, and worked on the docks and in other manual labor jobs. Their musical tradition came from work songs, blues, and the black church.

Around the turn of the century, music in New Orleans was undergoing a transformation. A new sound was being created by musicians like Buddy Bolden, the innovative cornet player famed for his ability to improvise, and Tony Jackson, considered by many "the best pianist they had." One man who helped bring about this musical revolution was Ferdinand La Menthe, a Creole of Color eventually known as "Jelly Roll" Morton. From early childhood, music was a vital part of Morton's family's life. "We always had some kind of musical instruments in the house, including guitar, drums, piano, trombone. We had lots of them, and everybody played for their pleasure." Other rich sources of inspiration that Morton described were the marching bands and the social clubs they represented. "New Orleans was very organization minded. I have never seen such beautiful clubs as they have there. The Broadway Swells, the High Arts, the Bulls and the Bears, the Tramps and the Iroquois. They'd have a great big band. The grand marshal would ride in front with all his aides behind him."

While still a teenager, Morton had been hired to play the piano at Lulu White's bordello in the Storyville section of New Orleans, the most famous red-light district in nineteenth-century America. "In Storyville, lights of all colors were glittering, glaring. Music was pouring into the streets from every house. Women were standing in the doorways, singing or chanting some kind of blues—some very happy, some very sad, some with the desire to end it all with poison, some planning a big outing, a dance or some other kind of enjoyment."

Storyville was a world of prostitution where white and black women were available to white men, and black men were restricted to black women in segregated establishments. Only black musicians were allowed in the whites-only houses. "You could play music there, but you couldn't play there," Morton said. "If a white man even suspected you showed too much interest in one of the ladies, well that could be too bad for you."

In Storyville, Jelly Roll Morton became one of the jazz greats. Jazz was not created in Storyville, but many jazz musicians perfected their own talents by providing musical entertainment for the prostitutes and their customers. Louis Armstrong, who helped make coal deliveries to Storyville as a child, remembered how enthralled he was at hearing the music: "There were all kinds of thrills for me in Storyville. On every corner I could hear music. And such good music. All those glorious trumpets—Joe Oliver, Bunk Johnson—It seemed that all the bands were shooting each other with these hot riffs."

Through their music, musicians could drop their masks and express their deepest feelings. Music provided a rich internal life in a Jim Crow world, which influenced their music but did not determine it. There were tears behind their sounds, but there was joy as well.

Many musicians were workingmen, and music was a part-time profession. Johnny St. Cyr saw work and music as being intimately connected. "To be a jazz musician you had to be a working class of man, out in the open all the time, healthy, strong. See the average working man is very musical. Playing music for him is just relaxing. The more enthusiastic his audience is, the more spirit the working man's got to play."

Black workers in New Orleans were often militant. Dockworkers helped organize one of the few interracial unions in the South, convincing white workers that racial cooperation, not racial conflict, was the only way to higher wages and better working conditions for all. They organized strikes together in the 1890s and won higher wages. One black dockworker commented, "We are tired of being used as an instrument to starve our brother workmen, the white men."

Blacks also fought for civil rights. When the state passed the Railway Separation Act in 1890, segregating public transportation, an organization of Creoles of Color challenged the constitutionality of the law. Rodolphe Desdunes, editor of *The Crusader,* a newspaper for the Creole of Color community, encouraged resistance. "It is more noble and dignified to fight than to show a passive attitude of resignation. Absolute submission augments the oppressor's power and creates doubt about the feelings of the oppressed. . . . No theory of white supremacy, no method of lynching, no class legislation, no undue disqualification of citizenship, no system of enforced ignorance, no privileged classes at the expense of others can be tolerated."

The man who volunteered to make history was Homère Plessy, a Creole of Color who could pass for white. Plessy deliberately seated himself in the white section of a train and then identified himself as "colored." When he refused to move, he was arrested. The case, known as *Plessy* v. *Ferguson,* worked its way up to the United States Supreme Court. In 1896, the Court—which several years earlier had ruled that a state did not have the power to forbid segregation—now decided a state had the power to require it. Segregation was now legal. Justice Henry B. Brown, characterized by one scholar as one of the "dimmer lights" on the Court, wrote in the decision, "If one race is inferior to the other socially, the Constitution of the United States cannot put them on the same level." Two years later, in *Williams* v. *Mississippi,* the Court once again approved white supremacy by allowing states legally to deprive blacks of their right to vote.

As blacks lost political and civil power, white hostility intensified. Whites like John Hearsey, the negrophobic editor and publisher of *The States,* the most influential white newspaper in New Orleans, maliciously stirred up nightmare visions of race war. "Under the dark, seething mass of humanity that surrounds us and is in our midst, all appears peaceful and delightful; we do not know, it seems, what hellish schemes of hate, of arson, of murder, of rape, are being hatched in the dark depths. We are under the regime of the free Negro, in the midst of a dangerous element of a servile uprising. If Negroes listen to the screeds of agitators of the North . . . the result will be a race war and race war means extermination. The Negro problem will be solved and that by extermination."

For Robert Charles, a workingman in New Orleans, the situation had become intolerable. Charles had come to New Orleans from Mississippi in the early 1890s seeking work and entertainment. He worked, as many blacks did, at a variety of jobs, most of which involved manual labor. Although he developed a reputation as a sharp dresser and enjoyed the company of women, he was a man not to be taken lightly, He was over six feet tall, weighed about 190 pounds, and carried a gun. An anonymous friend described him as a serious man. "He was a quiet, fine person, who was always studying and trying to improve himself. He believed that black people should defend themselves against lynching, and he was trying to overcome his anger against whites." That anger began to build as lynchings soared and segregation increased. After one particularly brutal lynching in Georgia, Charles told a friend, "The time has come for every black man to defend himself. It is the duty of every Negro to buy a rifle and keep it ready against the time they may be called upon to act in unison."

As New Orleans became increasingly segregated and opportunities for blacks became more limited, Charles despaired that African Americans would progress in America. He became a supporter of Bishop Henry Turner's back-to-Africa movement and sold Turner's nationalistic newspaper, *Voice of Missions,* in New Orleans. By 1900, Charles was determined to leave America for Liberia. It was not to happen. One evening in July, as Charles and his friend Leonard Price were seated on the steps of a house waiting for their lady friends, two policeman approached and began to question them. A fight broke out. Charles and one of the policeman exchanged shots; both were wounded. Charles fled the scene and returned home. When three policemen came to his home to arrest him, he shot and killed two of them and went into hiding.

Whites in New Orleans went wild. An estimated twenty thousand men searching for Charles were ready to kill any black person, man or woman, they saw. One mayor from a nearby town gave a speech inciting the mob. "I have come down tonight to assist you in teaching the blacks a lesson. I have killed a Negro before and I am willing to kill again. The only way you can teach these niggers a lesson is to go out and lynch a few of them—kill them, string them up, lynch them." Dozens of unsuspecting black men were killed, including the father of jazz, musician Louis "Big Eye" Nelson, who was playing that night. "We heard shooting. All them boys flung themselves out the back. We made it out the window of the gambling house in back, but man, that alley was loaded with folks. We might have been assassinated but we were lucky enough to get to a friend's house. Next day somebody said I better go down to the hospital. Man had been brought in about 2 A.M. in very bad condition and died around sunup. It was my daddy. They had snatched him off his meat-wagon at the French market and killed him."

Four days later, the final shootout took place. Charles was betrayed by an informer, and a mob estimated at twenty thousand gathered outside his hiding place. Jelly Roll Morton described the battle: "The man got into his house and he got his gun and fired from all the windows. Policemen came from all over. There was a mob of them ambushing his house. Every time he raised his rifle and got a policeman in his sights, there'd be another one dead." Before he was shot to death, Charles killed five more men and wounded seventeen. After Charles's death, an admirer wrote a letter to the famous anti-lynching crusader Ida B. Wells. "Dear Mrs. Wells-Barnett: It affords me great pleasure to inform you as far as I know Robert Charles, he has never given trouble to anyone in this city. He was a quiet and peaceful man and too much of a hero to die; few can be found equal to him." "Like many other bad men, Charles had a song originated about him," Jelly Roll Morton later said. "This song was squashed very easily by the police department due to the fact it was a trouble breeder. I once knew the Robert Charles song but I found out it was best for me to forget it and that I did in order to get along with the world on the peaceful side."

Charles had sought freedom and found death. The limits of freedom for musicians in New Orleans were clear. Many would leave the city and travel to the North and West. The sounds of the Delta and New Orleans would produce a new and great music that would enthrall audiences in almost every country in the Western world—and allow its creators to find some degree of the freedom they sought. Sidney Bechet, one of the New Orleans greats, expressed it best of all:

> The music, it was the onliest thing that counted. The music it was having a time for itself. It was moving. It was being free and natural. All the beauty that's ever been. The voice the wind had in Africa and the cries from Congo Square and the fine shouting that came up on Free[dom] Day. The blues and the spirituals and the waiting and the suffering . . . that's all inside the music. And when the music is played right, it does an explaining of all those things. Me, I want to explain myself so bad, I want to have myself understood. And the music, it can do that. The music, it's my whole story.

Chapter 6

The Worst of Times, 1900–1917

There were other sounds of music in the air.

> Coon, coon, coon, I wish my color would fade.
> Coon, coon, coon, I'd like a different shade.
> Coon, coon, coon, from morning, night and noon;
> I wish I was a white man instead of a coon.

As America entered the twentieth century, white Americans sang "coon" songs, the purpose of which was to ridicule and denigrate black people: "All Coons Look Alike to Me," "Coon, Coon, Coon, I Wish My Color Would Fade," "If the Man in the Moon were a Coon," "The Red Headed Coon." White supremacy, once considered a Southern idiosyncrasy, had become a national ideology. A malicious negrophobia—a pathological fear and hatred of blacks—had gripped the country. Respected academics claimed that the Negro was inferior biologically, psychologically, anthropologically, culturally, and historically, despite the fact that there was overwhelming evidence to the contrary. Edward Drinker Cope, a professor of zoology, claimed that black mental growth was permanently arrested at age fourteen. He recommended that blacks should be deported in order to protect from miscegenation "the finest race on earth, the whites of the South." Pseudo-scientific literature joined the cacophony of white supremacy. Their very titles reveal their malicious intent: *The Negro a Beast, The Negro a*

When W.E.B. Du Bois published *The Souls of Black Folk* in 1903, it caused a sensation in the black community. One of the essays in the book took Booker T. Washington to task for his acceptance of a subordinate status for blacks.

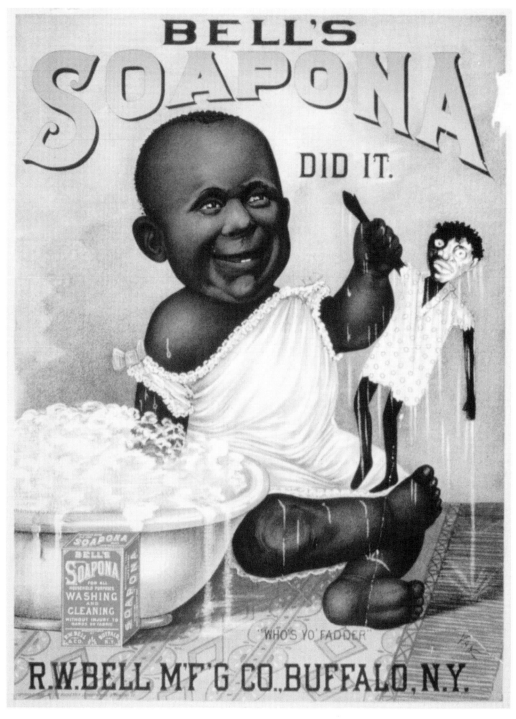

By the turn of the century, white supremacy had become a national ideology and was reinforced by the use of stereotypical images of inferior-looking blacks in advertising.

Menace to Civilization. Popular fiction denigrating blacks flooded the market. Novelist Thomas Dixon portrayed blacks with a racial antipathy in his turn-of-the-century trilogy *The Leopard's Spots: A Romance of the White Man's Burden 1865–1900, The Clansman: A Historical Romance of the Ku Klux Klan,* and *The Traitor: A Story of the Fall of the Invisible Empire.* The novels reviled blacks and glorified the Ku Klux Klan. *The Clansman* was adapted into an extremely popular play, and Dixon often appeared on stage praising the Klan to the exuberant applause of white audiences.

The beginning of the twentieth century witnessed a proliferation of Jim Crow laws in the South. Populists and Democrats, whatever their disputes, were now united in one thing: the total subjugation of blacks and their removal, as far as possible, from the mainstream of Southern life. During the nineteenth century, legal segregation had existed primarily on trains, although social segregation existed in many public places, including restaurants and theaters. Now the South blanketed its cities with Jim Crow laws. The Jim Crow waiting room, seen in only a few Southern states before 1900, was adopted by all. In 1901, North Carolina and Virginia segregated all public transportation, followed by Louisiana in 1902; South Carolina, Arkansas, Tennessee, Maryland, and Mississippi in 1903, and Florida in 1904. Signs proliferated: WHITE, WHITE ONLY, WHITE ONLY SERVED HERE, NO BLACKS ALLOWED, PARK RESERVED FOR WHITES. Separate water fountains and rest rooms were reserved for both races and so indicated. Separate entrances to buildings, separate elevators, separate cashier windows in amusement parks, separate cemeteries for the dead. In Atlanta, blacks and whites who testified as witnesses in court had to swear their oath "to tell the truth" on separate Bibles. Patients were racially separated in hospitals, mental institutions, jails and prisons, and homes for the blind, deaf, elderly, orphans, and the poor. Residential areas were segregated. In Oklahoma, state law required that the phone company install separate booths for the races. North Carolina and Florida required that school textbooks for black and white children be kept separate. In New Orleans, prostitutes were separated by race. Blacks were excluded from parks, swimming pools, beaches, certain neighborhoods, and even towns. Some towns posted signs that read, "Nigger, don't let the sun set on you here."

The proliferation of signs made Pauli Murray glad that her blind grandfather was spared from seeing them. "I saw the things which grandfather could not see—in fact had never seen—the signs which literally screamed at me from every side—on streetcars, over drinking fountains, on doorways: FOR WHITE ONLY, FOR COLORED ONLY, WHITE LADIES, COLORED WOMEN, WHITE, COLORED. If I missed the signs, I had only to follow my nose to the dirtiest, smelliest, most neglected accommodations, or they were pointed out to me by a heavily armed, invariably mountainous red-faced policeman who seemed more to me a signal of calamity than of protection."

The impact of segregation widened a gap within the black community. Middle-class blacks resented that the new laws applied to all black people equally. They could understand why whites would want to restrict "poor" blacks, and some argued that segregation and disfranchisement might be appropriate—even desirable—for them. But for educated, economically successful, and morally upright blacks—the mirror image of the ideal white model for

By the turn of the century, Booker T. Washington was the most influential black man in America. He socialized with rich philanthropists who funded black education and had the power to determine what schools received money.

acceptability in society—the laws were unfair. Their appeal to whites on the basis of their common identity of class interests fell on deaf ears. "Respectable whites" made no distinction between blacks. They would rather identify with poor whites on the basis of race than with successful blacks on the basis of class. What was particularly galling to middle-class blacks was that whites they considered their social inferiors—the bus driver, the elevator operator, the streetcar and train conductor, the theater usher—had power over them. These whites could arbitrarily dictate to blacks as they wished, and if a black person resisted, they had the authority to beat or even kill him.

Consumer products reinforced white supremacy on a national scale. Black stereotypes representing the "happy darky" figure became commonplace. Consumers were greeted by smiling mammies, Aunt Jemima, Uncle Mose, and the Gold Dust Twins on products they bought. These images were incarnations of blacks as Southerners had represented them during slavery days. Stereotypical racial figures appeared on ashtrays, tablecloths, postcards, sheet music, tourist souvenirs, figurines, and a seemingly infinite number of household items. Many images distorted the physical appearance of African Americans; they were never portrayed as real human beings. Images on cigarette packs showed blacks as having large heads, large hands, big lips, and bulging eyes. Some were depicted as playing croquet and hitting themselves instead of the ball. African Americans were represented as an inferior race, people not like white people but totally separate from them. One consequence of these stereotypes was that they helped deaden any national anger against lynching. Many Northerners accepted the Southern view that any black person who did not fit these images of servility was dangerous and probably deserved what he or she received.

At the extreme end of the spectrum of white supremacy were those who preached violence. White radicals rationalized their negrophobia as a response to the so-called regression of blacks toward bestiality. Freedom, they claimed, had made the black a savage creature. The solution was to kill the offender or castrate him and exterminate the race. The radical racists claimed that blacks were lynched because they raped white women, even though rape was not even an issue raised in most lynchings. United States Senator "Pitchfork" Ben Tillman ranted, "So far as I am concerned, he [the Negro] has put himself outside of the law, human and divine. Civilization peels off, any and all of us who are men and we revert to the original savage type whose impulse under any and all circumstances has always been to 'kill, kill, kill.'" Rebecca Felton, Georgia feminist and suffragette, added to the cacophony. "If a rapist was torn to pieces limb by limb and burnt with a slow fire, or hung by the thumbs until the buzzards swarmed around him, he would still be saved some of the revolting torture already inflicted upon a harmless victim. In dealing with such ravenous beasts the best thing to do is rid the earth of such vile and dangerous cattle."

In 1906, negrophobia arrived in Atlanta. For many whites as well as blacks Atlanta seemed to be the least likely place for white racial radicalism. Atlanta was a model city of the new South. The economy was booming. Its population was fast approaching the one-hundred-thousand mark. The number of factories had multiplied by 60 percent since 1900. The number of buildings constructed rose from 230 in 1900 to more than 1,300 by 1906. The Coca-Cola Company had been established. The city was proud of its major department stores, fancy residential areas, 11 major railroad lines, and 160 miles of streetcar lines.

Black businesses were springing up on Auburn Street, soon to be called "Sweet Auburn" because of its economic attractions. Among the successful businessmen were Alonzo Herndon, owner of a barbershop and a life insurance company, who became the richest black man in Georgia, and Moses Amos, the first black pharmacist in the state. There were plenty of jobs for workingmen and -women, although most of those jobs involved menial labor or domestic work at subsistence wages. The city also boasted numerous black publications, the most outstanding of which was the *Voice of the Negro* edited by J. Max Barber. The *Voice of the Negro* published articles by black leaders throughout the South, promoting what it called "higher culture"—literature and the arts. It examined world issues and criticized rabid racists like James Vardaman of Mississippi and "Pitchfork" Ben Tillman of South Carolina while careful not to offend Atlanta's whites.

At the center of its cultural life were the black colleges: Atlanta Baptist College, Gammon

As men were disenfranchised and lost political power, women stepped up their roles through women's clubs. They focused their energies on improving the education, health, and welfare of their communities as well as quietly working to achieve basic rights for all African Americans.

Theological Seminary, Atlanta University, Spelman Seminary, Clark University, and Morris Brown College. The colleges and churches provided much of the intellectual leadership for the black community. The dominating figure was the aristocratic scholar Dr. W. E. B. Du Bois of Atlanta University. Educated at Fisk, Harvard, and the University of Berlin, Du Bois was the first scholar to make the scientific study of African-American life part of the university curriculum. Among Du Bois's peers were John Hope, soon to be the first black president of Atlanta University, Professor J. W. Bowen of Gammon Theological Seminary, Bishop Henry McNeil Turner of the African Methodist Episcopal church and Henry Hugh Proctor, pastor of the Congregationalist church. When whites criticized the black colleges on the grounds that most of their students were enrolled in high school rather than college courses, Du Bois acknowledged that there were weaknesses but pointed out the college's strength. "Above the sneers of the critics stood one crushing rejoinder: in a single generation the colleges put thirty thousand black teachers in the South and wiped out the illiteracy of the majority of black people in the land."

These intellectual and moral leaders of the community, while circumspect in their behavior with Atlanta's whites, were not cut in the conciliatory mold of Booker T. Washington. In 1903, Du Bois had fired his first warning shot at Washington's policy of forgoing black civil and political rights in exchange for economic opportunities and due process of law. Du Bois published *The Souls of Black Folk,* a series of essays, one of which took Washington to task. While praising him from his contributions to the progress of the race, Du Bois criticized Washington for his failures to speak out in its behalf: ". . . so far as Mr. Washington apologizes for injustice, North and South, does not rightly value the privilege and duty of voting, belittles the emasculating effects of caste distinctions, and opposes the higher training and education of our brighter minds—so far as he, the South or the Nation does this—we must unceasingly and firmly oppose them." The following year, Du Bois organized the Niagara Conference at Niagara Falls, at which he invited a number of prominent black leaders to form a civil rights organization to challenge Washington's leadership. The movement ultimately failed but served as a precursor to the National Association for the Advancement of Colored People (NAACP), which was founded five years later. In a statement defining the movement's goals, Du Bois proclaimed, "We claim for ourselves every single right that belongs to a freeborn American, political, civil and social; and until we get these rights we will never cease to protest and assail the ears of America."

Du Bois was not the only voice speaking out. Bishop Henry Turner castigated the United States government when, in his judgment, it committed outrages against black people. After the United States Supreme Court ruled a congressional civil rights law unconstitutional, Turner thundered, "The Supreme Court is an organized mob against the Negro. What can all the people in the United States do when the Court declares that the Negro is a dog? That barbarous decision should be branded, battle-axed, sawed, cut and carved with the most bitter epithets and blistering denunciations that words can express . . . it absolved the allegiance of the Negro to the United States." When Turner said that he preferred ". . . hell to the United States" and called the American flag "a dirty contemptible rag," President Theodore Roosevelt threatened to charge him with treason. Turner retorted that he could prove "forty more times treason against my race under the shadow of the United States flag than they can against me."

Turner, along with Du Bois, Barber, and other leaders, attended a Georgia Equal Rights convention in 1905 that demanded black civil and political rights but carefully avoided the issue of social equality.

African-American women were also quite active in Atlanta. Many joined women's clubs, most of which were affiliated with the National Association of Colored Women, the dominant black women's organization in America. Women took it upon themselves to provide community services to poor blacks and instill in them middle-class standards and values. The race, they maintained, needed uplift by self-help, racial solidarity, temperance, thrift, chastity, social purity, patriarchal authority, and the accumulation of wealth; the instruments by which racial uplift were to be achieved were the churches, fraternal organizations, and, especially, the women's clubs.

The values the women expressed were those of the black middle-class world of the nineteenth century. They shared the belief that if blacks adopted white civilization—and by civilization was meant white middle-class Victorian standards—they would be accepted, or at least escape from the worst outrages of white supremacy.

One outstanding leader was Lugenia Hope, whose background was in social work. Her

Atlanta boasted an intellectual and cultural elite that performed and attended music concerts, plays, and the theater. Much of the intellectual activity was generated from the five black colleges in the city.

husband, John Hope, a severe critic of Booker T. Washington, had been hired to teach classics at Atlanta Baptist College. Lugenia Hope recognized that black women could have enormous influence when they organized. Her vision was to deliver services to every neighborhood in the city through a series of networks built in each community. Hope wandered through the back alleys of the slum areas. The roads were unpaved and full of holes. There were no water mains, and some areas were used as garbage dumps. She proposed that the kindergartens be transformed into community centers that would reach out to all people in the area with a variety of services. She championed such health services as antituberculosis clinics and shelters for the elderly, sewing and literature classes for young women, and playgrounds for children. She felt that women should lobby the city government for better streets, sewerage, and lights, and expose landlords who refused to provide minimum services and shopkeepers who cheated people.

Another activist deeply concerned about bettering her community was Carrie Steele Logan, who worked as a cook and volunteer probation officer for juveniles. Born in slavery, she single-handedly raised money to found the first black orphanage in Atlanta in 1898. "I have seen the hungry, half-clad ignorant children barefooted and crying for bread. I have seen them searching in vain for a place to lay their tired heads; and so I resolved to do something for the children of my race."

While Carrie Steele Logan relied on church groups, many black women worked for community betterment through women's clubs. Organizations like the Sisters of Friendship, Sisters of Love, Daughters of Bethel, and Daughters of Samara—all church related—played an active role in their neighborhoods in community organizations.

Men's organizations and lodges were also active. They provided health benefits for members, gave financial assistance to widows and orphans, worked for civic improvement, offered financial help to students in school, and held parades. Within their own organizations, religious and secular, blacks could run for and hold office, vote, administer the expenditures of moneys, wield power, and gain prestige that was forbidden to them in the white world. The black community had its own ball teams, dramatic societies, and social organizations. This frightened some whites who were afraid that the lodges would breed secret, antiwhite activities. One white state representative, E. H. McMichael, introduced a bill in the Georgia legislature that would have so severely restricted lodges that for all intents and purposes they would have had to shut down. The bill, he said, "would protect the 'good negro' from the wiles and wicked designs of a few scoundrels of his own race who would arouse ambitions that could never be gratified." Blacks rallied against the measure, and it was defeated.

By the turn of the century, Atlanta was becoming the leading black commercial center of the Southeast. Many black businessmen emphasized the importance of blacks patronizing black businesses as a matter of racial pride. As one newspaper noted:

> There is a singular group in Atlanta where a black man may get up in the morning from a mattress made by black men, in a house which a black man built out of lumber which black men cut and planed; he may put on a suit which he bought at a colored haberdashery and socks knit at a colored mill; he may cook victuals from a colored grocery on a stove which black men fashioned; he may earn his living working for colored men, be sick in a colored hospital, and buried from a colored church; and the Negro insurance company will pay his widow to keep his children in a colored school.

Although racial uplift benefited the black community in many ways, it also promoted an elitist philosophy. During emancipation, as blacks struggled for citizenship, material advancement, human rights, education, and democracy, the community as a whole worked together to achieve these ideals. During the Jim Crow years, many middle-class blacks drew class distinctions in which they often blamed the behavior of poor blacks for the "Negro problem." Their task was to uplift these people to middle-class respectability in order to free the race from discrimination. The problem was that the behavior of working and poor people was not the cause of racism. Their condition was the consequence of an oppressive and brutal Jim Crow society. Nor did the middle class always see that working-class people played a dynamic role in community life. They contributed their labor, time, and money to support

A riot had been building for weeks in Atlanta before it exploded. No one knows exactly how many blacks or whites were killed—many bodies were buried secretly. Most of the blacks who were killed had been caught unaware downtown.

schools and other community institutions and helped one another in hard times. Workers sporadically staged strikes and work slowdowns to protest their low wages. On several occasions, washerwomen refused to wash clothes and sanitation workers to clean streets until they were paid a living wage.

Despite the accomplishments of the black community, Atlanta remained one of the most segregated cities in the South. If W.E.B. Du Bois had a meeting with a white lawyer in town,

Walter White (bottom right) was a teenager in Atlanta when the riot took place and was downtown with his postman father, who was making his rounds. What saved his life was that he and his father could pass for white. The riot played a role in White's eventually becoming a civil rights activist.

he would either have to walk up the stairs to his office or take the freight elevator. He could not use the main elevator despite his accomplishments. He would also have to wait for the lawyer in the colored section of his office. If he went shopping in town and wanted to buy a hat in a white store, he could not try it on. If he rode a streetcar or went to a lake for recreation, he would encounter Jim Crow restrictions. As a result, Du Bois walked wherever he went and seldom, if ever, shopped in white Atlanta.

Even with rigid segregation, one historian wrote in 1902, "There has never been a race riot in Atlanta. The white man and the negro have lived together in this city more peacefully and in better spirit than in any other city, in either the north or south." Negrophobia, which was beneath the surface in Atlanta, began to surface in 1905 when Thomas Dixon's play version of his novel *The Clansman* arrived in Atlanta. The play reinforced the image of blacks as either loyal "Sambo"-type servants or vicious "beast-rapists." It glorified the Klan as saving the South from the Negro menace and protecting the honor of white women.

Not all Southerners agreed with Dixon. Joseph Cummings, a former Civil War officer and Klansman, condemned the play. "I regard this reverend gentleman's work in the 'Clansman' as not only nasty—like all his writings—but fiendish and cowardly, because it intends to incite our people to deeds of violence and cruelty towards a defenseless class of people who need our protection and encouragement."

The following year, tensions increased during the political campaign for governor. The candidates were Hoke Smith, a successful and usually racially moderate political leader, and Clark Howell, also a racial moderate, who was editor of the *Atlanta Constitution.* In order to win the election, Smith pandered to the racial hatred of the crowds, invoking the racial massacres in Wilmington. "We can handle them as we did in Wilmington, where the woods were black with their hanging carcasses. Shall it be ballots now or bullets later?" Smith enlisted the support of former Populist leader Tom Watson, who still had great influence over Georgia's white farmers. Watson had abandoned his advocacy of racial cooperation. The price for his support was Smith's promise to disfranchise blacks. Watson unleashed a vituperative campaign against blacks. "The Negro has no comprehension of virtue, honesty, gratitude, truth and principle. It is necessary to lynch him occasionally, and to flog him now and then, to keep him from blaspheming the almighty by his conduct on account of his color and smell."

Bishop Henry Turner struck back. "Disfranchisement is thievery," he said. "Disfranchisement cannot permanently settle the race or suffrage questions, for whatever the barbarism, the negro will climb over it. If the demand is property, we will buy it; if education, we will acquire it. We are determined to vote. Give us liberty, symbolized by the ballot, or give us death."

Even after Smith won, the mood remained tense as the press launched a newspaper war, using alleged assaults by blacks against white women as the ammunition. Although it turned out that most of the so-called crimes were fiction, the articles and editorials were maliciously inflammatory. "To think of the awful crimes being committed against our women is alarming. It seems that men are justified in adopting the most radical punishment for the perpetration of such deeds as can be devised this side of the region of fire and brimstone. Then to Arms Men of Georgia!" Another writer suggested, "Let's continue to kill all negroes who commit the unmentionable crime, and make eunuchs of all male issues before they are 8 days old."

In 1909, W.E.B. Du Bois, critical of Booker T. Washington's philosophy of accommodation, and his domination of funding for black education, exchanged his scholar's life for that of an activist's and joined the National Association for the Advancement of Colored People in New York.

Another target of white outrage was Decatur Street, a world of secondhand stores, pawnshops, cheap foods, pool halls, barber shops, moonshine, clubs and theaters, saloons and dance halls, vaudeville and minstrel shows, blues singers. Here black men and women sought to escape the harshness of the white world and find social dignity and entertainment they could afford. It was also a quarter in which poor whites and blacks drank and gambled together and shared the same prostitutes. The *Atlanta Journal* condemned it: "The whole street stunk. Odors of mullet, of week old beer, of corn and rye whiskey, of frying grease, of barber shops, of humanity rushed pell-mell. . . . Drunken and maudlin negroes, men and women, with the criminal white types, lounged on the sidewalk or staggered through the dense crowds."

Middle-class blacks also railed against Decatur Street. Reverend Proctor condemned the public dance halls as sinful. "The better element does not want them and the worse element should not have them. In the name of Anglo-Saxon civilization, remove these things that are ruining the character of our young men and stealing away the virtue of our young women."

Throughout the third week of September, the *Atlanta Evening News* and the *Atlanta Jour-*

nal, locked in a campaign to attract readers, published a number of special editions with hysterical headlines about black assaults on white women, almost every one of which was false. The headlines intensified the racial hostilities raised by Dixon's play and the political campaign. On Saturday, white crowds along Decatur Street, many of whom were drunk and inflamed by the headlines, began to gather. Men gave speeches about protecting white women from the black menace. Someone shouted, "Kill the niggers," and soon the cry was running along the crowded streets. Some ten thousand men and boys were in the mob. Whenever the whites would see a Negro, someone would cry, "There is one of the black fiends." In a few minutes the black would be dead or beaten unconscious. Men, women, and children were dragged off of streetcars and attacked without mercy. Two Negro barbers working at their chairs made no effort to resist. A brick hit one in the face and shots were fired. Both men fell to the floor. Their clothing was torn from them as souvenirs. Thirteen-year-old Walter White was accompanying his father, a postman, on his mail delivery rounds. They were able to pass through the mob because of their light skin color. White, writing of that night, said they witnessed the mob beat a crippled black man to death. "We saw a lame negro bootblack coming from Herndon's barber shop pathetically trying to outrun a mob of whites. We saw clubs and fists descending to the accompaniment of savage shouting and cursing. Its work done, the mob went after new prey. The body with the withered foot lay dead in a pool of blood in the street."

White and his father returned home, prepared to defend their family and property from the mob that was headed in their direction. With guns in hand, they waited inside the dark house. "We turned out the lights early as did all our neighbors. No one removed his clothes or thought of sleep. Apprehension was tangible. We could almost touch its cold and clammy surface. Toward midnight the unnatural quiet was broken by a roar that grew steady in volume."

When the mob appeared, White wrote that he heard the son of a grocer with whom his family had traded for many years yell, "That's where the nigger mail carrier lives! Let's burn it down. It's too nice for a nigger to live in!" White's father turned to him. "In a voice as quiet as if he was asking me to pass the sugar, he said, 'Son, don't shoot until the first man puts his foot on the lawn and then—don't you miss!' In that instant there opened up in me a great awareness. I knew then who I was. I was a negro . . . a person to be hunted, hanged, abused, discriminated against, kept in poverty and ignorance. It made no difference how intelligent, or talented, my millions of brothers and I were nor how virtuously we lived. A curse like that of Judas was on us."

As the mob advanced toward White's house, blacks in a neighboring house opened fire. The mob hesitated, then retreated. William Crogman, soon to be president of Georgia's Clark College, noted how the riot revealed the irony of racial uplift and its class distinctions. "Here we have worked and prayed and tried to make good men and women out of our colored population, and on our very doorstep the whites kill these good men. But lawless elements in our population, the element we have condemned fights back and it is to these people we owe our lives."

Officially, twenty-five blacks and one white died. Unofficially, more than one hundred may have died. Many were believed to be whites. David Howard, a black mortician, told a friend he had secretly buried a number of whites in the black cemetery. "You have no idea how many white people I had to bury in the Negro cemetery because they didn't want the white people to know who was getting killed by the Negroes in the riots."

The mayor ordered blacks to be searched for firearms. Blacks found ways to circumvent the order. Lugenia Hope, whose husband was guarding the campus of Atlanta Baptist with a rifle, reported, "The Negroes hid their arms and those of their neighbors who were not at home. We had enough to feel secure. It was said they came to the city in coffins. Some were carried in soiled laundry." W.E.B Du Bois, rushing home from Alabama to protect his family, wrote the highly emotional poem "A Litany at Atlanta," which questioned if the riot was not the amusement of a racist white God:

> Bewildered we are, and passion-tost, mad with the madness of a mobbed and mocked and murdered people; straining at the armposts of Thy Throne, we raise our shackled hands and charge Thee, God, by the bones of our stolen fathers, by the tears of our dead mothers, by the very blood of Thy crucified Christ: *What meaneth this?* Tell us the Plan; give us the Sign!
>
>   *Keep not Thou silent, O God!*

After the riot, the white business leaders, shocked at what had happened, agreed to meet with black leaders. They were startled to find themselves confronted by one businessman: "If living a sober, industrious, upright life, accumulating property and educating his children is not the standard by which a colored man can live and be protected in the South, what is to become of him? When we aspire to be decent and industrious, we are told we set bad examples to other colored men. Tell us your standards for colored men. What are the requirements under which we may live and be protected?" Whites had no answer.

Booker T. Washington was pleased when whites offered to fire some police officers and arrest some mob leaders. He condemned black rapists along with white rioters and praised the interracial council for its conciliatory efforts. "I would especially urge the colored people in Atlanta not to make the fatal mistake of trying to retaliate. What is needed now is to get the best element of both races together and try to change the deplorable state of affairs. The Atlanta outbreak should not discourage our people but should teach a lesson from which we all can profit." His stance angered many black residents of Atlanta. Some pointed out that they had taken his advice on business and education and did not try to push too hard for their rights. And yet a race riot still happened. Washington's moral authority was shaken.

White conciliation had its limits. The leaders of the city refused to accept responsibility for the riot. When J. Max Barber published an article in a Northern journal blaming whites for the riot, claiming that better-class whites were also members of the mob, he was told either to leave town or face a criminal trial. "Not wanting to be made a slave on a Georgia chain gang, I departed for the North," he said.

Thomas Dixon, whose play *The Clansman* had helped ignite the riots, had no regrets. Race war, he said, was inevitable. "The insolence of the Negro in Atlanta has grown greatly. The outbreak of whites against the Negro was inevitable. There will be many outbreaks as long as the Negro continues to live in the same community as the white man."

The Atlanta riot was followed by disfranchisement, despite black efforts to block it. Du Bois was now determined to give up the scholar's life for that of an activist. In 1909, he traveled to New York to help found the interracial National Association for the Advancement of Colored People. The NAACP would become the foremost champion of black rights in America for the next fifty years.

When World War I began, the black soldiers seen here handcuffed together were sent to Fort Logan, Texas, outside of Houston. Harassed by the police, they struck back, killing sixteen whites.

Du Bois resigned from Atlanta University and became editor of the NAACP's magazine *The Crisis,* which would become the voice of a new generation of black militants. *The Crisis* battled racial discrimination, exposed atrocities and outrages against blacks, supported women's rights, and promoted race pride in the arts and literature. Within four months, the number of subscribers jumped from one thousand to six thousand and eventually soared to more than one hundred thousand.

Du Bois startled his readers in 1912 when he supported Woodrow Wilson for President even though Wilson was a Democrat and a Southerner. Wilson, he said, had promised fairness and justice for blacks, and he seemed a man of his word. In a letter to a black church official, Wilson wrote, "Let me assure my fellow colored citizens the earnest wish to see justice done the colored people in every manner and not merely grudging justice, but justice executed with liberality and cordial good feeling. Should I become President of the United States they may count upon me for absolute fair dealing for everything by which I could assist in advancing their interests of the race." Du Bois had no illusions about Wilson and the Southern Democrats, but he was aware that Northern Republicans had lost interest in supporting black rights. He also perceived that blacks who had migrated to Northern cities were voting and might be willing to vote for Democrats—if Northern Democrats proved sympathetic to demands for their rights.

Du Bois articulated what blacks expected from Wilson: "We want to be treated as men. We want to vote. We want our children to be educated. We want lynching stopped. We want no longer to be herded as cattle on street cars and railroads. We want the right to earn a living and own property. Be not untrue, President Wilson, to the highest ideals of American Democracy."

Du Bois underestimated the political power of the Southern demagogues in the Senate. Mississippi's James Kimble Vardaman and John Sharp Williams, Georgia's Hoke Smith, and South Carolina's Ben Tillman used Wilson's own racial prejudice to their advantage. They persuaded him to dismiss fifteen out of seventeen black supervisors who had been previously appointed to federal jobs and replace them with whites. He also refused to appoint black ambassadors to Haiti and Santo Domingo, posts traditionally awarded to them.

Postmaster General Albert Burelson and Treasury Secretary William McAdoo, both Southerners, issued orders segregating their departments, backed with an executive order from Wilson. They were determined to put blacks "in their place" by forcing them out of positions of competence and authority and into menial jobs. They could be doormen or messengers but not auditor for the navy nor recorder of deeds, two positions that had been held by blacks since Grant was President.

Throughout the country, blacks were segregated or dismissed. In Georgia, the head of the Internal Revenue Division fired all black employees. "There are no government positions for Negroes in the South. A Negro's place is in the corn field," he said. The President's wife, Ellen Wilson, was said to have a hand in expanding the segregation of federal employees in Washington. Black were shunted off into dimly lit and poorly ventilated rooms away from whites, forced out of lunchrooms, and required to use separate toilets. Salaries were reduced, in some cases drastically. W. P. Napper's salary was cut from $1,400 to $720; Julian Ross's was slashed from $1,600 to $600. Experienced clerks were reassigned as messengers and watchmen.

To justify segregation, officials publicized complaints by white women. The standard complaints were made: Women clerks were supposed to be afraid of black men's sexuality and disease. According to one woman, "Several years ago, I was compelled to take dictation from two negro men. I worked for a dark skinned woolly-headed negro. I then felt if a human being would ever be justified in ending her life, I would then for I was a Southern woman, my father a distinguished officer and my mother a woman of greatest refinement." Another woman testified, "The same toilet is used by whites and blacks and some of said blacks have been diseased. That one Negro woman, Alexandria, has been for many years afflicted with a private disease and for dread of using the toilet after her, some of the girls are compelled to suffer physically and mentally."

When a group of black women refused to sit in special lunchrooms reserved for them, they were warned of the consequences by Mrs. Archibald Hopkins, a white woman. "Why do you go where you are not wanted? Do you know that the Democrats are in power? If you people will go along and stay away from places where you are not wanted, we may let you hold your places."

African-American women fought back as best they could. Mary Church Terrell, a member of the highly influential Church family of Memphis and married to one of the few African-American judges in Washington, was one of several women who protested against Jim Crow in the government. "One of the young women came to tell me that an order had been promulgated whereby the colored women clerks in our section would no longer be allowed to enter the lavatory. Then and there I made up my mind I would do everything in my power to prevent that order from being executed." She embarrassed officials by offering a strongly

Despite the intense racial prejudice against them, black soldiers served their country during World War I. Some fought in France alongside French troops, since American generals did not want them serving with white American soldiers. The French people treated them warmly and without prejudice.

worded letter of resignation. In return for moderating her letter and not releasing it publicly, her department agreed to cancel the order.

Despite Wilson's protest that he was under pressure from Southern senators to segregate the government, the President was sympathetic to their demands. "I do approve of the segregation that is being attempted in several of the departments," he wrote to a minister. "It is distinctly to the advantage of the colored people themselves that they should be organized, so far as possible and convenient, in distinct bureaus where they will center their work."

Booker T. Washington, deeply saddened by what was happening, said little publicly. For years he had labored in the vineyards of accommodation, but all it had borne were the bitter fruits of white supremacy. The Wilson administration made him even more despairing. "I have never seen the colored people so discouraged and bitter as they are at the present time. I can't believe President Wilson realizes what harm is being done to both races on account of the recent policy of racial discrimination in the departments." Washington remained publicly silent even though people begged him to speak out. One woman wrote, "We all love and revere you for what you have achieved but we could love and honor you so much more if you would speak out for your people."

Du Bois sharply criticized Wilson in *The Crisis.* "The federal government has set the colored apart as if mere contact with them were contamination. Behind screens and closed doors they now sit as though leprous. How long will it be before the hateful epithets of 'Nigger' and 'Jim Crow' are openly applied?" The NAACP publicly exposed the segregationist policies of the Wilson administration and organized a national campaign of protest. Its efforts checked the spread of Wilson's Jim Crow campaign but did not root out procedures that were already in place.

On the evening of March 21, 1915, President Wilson attended a special screening at the White House of *Birth of a Nation,* a film based on *The Clansman* and directed by D. W. Griffith. The film presented a distorted portrait of the South after the Civil War, glorifying the Ku Klux Klan and denigrating blacks. An enthusiastic Wilson reportedly remarked, "It is like writing history with lightning, and my only regret is that it is all so terribly true." African-American audiences openly wept at its malicious portrayal of blacks while Northern white audiences cheered. Violence erupted in many cities where the film was shown. Gangs of whites roamed city streets attacking blacks. In Lafayette, Indiana, a white man killed a black teenager after seeing the movie. Thomas Dixon reveled in its triumph. "The real purpose of my film," he confessed gleefully, "was to revolutionize Northern audiences that would transform every man into a Southern partisan for life."

As the NAACP fought against the film and tried unsuccessfully to get it banned, the Ku Klux Klan used it to launch a massive recruiting campaign that would bring in millions of members.

In the midst of the battle over *Birth of a Nation,* Booker T. Washington died. Du Bois tactfully praised him for his greatness but also pointed out his weaknesses. "He was the greatest Negro leader since Frederick Douglass and the most distinguished man, white or black, who has come out of the South since the Civil War. Of the good he accomplished there can be no doubt . . . On the other hand, we must lay on the soul of this man, a heavy responsibility for the consummation of Negro disfranchisement, the decline of the Negro college and public school and the firmer establishment of color caste in this land."

Du Bois's battle with Washington was over, but his quarrel with Wilson continued. Although he supported the President when Wilson declared war on Germany in 1917, he did so reluctantly. Black soldiers, he knew, would suffer in America's Jim Crow army.

In 1917, soldiers of the all-black Third Battalion, Twenty-Fourth Infantry were assigned to Fort Logan outside of Houston, Texas. Houston had the largest black community in the state at the time, with a police force that was particularly aggressive toward black people. Clashes developed between the police and the soldiers, many of whom were not Southerners and not used to segregation. Black soldiers suffered beatings and unjustified arrests by the police. When a rumor spread that one of the soldiers, Corporal Charles Baltimore, had been killed by the police, his company prepared to march into town and take revenge. Baltimore had been beaten by the police but not killed, and then returned to camp. But the soldiers had passed their emotional point of no return. They marched into town and opened fire. When the shooting stopped, sixteen whites and four black men were dead. In a rushed and secret court-martial, nineteen men were sentenced to death and forty-three to life imprisonment. The first thirteen to die were not told their sentence or the date of their execution until hours before they were to die. They were denied their right to appeal to the president. The men requested to be shot as soldiers. The army refused their request.

On the night before his execution, on December 11, 1917, Baltimore wrote a farewell letter to his brother.

I write you for the last time in this world. I am to be executed tomorrow morning. I know this is shocking news but don't worry too much as it is God's will. I was convicted at the general court-martial held here last month; tried for mutiny and murder. It is true that I went downtown with the men who marched out from camp.
But I am innocent of shedding any blood.
Goodbye and meet me in heaven.
Your brother.
Charles Baltimore

C. E. Butzer, a white soldier, witnessed their deaths:

The prisoners were sitting in two rows, back to back on folding chairs and the hangman's knots were being adjusted. The men were droning a hymn, very soft and low. All I could make out was "I'm comin home, I'm comin home." Colonel Millard Waltz, the army officer in charge gave the command "Attention!" The prisoners snapped to their feet and stood on trapdoors. Then, as if by preconcerted plan, they broke into a song. It was a dolorous hymn chanted in a nasal monotone. Their last words were addressed to their white guards with whom they had become friendly. And the men of the 24th could be heard to say "Goodbye Boys of Company C."

Du Bois was deeply saddened and angered by the executions. In one of his most powerful editorials, he condemned the system that enabled this tragedy to happen.

Houston was not an ordinary outburst. They were not young recruits; they were not wild and drunkard wastrels. They were disciplined men who said—"This is enough—we'll stand no more." They broke the law. Against their punishment, if it were legal, we cannot protest. But we can protest and we do protest against the shameful treatment which these men and which we, their brothers, receive all our lives, and which our fathers received and which our children await. And above all we raise our clenched hand against the hundreds of thousands of white murderers and rapists and scoundrels who have oppressed, killed, ruined and robbed, and debased their black fellow men and fellow women and yet today walk scot free, unwhipped by justice, and uncondemned by millions of their white fellow citizens and unrebuked by the President of the United States.

While the war reinforced racial prejudice, it also set in motion social forces that would challenge that prejudice. Hundreds of thousands of blacks migrated north to work in factories, while some two hundred thousand African Americans served their country in Europe in a segregated army.

The army went out of its way to discriminate against blacks, especially in France where French citizens were not obsessed with racial distinctions. General John Pershing, commander in chief, sent a directive to the French Military Mission stationed with American troops. It read in part, "We must prevent the rise of any pronounced degree of intimacy between French officers and black officers. . . . We must not eat with them, shake hands with them, seek to talk to them and meet with them outside the requirements of military service. . . . White Americans become very incensed at any particular expression of intimacy between white women and black men."

One all-black regiment, the 369th, fought side by side with French soldiers as equals. The men of the 369th earned an unprecedented number of French military honors: 171 Croix de Guerre, France's highest military medal. African-American soldiers hoped that their patriotic service would earn them recognition, acceptance, and equality in American society on their return. The world war had created a new impetus and a new confidence in those the writer Alain Locke called the "New Negro."

As black soldiers returned home from France, W.E.B. Du Bois summoned them to prepare for what they were about to confront at home. "Make way for democracy. We saved it in France and by the great Jehovah we will save it in the United States or know the reasons why. This country of ours, despite all its better souls have done and dreamed is yet a shameful land. It gloats in lynching, disfranchisement, caste, brutality, and insults. By the gods of heavens we are cowards and jackasses if we do not now marshal every one of our brains and brawn to fight a sterner, longer, more unbending battle against the forces of hell in our own land. We return. We return from fighting. We return fighting."

Chapter 7

Prelude to Change:
Between Two Wars, 1918–1931

It was Walter White's favorite joke. When traveling through the South, he would board the train, seat himself in the "white" section, order a drink, and sometimes have a conversation with his fellow passengers about crops, the weather, the heat—or race. Once, one of his traveling companions expressed anger about "nigruhs" trying to pass for white. "However,"

the man added confidently, "they can't fool me." Walter White asked how he could tell. "By their fingernails," the man replied. "They're always shaped like half-moons." Looking directly at his traveling companion, his blue eyes calm as lake water, White held up the back of his hand and asked what race he belonged to. The Southerner laughed and said he was definitely a white man. Walter White grinned. He might have burst out laughing, but then he would risk someone discovering that he was a black man. Discovery would get him killed.

Walter White was not playing a practical joke. Nor was he trying to cross the color line for his own advantage. He was on a deadly mission for the NAACP, and his fair complexion was his cover. In 1918, White had become the NAACP's chief investigator of lynching. He would travel to a town where a lynching had occurred, pretend he was a salesman or newspaperman, interview

Lynchings continued in the 1920s. In this image, one of the mob is cutting off the toe of one of the victims to take as a souvenir.

In the 1920s, the NAACP began an extensive anti-lynching campaign in order to get Congress to pass a law making lynching a federal crime. But Southern Senators were able to block the bill from passing.

local whites about the event, gather the names of some of the members of the mob, and then publish the facts in *The Crisis* and other Northern newspapers.

In May, White journeyed to south Georgia to find out why black tenant farmers Hayes and Mary Turner had both been lynched. White casually engaged local people in seemingly unrelated conversations until they freely offered to talk about the Turner lynchings. White discovered that the Turners had worked for a white planter who had been murdered by one of his black tenants. The tenant had fled, and the mob lynched Hayes Turner, accusing him of being an accomplice solely on the grounds that he knew the killer—not a surprising fact since both worked for the same man. Turner's wife, Mary, eight months pregnant, angrily announced that if she ever found out who lynched her husband, she would swear out a warrant for their arrest. The mob went wild and tracked her down. Walter White later reported what happened next.

Securely they bound her ankles together and, by them, hanged her to a tree. Gasoline and motor oil were thrown upon her dangling clothes; a match wrapped her in sudden flames. Mocking, ribald laughter from her tormentors answered the helpless woman's screams of pain and terror. "Mister you ought to have heard the nigger wench howl," a member of the mob boasted to me a few days later as we stood at the place of Mary Turner's death. The clothes burned from her crisply toasted body, in which, unfortunately life still lingered. A man stepped forward towards the woman and with his knife, ripped open the abdomen in a crude Cæsarean operation. Out tumbled the prematurely born child. Two feeble cries it gave—and received for answer, the heel of a stalwart man, as life was ground out of the tiny form. Under the tree of death was scooped a shallow hole. . . . An empty whisky bottle, quart size, was given for a headstone. Inside its neck was stuck a half-smoked cigar—which had saved the delicate nostrils of one member of the mob from the stench of burning flesh.

The Turner lynchings were a prelude to the racial storms about to sweep across America at the end of World War I. In the summer of 1919, the racial time bomb exploded. Lynchings were brazenly carried out and advertised in newspapers before the event. In Ellisville, Tennessee, local newspapers announced the lynching in advance: "Three Thousand Will Burn Negro," "John Hartfield Will be Lynched by Ellisville Mob at 5 This Afternoon," "Negro Sulky as Burning Nears." Thousands came to watch or participate, jamming trains, bringing their dinners, and turning the event into a festive occasion.

In 1919, twenty-three race riots occurred, in mostly Northern cities. As Chicago sweltered in a blaze of summer's heat, racial temperatures were climbing. On Sunday, July 27, Eugene Williams, a seventeen-year-old black youth, went swimming in Lake Michigan to cool off. Blacks and whites used separate sections of the beach. When Williams mistakenly swam across the color line, screaming white youths hurled rocks at him. Williams frantically tried to swim to safety but drowned before he could make it back to the black section of the beach. The incident triggered a race riot. That night, bands of whites roamed the city streets beating and killing unsuspecting blacks. Blacks fiercely fought back. When the riot finally ended, some fifteen whites and twenty-three blacks were dead.

The Chicago riot was part of a racial frenzy of clashes, massacres, and lynchings throughout the North and the South. All were started by whites. In Washington, D.C., four whites and two blacks were killed. Whites were astonished that blacks dared to fight back. The *New York Times* lamented the new black militancy: "There had been no trouble with the Negro before the war when most admitted the superiority of the white race." A "southern black woman," as she identified herself in a letter to *The Crisis*, praised blacks for fighting back. "The Washington riot gave me a thrill that comes once in a life time . . . at last our men had stood up like men. . . . I stood up alone in my room . . . and exclaimed aloud, 'Oh I thank God, thank God.' The pent up horror, grief and humiliation of a life time—half a century—was being stripped from me."

In October 1919, a race war exploded in Phillips County, Arkansas. On the night of September 30, a small group of black men and women were gathering at a rural church to organize the Progressive Farmers and Household Union of America. They had hired a white lawyer, U. S. Bratton, and were planning to sue their landlords for money owed them for their crops, and for an itemized accounting of their charges at the store. When two white law enforcement officers arrived at the church, one later claiming they were looking for a bootlegger, shots were exchanged. One officer was killed and the other wounded.

As word of the shootings spread throughout the county, the local sheriff sent out a call for men "to hunt Mr. Nigger in his lair." The call went out to Mississippi to come to the aid of white men in Phillips County. Hundreds of armed men jumped into trains, trucks, and cars and crossed into Arkansas, firing out of windows at every black they saw. Some said that if it was black and moving, it was target practice. Frank Moore, one of the farmers at the church, saw the massacre as it unfolded. "The whites sent word that they was comin down here and kill every nigger they found. There were 300 or 400 more white men with guns, shooting and killing women and children."

Farmers were not the only target for the mob. Dr. D.A.E. Johnston, a prominent dentist from Helena, Arkansas, and his three brothers were seized as they returned from a hunting trip. They were chained together in a car and shot to death.

Soldiers from the United States Army eventually restored order, although some claimed they participated in the killings. By the time the shooting ended, twenty-five blacks and five whites were listed as officially dead. Many blacks believed that perhaps as many as two hundred blacks were killed, their bodies dumped in the Mississippi River or left to rot in the canebrake. The stench of the dead could be smelled for miles.

The white establishment charged that blacks had been in a secret conspiracy to rise up and overthrow the white power planters, take their land, and rape their women. No evidence was produced to substantiate the charge. Since five white men were killed during the riot—some probably shot by accident by other whites—more black men had to die. More than seven hundred were arrested. Sixty-seven were sent to prison. Twelve farmers were tried by an all-white jury for the murder of whites. During the trial, a mob surrounded the courthouse, shouting that if the accused black men were not sentenced to death, the mob would lynch them. Prisoners were tortured to confess or to testify against others. Alf Banks, one of the twelve, told his lawyer, "I was frequently whipped and also put in an electric chair and shocked and strangling drugs would be put in my nose to make me tell that others had killed or shot at white people and to force me to testify against them."

The all-white jury debated the charges fewer than eight minutes per man. Each defendant was found guilty. The judge dutifully sentenced all twelve to death. The mob cheered. As far as Arkansas was concerned, the case was closed.

For Walter White the case was far from closed. As far as he was concerned, the trial was a

One reason W.E.B. Du Bois was protective of Fisk was because it was his alma mater. This is his graduation photo in 1887—he is seated at the left.

lynching that wore the mask of law. White traveled to Arkansas posing as a newspaper reporter, first interviewing the governor, who called White "one of the most brilliant newspapermen he had ever met," and then traveling to Phillips County, the scene of the massacre. During his investigation, a black man approached White and warned him that a lynching party was being prepared for him. His identity had been discovered. White immediately boarded the first train out of Helena. As he anxiously waited for the train to leave the station, the conductor approached him. "You're leaving just before the fun is about to start. There's a damned yellow nigger down here passing for white and the boys are gonna get him. . . . When they get through with him, he won't pass for white no more." White later wrote, "No matter what the distance, I shall never take a train ride as long as that one. Later in Memphis, I learned that news had been circulated there that I had been lynched in Arkansas that afternoon."

White published the real story behind the massacre that challenged Arkansas's version of the events. He wrote that the attempt of blacks to form a union to control their own labor angered whites who were determined to destroy it by any means.

The NAACP hired local lawyers to appeal the death sentence of the twelve convicted farmers. Among them was Scipio Africanus Jones, a black lawyer from Little Rock born in slavery, who argued that the presence of the mob outside the courthouse during the trial made it impossible for the defendants to receive a fair trial. After several years of fighting to have the twelve men freed, the United States Supreme Court agreed to hear the case. On February 19, 1923, in a landmark decision (*Moore* v. *Dempsey*) that became a major step in defending the rights of black defendants, Justice Oliver Wendell Holmes wrote, "If the whole case is a mask—that counsel, jury and judge were swept to the fatal end by an irresistible tide of public passion—and the state courts refuse to correct the wrong, then nothing can prevent this court from securing to the petitioners their constitutional rights."

More and greater violence was yet to come. In 1921, the worst race riot in America occurred in Tulsa, Oklahoma, a city that boasted one of the most prosperous African-American communities in the country. The city had three black millionaires and numerous prosperous black businessmen. When a young woman elevator operator charged a black youth with assault—it seemed that he accidentally stepped on her toe—the youth was arrested. Seventy-five armed blacks went to the jail to protect him from a mob, but no mob had gathered. As the men were about to leave, a white man tried to take away the gun of a black man. The confrontation suddenly escalated into a gun battle. Several whites were killed and injured and two blacks were killed. Mobs of enraged white men roamed the black section of Greenwood, breaking into houses, gunning down blacks in their beds, and setting fire to houses and businesses. By the next morning, the black section of Greenwood lay in ashes. Thirty-five city blocks had been burned to the ground. Six thousand blacks had been rounded up by the mob, and more than eight hundred were wounded. Anywhere between seventy-five to three hundred African Americans might have been killed. Not a single white was ever prosecuted.

The NAACP urgently tried to stem the violence by focusing national attention on what was happening in the South and lobbying for federal anti-lynching laws. Supported by Congressmen L. C. Dyer of Missouri, the NAACP pushed to make lynching a federal crime, emphasizing that more than 50 percent of those people lynched were already in the custody of law enforcement officials. The NAACP charged that a good many sheriffs had arranged for their prisoners to be handed over to the mob.

* * *

For W.E.B. Du Bois, there were other battles to be fought in addition to lynching. The training grounds for what he called "the talented tenth," that 10 percent of the race that he believed would lead the fight against Jim Crow, were the liberal arts black colleges like his beloved alma mater Fisk University in Nashville. In the mid-1920s, Du Bois saw that the liberal arts tradition in general, and Fisk University in particular, was threatened. Using *The Crisis* as his platform, Du Bois clashed with some of the most powerful and influential men in America.

Du Bois had graduated from Fisk in the 1880s, and he cherished the university that had intellectually nourished him. He considered Fisk the crown jewel of the black colleges. It had an integrated faculty and more than six hundred students, many of whom came from the elite families of the black middle class. "Fisk is the college—the shrine of my young years of high idealism and infinite faith," he wrote. "I have known it in the great days of its leaders—Cravath, Spence, Morgan—firm, splendid souls to whom compromise with evil was death. They were men radical in their belief in Negro equality."

The churches that had once financially supported Fisk and other black colleges had run out of money. In their place emerged a new breed of philanthropists who no longer believed in black equality. They were businessmen of great wealth—men like Andrew Carnegie, John D. Rockefeller, George Foster Peabody, and Julius Rosenwald—whose foundations supported black and white schools in the rural South. They did not want to transform the South but to make it run more efficiently. Black education for them was primarily a means to socialize black children to accept a subordinate status, not a means of improving their lives.

The most powerful of the philanthropic foundations was the General Education Board, founded by John D. Rockefeller. Its first president, William Baldwin, perfectly incarnated its philosophy. Baldwin, the son of a former abolitionist who fought to end slavery, despised abolitionism. He was described as a nervous, impatient man, intolerant of dissent and convinced that African Americans were innately inferior. He hated black intellectuals, "especially those who have been educated at Harvard," pointedly referring to the Harvard-educated Du Bois. He charged, "Their problem was that it was purely an attempt on their part to be white people." He believed that blacks could not be educated much beyond the three R's, that they were a child race two hundred years behind the Anglo-Saxon in development.

In the 1890s, Baldwin paid a surprise visit to Tuskegee and became a disciple of industrial education. He enthusiastically embraced Booker T. Washington's plan to train black teachers to instruct their students to accept Jim Crow and Southern whites as "their best friends." Aware that Southerners were suspicious of Northern white support for black schools, Baldwin reassured them that the General Education Board intended to reinforce the Southern way of life, not challenge it. He told one audience, "Time has proven that the Negro is best fitted to perform the heavy labor of the South. The Negro and the mule is the only combination to grow cotton. He will willingly fill the more menial positions and do the heavy work at less wages than the white man."

Baldwin issued a warning to black educators. "Avoid social questions; leave politics alone; continue to be patient; live moral lives; learn to work; and know that is a crime for any teacher, white or black, to educate the negro for positions that are not open to him." These remarks led Du Bois to reply, "There are those rich and intelligent people who masquerade as the Negro's friend in order to educate a race of scullions and then complain of their lack of proven ability."

Baldwin and his fellow philanthropists wanted to dismantle liberal arts instruction in African-American schools and colleges. Their goal was to bring social harmony and industrial progress to the South by making black schools vocational institutions like Tuskegee and Hampton. They felt that vocational training would be good for blacks, good for the South, and good for business, as it would keep labor unions out. Fisk was on their list. They agreed with Robert L. Jones, Tennessee's superintendent of education, who commented, "I would have his academic education limited, for I am inclined to think that the negro can best be utilized on the farms, in the shops and, in fact, in all lines of trade."

In 1915, the trustees of Fisk hired Fayette McKenzie, a white educator, as president of the university. Du Bois welcomed him at first. "I saw in him a new type of young, scientific philanthropist come to help and re-establish training among Negroes."

McKenzie's motto was, "Let Us Dare to Be a University. . . . A Negro is . . . capable of the highest scholarship . . . and a Negro college . . . can measure up at every point with the standard colleges of the land." Part of McKenzie's plan was to raise a million-dollar endowment from Northern foundations in order to upgrade the quality of education at Fisk and make it free from financial worries. Although there was some concern among board members about liberalism at Fisk, some recognized that a few black colleges were needed to train the ministers, doctors, and lawyers who would serve the black community. The board wanted to see that McKenzie had the support of Nashville's white community and that the school produced students who would accommodate the realities of white supremacy and accept "complete separation" of the races.

The board soon discovered that McKenzie was their kind of educator. Convinced that black adolescents were extremely sensual beings who had to be controlled, McKenzie imposed strict rules of behavior on men and women, regulating almost every moment of their lives. He banned dating and most contact between men and women. He imposed a strict dress code for women. They were required to wear high-necked gingham dresses with long sleeves, white between April and November, blue the rest of the year. "The skirt could be gathered but could have no more than three tucks or ruffles. No lace or embroidery trimming was allowed. . . . Chiffon, georgette, organdy or other thin waists were proscribed."

Smoking was not allowed. Jazz playing was forbidden on the piano. He ended intercollegiate baseball and track, barred fraternities and the NAACP from campus. McKenzie abolished student government and the student literary magazine, *The Herald*. He even censored Du Bois's magazine, *The Crisis*. He monitored all student oration and debates, expelled students without due process, and fired faculty members he felt were disloyal. He encouraged snitching, preferred docile students, and ignored Nashville's black community. To McKenzie and his supporters, the spirit of Fisk University was incarnated in its famous choir, which for fifty years had entertained white audiences around the world with mournful spirituals rooted in slavery days.

In the 1920s, jazz, not spirituals, was the soul of black music. Jazz was the voice of rebellious youth demanding new freedoms from old ways. On the Fisk campus, the irresistible forces of the new jazz age collided with the immovable resistance of the old ways. At Vanderbilt University across town, white students dressed in the styles of the day, drank from hip flasks, petted in the back of cars, smoked, danced, and listened to jazz music. Fisk's black students complained to Du Bois. Some expressed serious concerns about censorship and paternalism. Others were more troubled by the limits on their personal freedom. One coed wrote, "The girls of the student body might have been able to get along with the orders forbidding them to talk to boys. They may have been peaceful with the orders which forbade dancing, but when they keep wearing cotton stockings and gingham dresses, it is too much."

The white citizens of Nashville, impressed with McKenzie's rule, pledged fifty thousand dollars to the endowment fund, the first time a Southern community had done so for a black college.

In 1923, Julius Rosenwald visited Fisk. The founder of Sears Roebuck had contributed millions of dollars for black elementary and secondary schools throughout the South. Known as Rosenwald schools, they were built mostly by local people who contributed their labor and often raised part of the money. Rosenwald and the state contributed the rest. Thousands of Rosenwald schools were constructed in the 1920s and 1930s, and they provided much of the education for black children. In 1927, Tennessee spent $21.02 for every white child and only $11.88 for every black child.

Rosenwald was far more liberal and sympathetic than other philantropists to black aspirations, yet Fisk's students troubled him. "There seems to be an air of superiority among them and a desire to take on the spirit of a white university rather than the spirit which has always impressed me at Tuskegee."

Despite the concern, the board agreed to the endowment. They felt that McKenzie would see to it that Fisk students accepted the Southern way of life rather than challenged it. They expected Fisk not to produce any more Du Boises. To Du Bois, the issue was the soul of the university. "Suppose we lose Fisk; suppose we lose every cent that the entrenched millionaires have set aside to buy our freedom. They have the power, they have the wealth but Glory be to God, we still have our own souls and led by young men as these let us neither flinch nor falter, but fight and fight and fight again." Du Bois saw that McKenzie was accommodating to the South and had accepted white supremacy in exchange for an endowment. Instead of producing the "New Negro," a militant youth who would insist on his full rights as an American and be a race leader, Fisk was in danger of producing Booker T. Washingtons who would accept Jim Crow. This betrayed the ideals of democracy and equality of the abolitionist founders of Fisk.

At the end of May 1924, a deeply troubled Du Bois boarded a train to visit Fisk in Nashville. His daughter Yolande was graduating and he had been invited by McKenzie to address the alumni the following day. On June 2, with the president of the university, the trustees, students, and alumni packing Cravath Memorial Chapel and no doubt expecting a eulogy of McKenzie, Du Bois lowered the boom on him. *"Duiturni Silenti,"* he began, quoting "To My Long Continued Silence," Cicero's great oration before the Roman Senate almost two thousand years earlier. The smiling faces of McKenzie and his supporters turned to startled ones as Du Bois lashed McKenzie with fierce words of criticism. "I have never known an institution whose alumni are more bitter and disgusted with the present situation in this university. In Fisk today, discipline is choking freedom, threats are replacing inspiration, iron clad rules, suspicion, tale bearing are almost universal." Expecting to hear his praises sung by the man whom many considered the voice of black America, McKenzie was scolded like a naughty child in front of the whole world. Du Bois blasted him for his tyrannical rule, for selling out Fisk's birthright to wealthy philanthropists, and for subjecting female students to Jim Crow humiliations. "I am told the president of Fisk University took fifteen girls from the glee club, girls from some of the best Negro families in the United States, carried them down town at night to a white men's club, took them down an alley and admitted them through a servant's entrance, and had them sing in a basement while these white men smoked and laughed. If Erastus Cravath, one of our founders knew that a thing like that happened at Fisk

University, he would rise from the grave and protest against this disgrace and sacrilege." The students and some teachers broke out in thunderous applause. McKenzie spied one young lady furiously clapping from a seat in front of the chapel. Shortly afterward, she was charged with cheating and suspended.

Du Bois's speech added fuel to the fires of protest that had been burning on campus. George Streator, a returned World War I veteran, and one of the student leaders, kept Du Bois informed by mail of what was happening. In one letter, he reported how a teacher was using the classroom as a forum to support McKenzie. "Miss Chasin, a professor in English, assigned a 5000 word essay on the subject 'Why Dr. McKenzie should be retained at Fisk.' You know the predicament of the students. Say 'no' they'll flunk. Say 'yes' they'll surely get a good grade."

In November 1924, the board trustees arrived on campus and were immediately greeted by students chanting anti-McKenzie and pro–Du Bois statements: "Away with the Tsar" and "Down with the Tyrant." Streator presented a list of grievances to the trustees. The trustees recommended to McKenzie that he make a few minor concessions. McKenzie seemed to have agreed. Then, during a chapel service in February 1925, he revealed that the conciliatory hand masked an iron fist. He told the students, "A complete ignoring of the charges made against the university will be the policy of the board of trustees of Fisk University. The policy is unchanged. Those who don't like it can go." The battle escalated. Students responded with a brief but noisy demonstration. The students overturned chapel seats and broke windows, all the while keeping up a steady shouting of "Du Bois, Du Bois" and singing "Before I'll be a slave, I'll be buried in my grave."

McKenzie immediately retaliated by summoning the feared Nashville police to campus. Nashville blacks had continually suffered at the hands of the local police. A black minister had recently been killed by them, and a black youth was dragged out of his hospital bed and lynched without police interference. Two black women had been beaten by whites and a black merchant gunned down by a white saloon owner.

Eighty policemen armed with riot guns broke down the doors to the men's dormitory, smashed windows, and beat and arrested six of the seven students whom McKenzie had claimed were the ringleaders of the demonstration. The students were charged with a felony, a crime for which they could be sent to prison. McKenzie confessed that he lacked proof that the arrested men were guilty of any of the charges he made. "These men have spoken against my policies all throughout the year," he weakly explained. "While I had no proof these were the disturbers, I felt that they might be behind it." The charges against the students were dropped and after they were released, they left the school.

In response to the arrests, the students called a strike that polarized the Nashville community. Du Bois cheered them on. "I thank God that the younger generation of black students have the guts to yell and fight when their noses are rubbed in the mud." The white community completely supported McKenzie; the black community, the students. McKenzie mobilized Nashville's white civic clubs, which honored him with a luncheon. "When I was introduced, everybody in the room rose to his feet and a great many yelled as well as a great many cheered. I feel that never before in the United States has a white man in our work had such a hold on the city as I have in Nashville." He implied that should he not

The Great Depression hit the rural South with all the force of an economic tornado, destroying the lives and dreams of many sharecroppers and their children.

receive unconditional support from the black community and the trustees, "Not only will the white citizens and money of Nashville be turned into other directions, but the same will perhaps be true of a considerable part of the North."

The students struck, with Du Bois's blessing and moral support and with the alumni and the local black community behind them. They held fast for eight weeks despite pressure. Local white banks and the post office no longer would cash their checks. The black community stepped in to the rescue. They housed and fed them, advanced money, and were unwavering in their support. Coeds showed their rebellion by wearing flapper dresses, silk stockings, and high heels.

Du Bois now tried to rally the black community in support of his war against McKenzie and the General Education Board. To Du Bois's disgust, McKenzie received support from hundreds of parents of students. "We are heartily in accord with you and denounce this unbridled uprising among the students," wrote Mr. and Mrs. Alpha O. Young. "I hope you will continue strict rules and regulations for by such we feel our boys and girls are safe there," James T. Wright, a father of a student, wrote. "Get more machine guns and stay on the job. We need you and the sacrifices you are making for our people," W.L.B. Johnson agreed. Du Bois would later respond,

> "There were parents and alumna who insisted that even if the school authorities are wrong, it was the business of black boys and girls to submit. When students are willing to jeopardize their whole lives in an appeal for justice, the business of parents is to encourage and uphold their protesting children instead of cowing and disgracing them."

Despite having the trustees' support, McKenzie's rule was finished. Two months later, he resigned.

The victory had repercussions on other black campuses. At Howard University, a confrontation between the white president and the black faculty and student body led to the president's resignation and the appointment of the school's first black president. At Hampton, the battle was between the students and a white autocratic president supported by a condescending white faculty. Hampton was little more than a technical high school. Philanthropists lavished a great deal of money on the school because it was the embodiment of their ideal of black education. Du Bois sarcastically remarked that it had everything money could buy—except racial integrity. The strike was defeated, but it forced changes in the curriculum.

For many students, graduation from college was no guarantee of a good job in the South. Many of the best and brightest joined the mass migration that had begun before World War I and continued throughout the 1920s. The *Chicago Defender* continued its campaign to encourage blacks to leave. For millions of blacks, the paper kept alive the vision of the North as the land of freedom, a dream that had been in the hearts of black men and women since slavery time. Young Richard Wright, who became a nationally acclaimed writer, remembered how the North kept hope alive during the dark days of his childhood in the Deep South. "The North symbolized to me all that I had not felt or seen; it had no relation to what actually

The Scottsboro Boys were nine black youths who were riding a freight train when they were arrested for fighting with whites. When two women hoboes were discovered on the train, the boys were charged with rape and sentenced to death, although no rape had occurred. Their lives were saved by the legal campaign of the Communist Party.

existed. Yet by imagining a place where everything is possible, it kept hope alive inside of me."

The newspaper was banned in certain towns and counties of the South because whites feared its articles would cause their black laborers to leave for Chicago. Whites burned any copies of the paper they found. Blacks caught reading the newspaper could be flogged. Those bringing it in could be killed. Despite the censorship, blacks smuggled or sold the paper in almost every Southern city and town. Preachers read it to their congregations, barbers to their customers, the literate to the illiterate. One man commented, "My people grab it like a mule grabs a mouthful of fine fodder." Memphis Slim, a blues musician, recalled, "I was in a place called Marigold, Mississippi. They had a restaurant there and in the back, they had a peephole. And can you imagine what they were doing? They were reading the *Chicago Defender* and they had a lookout man at the door with a peephole. If a white man came into the restaurant, they'd stick the *Defender* into the stove and start playing checkers."

Blacks saw the exodus as a fulfillment of God's promise. A Birmingham minister offered the following prayer to his congregation: "We feel and believe that this great Exodus is God's hand and plan. In a mysterious way God is moving upon the hearts of our people to go where He has prepared for them."

Among those who migrated were the most creative people in the South. Jazz musicians came from New Orleans to play in Chicago, Kansas City, and New York. Blues players came from the Delta. The New York–based NAACP welcomed writer Zora Neale Hurston, poets Langston Hughes and Countee Cullen, and sculptor Augusta Savage. They, along with other black artists, created a cultural florescence known as the Harlem Renaissance.

The Harlem Renaissance was part of the Roaring Twenties, an age of sexual liberation, bootleg liquor, mobsters, and speakeasies. The country was swept up in a frenzy as stock prices reached astronomical figures.

In 1929, hard times came to America with the Great Depression. No group of people was hit harder than rural blacks. The price of cotton spiraled downward from eighteen to six cents a pound. Two-thirds of some two million black farmers made no money or went into debt. Those who could find work might do so for fifteen cents a day worth of credit at a landlord's store. There was no money to pay teachers. Black maids were fired by the thousands. Hundreds of thousands left the land for the cities, abandoning their fields and homes. Even traditional "Negro jobs"—busboys, elevator operators, garbage men, porters, maids, and cooks—were sought by desperate unemployed whites. In Atlanta, a Klan-like group called the Black Shirts paraded, carrying signs that read, "No jobs for niggers until every white man has a job." In other cities, people shouted, "Niggers back to the cotton fields. City jobs are for white men." In Mississippi, where blacks traditionally held certain jobs on trains, unemployed white men, seeking their jobs, ambushed and killed them as the train passed by their hiding places.

On March 2, 1931, as the Depression deepened, a number of unemployed white and black youths seeking work were riding separately on a freight train passing through Alabama. When a white man stepped on the hand of a black rider, the incident escalated into a fight. The whites were thrown off the train and immediately notified a local sheriff, who telegraphed ahead to the town of Paint Rock to stop the train and arrest all blacks on it.

An angry sheriff's posse met the train an hour later and seized nine black youths, some of whom had never seen each other until that moment. One of the youths was nineteen-year-old Clarence Norris. "They made all us boys come out of the train and line up. There was these men with guns, I don't know what they are—policemen, firemen. They had uniforms. All I remember was they had brass buttons. Some are yellin, 'let's take these niggers to a tree. Let's take these niggers and hang them.'"

As the sheriff's deputies continued to search the train, they discovered what seemed to be two white youths who turned out to be two young women, Ruby Bates and Victoria Price, dressed in boys' clothing. Suddenly the assault charge escalated into a rape case, although Clarence Norris swore that none of the youths had seen the women on the train. "And we didn't see no womens until they brought them to the jailhouse. And then one of the police asked—Victoria Price—which ones had you? And she pointed out five of the boys and said, 'this one-this one-this one-this one and that one.' Then they asked Ruby Bates. And she didn't say nothin. Then one of the white men's say, 'no need of askin her nothin'. The other four must of had her.' And that's the way a rape charge was framed against us. I never will forget it."

Bates and Price were mill workers and semiprostitutes, who were also riding the train seeking work. They had dressed as boys for protection, although the night before they had slept with some white men who were also riding trains.

The sheriff encouraged the women to bring rape charges against the nine black youths. Both women agreed. The nine youths were quickly tried and convicted of rape in the town of Scottsboro, Alabama. Eight of the nine were sentenced to death, the other to life imprisonment because he was only twelve years old. Immediately after their sentences, the American Communist Party burst on the scene, announcing it would fight to free all the boys.

The Communist Party USA was the only political organization in America before 1930 that championed black rights and full political, social, and civil equality. Their slogan, "self-determination in the black belt," meant that blacks should have their own "nation" in the South because this was where the greatest number of them lived. This idea came as a directive to the American party from Stalin and the Soviet Union. The Soviet Union had regarded American blacks as an oppressed colonial people rather than as an oppressed minority. Many American Communists simply ignored the directive or considered it a long-range goal.

The party had arrived in Alabama in 1930 and organized workers in the steel industry and coal mines around Birmingham. The dramatic entrance of the Communists into Alabama electrified blacks. They were amazed that the party advocated and practiced complete racial equality. When Communists formed a sharecroppers' union, they were surprised to receive thousands of responses from black tenant farmers.

The union then made a major effort to involve the local black community. Organizers visited churches and spoke—often over the objections of conservative ministers—about the party's vigorous defense of the Scottsboro defendants. Union organizers often preached to their audiences in biblical terms, or they combined the teachings of Marx and Lenin with the Gospels of John and Paul. They began and concluded their speeches with a prayer and saw no contradiction between being a Baptist and a Communist. For them, Jesus, Marx, and Lenin were fellow revolutionaries. The Communist organizers gave old songs new verses. "Give Me That Old Time Religion" became a vehicle for a Scottsboro Boys song.

> The Scottsboro Verdict
> The Scottsboro Verdict
> The Scottsboro Verdict
> Is not good enough for me.
>
> It's good for the big fat bosses
> For the workers' double crossers
> For low down slaves and hosses
> But it ain't good enough for me.

Ned Cobb was an Alabama tenant farmer who had managed to succeed despite the Jim Crow world in which he lived. In 1931, he joined the Sharecroppers Union to fight for the rights of all sharecroppers and farmers. He was involved in a shootout, was wounded, and was imprisoned for thirteen years, leaving his wife and children to run the farm.

Under the guise of sewing circles, the union organized farmers' wives. They met and discussed political and economic issues, read the Communist *Daily Worker* and *Working Women,* carried out union correspondence, and wrote letters to newspapers to encourage others. The union tried to organize white farmers as well. Lemon Johnson, an organizer and colleague of Ned Cobb, discovered that though many were sympathetic to the union, few dared risk crossing the racial divide. J. C. Davis, a white sharecropper, was lynched for his sympathies to the union.

Organizing was highly dangerous work. Union members were frequently murdered, their bodies dumped into the swamp. Some union leaders hid in the woods at night. Posses scoured the countryside for Albert Jackson, a Northern secretary of the union. He wrote of the constant fear he and his fellow union members had of being caught: "The terror drive continues. As I write, there is a lookout to warn me of the approach of lynchers. Constant vigil is kept at all times. Sleep is tortured with nightmares of lynching, terror and murder. Food settles with lumps in your stomach. But the struggle must go on!"

In Camp Hill, Alabama, a shootout had occurred between a black union leader, Ralph Gray, and a sheriff. Gray was standing guard while union members were meeting in a vacant house nearby. When the sheriff came to break up the meeting and make arrests, Gray intercepted him, and the two men confronted each other. An angry quarrel escalated into a shootout in which both men were wounded, the sheriff in the stomach and Gray in the legs. Gray was taken to his home and decided to remain there. His brother Tom later said that when the posse arrived, one member "tore the furniture all apart, broke the butter churn, spilt the milk out and even burned the mattresses." One of the posse "poked a pistol into Brother Ralph's mouth and shot down his throat." Gray's wife and children were in the room. The mob then burned down his house and dumped his body on the steps of the Dadeville courthouse where groups of angry whites shot and kicked the lifeless body. "Other blacks were arrested and mobs attacked sections of the black community, beating and killing farmers and terrorizing their families. Many fled into the woods for safety."

Despite the dangers, others continued to join the sharecroppers' union. Among them was Ned Cobb, a black farmer in Tallapoosa County, and a number of his friends and neighbors. Cobb was drawn to communism not because Marxism-Leninism appealed to him but because he regarded the Communists as the descendants of the Northern abolitionists who once brought Reconstruction to the South but failed to carry it through. Cobb remembered that his grandmother had predicted their return. "My Grandam Cealy used to say what used to be will come again. Colored people once knowed what it was like to live in freedom before they came to this country and they would know it again. I heard them words when I was a boy. It was instilled in me many a time, 'The bottom rail will be on the top. The poor will banish away their toils and snares.'"

Ned Cobb was a relatively prosperous tenant farmer who had successfully navigated the treacherous waters of race relations in rural Alabama. He was also deeply aware of the injustices of the South. "Ever since I've been in God's world, I've never had no rights, no voice in nothing that the white man didn't want me to have—even been cut out of book learning.

They'd give you a good name if you is obedient to them and didn't question them. You begin to cry about your rights and the mistreatin' of you and they'd murder you."

One of Cobb's major activities was persuading others to join the union. "I talked it over with folks. I told them it was a good thing in favor of the colored race. I told them that the organization would back you up and fight your battles with you. Some of them was too scared to join and some of them was too scared not to join; they didn't want to be left alone when push comes to shove."

In December 1932, Cobb received word that the sheriff was coming to foreclose on the property of his friend and fellow union member Clifford James. Cobb, putting his pistol in his pocket, decided to intervene. "I thought an organization is an organization and if I don't mean anything by joinin', I ought to keep my ass out of it. I had swore to stand up for poor black farmers—and poor white farmers if they'd taken a notion to join."

When Cobb arrived at the farm with several other union members, the foreclosure was just beginning. He politely asked the deputy to delay the process and give James a little time to pay his debt. The deputy refused. "I got orders to take it and I'll be damned if I ain't going to take it," Cobb quoted him as saying. Cobb replied that the only way he would allow him to take it was over his dead body. As Cobb later said, he was ready to start "a shooting frolic" if the foreclosure continued. The deputy left to gather reinforcements. Cobb, Clifford James, and several other union members remained. When the sheriff returned with a group of officers, Cobb stayed outside for a few moments while the posse spread out. As Cobb slowly walked back to the house, a deputy named Platt raised his shotgun. "I started in the house. Took one or two steps—BOOM—Mr. Platt threw his gun on me. BOOM BOOM. Shot me two more times before I could get in the door. He filled my hind end up from the bend of my legs to my hips with shot. My feet is just sloshing with blood. I snatched out my .32 Smith and Wesson and I commenced shooting at Platt. Good God, he jumped behind a tree, soon as that pistol fired. Every one of them officers run like the devil away from there. That Smith and Wesson is barking too much for them to stand."

When the shooting stopped, one union man was dead and several others were wounded, including Clifford James and Milo Bentley. Cobb escaped, and his family rushed him to the hospital at Tuskegee. James walked seventeen miles to the hospital, where he was treated for gunshot wounds. His doctor turned him in to the police. Cobb was not kept at the hospital, because the staff feared what might happen if whites discovered his presence there.

Vigilantes began to terrorize the black community, breaking into homes and beating and shooting people. One of the reported victims pistol-whipped was an elderly, blind black woman who was close to a hundred years old.

Cobb and the others were captured. The police threw the wounded James and Bentley into a damp jail cell and refused them medical treatment. They died of their wounds and pneumonia.

Ned Cobb was tried and found guilty. He was offered a lighter sentence if he supplied the names of other union members. He refused and was sent to prison for thirteen years. "Something done in your behalf, you've got to risk," he said. "You take such work as this. I see more good of it than I can really explain."

Despite the violence, union organizing continued. In 1933, the political landscape dramatically changed with the election of Franklin Delano Roosevelt. A new era in civil rights was about to begin that would radically transform America.

Chapter 8

Center Stage for Civil Rights, 1932–1944

In 1932, Franklin Delano Roosevelt was elected President of the United States by an over-whelming majority—of white votes. While more than 60 percent of the white community supported him, more than 60 percent of the black community voted against him. Although Roosevelt was a Northerner, his sympathies seemed to lie with the white supremacist South. As assistant secretary of the navy under Woodrow Wilson, Roosevelt had helped segregate his department. As governor of New York, he neither supported black civil rights nor appointed blacks to office. He boasted of his Southern roots and considered himself an honorary citizen of Georgia, where he owned property. During the election campaign, when the NAACP sent him a questionnaire about his position on civil rights for blacks, he did not respond. Expecting no consideration from Roosevelt or the Democratic Party, most blacks voted for Herbert Hoover, even though Hoover had supported a lily-white policy within his party, appointed few blacks to office, and refused to be photographed with any black leaders. African Americans voted Republican not because they had any illusions about Hoover but because they felt that the Republicans would do less damage to their few rights than the Democrats.

In the early years of Roosevelt's first term, their suspicions seemed justified. The President had no intention of angering the Southerners who controlled Congress by challenging established racial policies. His first priority was to end the Depression, and he needed the support of the Southern politicians who had the power to block his efforts. Federal agencies took their cue from the President during the early years of his first term. Many of them were run by men who held deep prejudices against blacks. When relief efforts got under way, blacks had to wait at the end of the line and received less money than whites. They received fewer jobs, less access to federal programs, and less relief money for equal work. When Congress passed the National Recovery Act, mandating that all workers be paid equally for the same work, Southern employers, used to paying blacks less, fired them and hired white workers to replace them. In 1933, the Agricultural Adjustment Administration was established. One of its purposes was to revive the dying cotton economy. Planters were paid to reduce the

At the beginning of his first term, President Franklin Delano Roosevelt did not give any consideration to the problems blacks were suffering as a result of the Depression. However, his wife, Eleanor, an advocate for black rights, convinced the President to include African Americans in the New Deal programs.

amount of land on which they would grow cotton. Part of that subsidy was supposed to be paid to their sharecroppers, though few sharecroppers received any benefits, and no action was taken against the planters. Having reduced their acreage, landlords then proceeded to evict their tenants from the land, adding to their misery. The Civilian Conservation Corps, established the same year, was designed to provide training and employment for youths. Out of the first two hundred fifty thousand recruits, only seven thousand five hundred were black despite the fact that twice as many black youths were out of work as white. As historian Harvard Sitkoff pointed out, white America was receiving a New Deal, while blacks were getting the same old raw deal.

Eleanor Roosevelt was one of the few who championed their cause in the White House. Mrs. Roosevelt had become increasingly aware of the injustices suffered by African Americans. She began to speak out publicly against race prejudice. She supported anti-lynching campaigns and anti–poll tax measures. She attended conferences with black speakers and spoke out urging justice and greater equality for blacks. She became a go-between between civil rights activists and the President, despite opposition to her efforts by many of Roosevelt's pro-Southern White House staff. The President began to respond to his wife's pleas for his administration to take action on behalf of blacks. His motives were not altogether altruistic. Roosevelt had noticed that the black vote in a number of key cities in the North had become significant, and could make the difference in a close election.

The President allowed black leaders access and became the first Democratic President to have his picture taken with them. He spoke out against lynching and called it murder. He appointed William Hastie as the first black federal judge and consulted with black leaders. He promised fair treatment of blacks by the federal government. And while his powers were limited by a Congress that was virtually held hostage by segregationist senators, Roosevelt gave hope and encouragement to black people everywhere.

As the President and Mrs. Roosevelt publicly addressed black concerns, the federal agencies followed suit. The Works Progress Administration, under the leadership of Harry Hopkins, and the Public Works Administration, led by Harold Ickes, swung into action. Both Hopkins and Ickes were, like Mrs. Roosevelt, pro–civil rights. They had hired many highly qualified young men and women on the basis of their professional abilities. Ickes and Hopkins wanted to bring not only blacks but also poor whites and workingmen and -women into the mainstream of American life. They built schools and libraries for blacks, and created federally subsidized housing.

Having received the green light to translate their beliefs into action, the New Dealers set out to incorporate blacks into federal programs. The government opened tens of thousands of jobs to blacks on public works projects and in the federal government at the same salaries as whites. Although most blacks filled unskilled positions, many black professionals were hired, from librarians to lawyers, economists to engineers. The Federal Theater Project hired black actors, directors, and stagehands. Tens of thousands of black youth were admitted into training programs including the Civilian Conservation Corps. Unemployed and disabled blacks became eligible for federal relief. The Farm Security Administration, led by Henry Wallace, distributed benefits to Southern black farmers, although still far short of that received by whites. As a result of the New Deal's policies, blacks received better health care, better education, better jobs, and increased benefits.

Many federal programs were directed by coalitions of blacks and liberal Southern whites. Outstanding black administrators like Robert Weaver worked with liberal Southerners, including Aubrey Williams, Virginia and Clifford Durr, Clark Foreman, and Will Alexander. Other young white Southerners, like Joseph Gelders and Palmer Weber, lobbied for legislation providing for federal protection of voting rights. For black and liberal whites, what the South needed was a second Reconstruction—one that would complete the first.

For some whites, the journey to liberalism began with a personal journey to overcome their own prejudices. Virginia Durr, who came from a prominent Alabama family, recalled that her moment of truth began when she was at Wellesley College in Massachusetts. She went to the dining room the first night she was there, and a black student was sitting at her table. She got up, marched out of the room, went upstairs, and waited for the head of the house. She told her she couldn't possibly eat at the table with a Negro girl. The house supervisor replied, "Wellesley College has rules. If you can't obey the rules, then you can withdraw." Durr said that if her father heard of her eating at the same table with a black person, he would be furious. She had been taught that to eat at the table of a Negro would be committing a terrible sin against society. This was the first time she became aware that her attitude was considered foolish by some people. It undermined her faith, her solid conviction of what she had been raised to believe. From that night on, she sat at the table without further complaint. It was the first small step on her long march supporting integration.

Perhaps the single most influential person in Washington on behalf of black civil rights was Mary McLeod Bethune. Bethune began life as a sharecropper's daughter, educated herself before attending Moody Bible Institute in Chicago, became a teacher, and founded one of the outstanding black schools for girls in the South (Daytona Normal and Industrial Institute for Negro Girls, now Bethune-Cookman College). She told her students, "You enter to learn and depart to serve." She then became a leader in the women's club movement. Bethune played a major role in helping develop the deep humanism of the President's wife and focusing it on the African-American struggle for freedom. Bethune became the unofficial leader of Roosevelt's "kitchen cabinet," a group composed of high-ranking black officials who sought to coordinate government policy regarding African Americans.

Bethune did not tolerate racial slurs. According to legend, she was walking across the lawn of the White House on her way to meet with the president and Mrs. Roosevelt when a white gardener from the South called out, "Aunty, where do you think you're going?" Bethune stopped, whirled about, fiercely looked the gardener dead in the eye, and then suddenly smiled. "Oh," she said. "I'm sorry I didn't recognize you. Which of my sister's children are you?"

The push for social change in race relations came from below as well as above. Civil rights activists organized boycotts against segregated facilities and demonstrations against white store owners in Northern cities who refused to hire blacks. Their slogan was, "Don't buy where you can't work."

The leading radical group of the era was the Communist Party. Its emphasis on interracial unity, the visibility of black leaders in the struggle, and its willingness to confront the police and politicians transformed the civil rights movement. The party's militant defense of the Scottsboro Boys inspired the respect and admiration of the black community. African Americans enthusiastically welcomed black and white Communists battling the police for black rights, leading hunger marches, and demonstrating for relief for the needy, an end to evictions, and jobs for the unemployed.

The agitation even won the support of members of the black establishment. Mordecai Johnson, the first African-American president of Howard University, publicly stated, "I don't mind being called a Communist. The day will come when being a Communist will be the highest honor that can be made to any individual." The *Chicago Defender* editorialized, "How can we go to war with the Communist Party? We may not agree with its entire program but there is one item we do agree with, and that is the zealousness with which it guards the rights of the race." Charles Houston, then dean of the Howard University Law School, saw the consequence of the Communist Party's militancy. "Communists are offering Negroes full and complete brotherhood without condition of race, creed or previous condition of servitude.

They are the first to fire the masses with a sense of their raw potential power and the first to openly preach the doctrine of mass resistance and mass struggle. . . . The Communists have made it impossible for any aspirant to Negro leadership to advocate anything less than full economic, social and political equality."

The Communists were not the only organization that preached and practiced integration. During the 1930s, in Arkansas, the Southern Tenant Farmers Union brought black and white sharecroppers and tenant farmers together in a struggle to get money owed them by their landlords. The United Mine Workers, the Steel Workers Organizing Committee, and the Mine, Mill and Smelter Workers sent organizers to Birmingham to form unions in their respective industries. Mine workers had had interracial unions since the turn of the century.

W.E.B. Du Bois, long an advocate of integration, suddenly shifted gears. In 1934, Du Bois, responding to the deep entrenchment of Jim Crow in the North, proposed that African Americans voluntarily segregate themselves, build their own businesses, and run their own schools. He was not suggesting segregation as a permanent move but as a tactic that would help the black community to gain parity with whites. "I know that this article will forthwith be interpreted by certain illiterate nitwits as a plea for segregated Negro schools. It is not. It is saying in plain English that a separate Negro school where children are treated like human beings, trained by teachers of their own race, who know what it means to be black, is infi-

nitely better than making our boys and girls doormats to be spit and trampled upon and lied to by ignorant social climbers whose sole claim to superiority is the ability to kick niggers when they are down."

The article sent shock waves through the NAACP leadership. The organization's mission had always been to achieve full integration of blacks in every aspect of American life. What Du Bois was suggesting was heresy. The NAACP board confronted Du Bois and told him that integration was the organization's goal and he had to accept it.

For twenty-four years, Du Bois, as editor of *The Crisis,* was the militant voice of the NAACP. His control over *The Crisis* had been challenged, but he had always prevailed. In 1929, when Walter White was appointed to succeed James Weldon Johnson as head of the organization, a conflict between the two strong-willed men seemed inevitable. White was not concerned with the broader issues that sometimes preoccupied Du Bois. He wanted *The Crisis* to cover what the NAACP

In the 1930s, Walter White became the head of the National Association for the Advancement of Colored People. Under his leadership, the NAACP launched a campaign to have Congress pass a federal anti-lynching law and attack segregation in the courts.

The leader of the NAACP's legal strategy to challenge the constitutionality of segregation in the federal courts was Charles Houston, seated at right. Standing is his protégé, Thurgood Marshall. They are arguing that their client, Donald Gaines Murray, seated between them, was illegally denied entrance to the University of Maryland law school because of his race. The Maryland court agreed.

was doing. White made a play to gain control of *The Crisis*, a move that angered Du Bois. He withstood the challenge. But now he was told either to retract his position or step down. Du Bois chose to resign.

As Du Bois left the NAACP, Charles Hamilton Houston, a black lawyer from Washington, D.C., and dean of Howard's Law School, arrived to help lead the fight against Jim Crow. Houston had dedicated his life to fighting race prejudice. During World War I, he had witnessed hundreds of black soldiers unjustly prosecuted by the military establishment without cause. "I made up my mind that if I ever got through this war, I would study law and use my time fighting for men who could not strike back."

Setting up a law practice with his father in Washington, D.C., Houston was one of approximately one thousand black lawyers, less than 1 percent of the total number of lawyers practicing in America. He was determined to help remedy this situation. Appointed dean of Howard University Law School in 1929, Houston transformed the school into a first-rate institution. He trained a cadre of young lawyers in civil rights laws, a course seldom if ever offered in law schools anywhere. His students included Thurgood Marshall, Spottiswood

Robinson, and Oliver Hill, all of whom would play major roles in challenging Jim Crow in the courts. Hill recalled that Houston was so tough as a teacher that his students, among themselves, called him " 'Iron Shoes' and 'Cement Pants' . . . and a few other names that don't bear repeating. He was harder on himself than he was on us. But he had to be. He was preparing us for war. He had a soldier's faith that every battle must be fought until it is won and without pause to take account of those stricken in the fray—even if it meant himself."

Houston felt that if black people were ever to achieve equal justice under law, they would have to act in their own behalf. He had watched with growing optimism as the Supreme Court began to make decisions favorable to black rights regarding criminal procedures, especially in the Scottsboro case. When Roosevelt began to appoint liberal judges to the Court, Houston felt the time had come to challenge segregation itself.

Houston was convinced that the battle for civil rights had to be won in the schools but fought in the courts. He understood that judges were not going to make decisions that would overturn rulings having to do with constitutional interpretation unless absolutely necessary. He felt that if he confronted the "separate but equal" doctrine laid down in *Plessy* v. *Ferguson* in 1898, the court would most likely reject the challenge. If, however, he insisted that *Plessy* be enforced—that is, if the NAACP sued a state to make its schools for black children equal to those for whites—then he could chip away segregation. The states would either have to build new schools for blacks, which they could not afford, or admit blacks into white schools. If the courts agreed with his argument, he could prepare to challenge the legal basis of segregation itself.

Houston decided that the NAACP had to carefully select cases that stood a good chance of winning. Those cases would establish a precedent that "would make plain the inequality that existed in educational opportunities of blacks and whites. And would make true equality too expensive for states to maintain." The ultimate goal was always integration. As Houston told one audience, "The NAACP will never compromise with segregation. It is not a question of wanting to sit in class with white students. It is a question of vindicating one's citizenship."

In 1934, Houston traveled to South Carolina county by county with a movie camera and filmed the profound inequality between black and white schools. He documented the abysmal conditions that young black children experienced and made notes. "Moore's Pond School. The nearest drinking water is across the highway at an abandoned gasoline station. The children sit inside on crowded benches. No desks, no chairs, one old piece of blackboard. The cracks in the floor are so wide that pencils often roll through to the ground when dropped. No pit. No lime. Just ashes from the stove to cover the [human] waste."

Houston also spoke at black colleges, churches, and union halls, met with teachers' groups, consulted with black lawyers, and addressed local NAACP chapters. His message was the same: Black people must lead their own struggle for civil rights and not wait for the white man to do it for them. "I have confidence in the capacity within the black community and the Negro race to bring about change. The struggle is always greater when it springs from the soil than when it is a foreign growth." He felt that black lawyers should take the lead in securing the full rights of citizenship guaranteed to African Americans by the Reconstruction amendments.

Houston also discovered that local leaders like Modjeska Simkins were organizing voters in an effort to breach the walls of the all-white primary. Simkins had used Roosevelt's popularity with black voters. "Roosevelt took the jug by the handle," she said. "He tried to give the people who were shot down and had nothing, something. It was a shot in the arm for Negroes." Her strategy was get people to pay their poll tax and register to vote in the general election first before tackling the primary. "Voting in the general election was a way of getting people's feet wet. . . . But we knew that nothing would come of this until we could vote in the primary, which was the only real election." Ralph Bunche, while working as a chief investigator for the Myrdal-Carnegie monumental study of the Negro (which formed the basis for Gunnar Myrdal's *An American Dilemma*), visited South Carolina and was favorably impressed. "Despite the hardships frequently imposed by registrars, increasing numbers of Negroes in the South are demonstrating an amazing amount of patience, perseverance and determination, and keep returning after rejections until they get their name on the registration books." In a number of Southern cities, blacks held mock elections with posters and meetings to elect a "bronze" mayor, that is, an unofficial mayor of the black community.

As voter registration drives slowly moved forward in the South, Houston prepared his challenge to segregation in the courts. There were major changes taking place in the Supreme Court concerning due process of law. The Court asserted its power to supervise administration of justice by examining evidence of discrimination for itself. The Court overturned convictions in which black defendants had been mentally and physically tortured to extract confessions or had been denied competent attorneys. The Court also ruled that if black citizens were deliberately excluded from jury rolls by a county, subsequent convictions were invalid. Other rulings struck down restrictive covenants that made it illegal to sell a house to blacks and peonage laws forcing blacks to work as virtual slave labor in order to pay off debts. The Court also mandated that black and white teachers be paid equal salaries.

Houston felt that his strongest case of inequality in education would be at the graduate school level. Most Southern states did not provide graduate studies for blacks and did not allow them into white graduate schools. He found the case he wanted in Missouri. Lloyd Gaines, a college graduate, had been denied entrance to the law school at the University of Missouri because of race. Houston argued that the state was obligated either to build a law school for blacks equal to that of whites or admit Gaines to the University of Missouri. The Supreme Court agreed. The Gaines decision breached the walls of segregation. It meant that every state must either build a separate graduate school for blacks or integrate. And if this were true for graduate schools, then why not high schools? And elementary schools?

Walter White supported Houston's strategy in the courts, but he had his own agenda. Throughout his career with the NAACP, he had been determined to see Congress pass a federal anti-lynching law. Lynching, he charged, was still a part of Southern culture and would not be eradicated without a federal law. He noted that the number of lynchings had risen during the Depression from a low of 7 in 1929, to 21 in 1930, to a high of 28 in 1933.

Despite the growing public revulsion against lynching, Roosevelt would not fight for an anti-lynching bill. He admitted to White that he was personally in favor of it, and he let that be known to Congress. He would not, however, challenge the Southern bloc of senators, who could defeat his programs for economic recovery. White met with the President on several occasions to discuss his support. White later revealed that the Roosevelt was unwilling to challenge the Southern leadership. "I did not choose the tools with which I must work," he reportedly told White. "If I come out for the anti-lynching bill they will block every bill I ask Congress to pass. I just can't take that risk."

To pressure Congress, White and the NAACP launched a major publicity campaign to organize grass-roots support for the bill. They published an account of the horrific lynching of Claude Neal by a mob from Alabama that seized Neal from a jail in Florida—with the cooperation of local law enforcement officials. The NAACP official filed a report describing how Neal was killed.

An eye witness told the NAACP investigator that parts of Neal's body [i.e., his genitals] were cut off and he was made to eat them. Then they sliced his sides and stomachs with knives and every now and then somebody would cut off a finger or toe. Red hot irons were used on the 'nigger' from top to bottom. From time to time during the torture, a rope would be tied around Neal's neck and he was pulled up over a limb and held there until he was almost choked to death when he would be let down and the torture begin again. After several hours of this unspeakable torture, "they just decided to kill him."

Churches and synagogues sent letters to congressmen urging them to pass the bill. Whatever the national feelings on black civil rights might have been, a consensus against lynching was developing in the South as well as the North. Southern newspapers editorialized against lynching. Southern churches condemned it. Scholars published studies exposing that rape—the Southern rationale for lynching—was seldom involved in most lynchings. A widely circulated brochure of the NAACP reminded the nation of the potential damage to all children. "Do not look at the Negro, look at the white children," it said. "What havoc is being wrought in their minds?"

In 1936, a bill was introduced in the House of Representatives allowing the federal government to intervene in lynchings, if local officials failed to act. As debate began, Governor Henry Lamar White of Mississippi publicly boasted that there was no need for a federal anti-lynching bill as Mississippi had not had a lynching in fifteen months. The following day, during a debate on the bill, Representative Arthur Mitchell of Illinois rose and read to his fellow congressmen an article from a Southern newspaper published the day after the governor's statement, describing what happened to two young black men in Duck Hill, Mississippi. They were taken from the custody of the sheriff, tied to trees, horsewhipped, their bodies mutilated with blowtorches, castrated, and shot to death. Their bodies were burned to ashes. The House listened to the report in total silence and then voted two to one in favor of the bill. Only one representative from a Southern state, Maury Maverick, a liberal congressmen from Texas, voted for the bill.

Even though the bill sailed through the House, it still had to pass formidable opposition in the Senate. Every attempt made to pass such a law foundered on the reefs of a filibuster by Southern senators, who prevented the issue from coming to a vote. Although a majority of

Women played a major role in the anti-lynching and voter registration drives in the 1940s and 1950s.

senators were in favor of the bill, and the president had made it clear he would sign it if passed, Southern senators were determined to kill it. In 1938, the bill finally reached the Senate floor. As Walter White sat in the gallery, Southern senators rallied around the battle flag of states' rights for seven weeks. Senator Allen Ellender proclaimed his allegiance to white supremacy on the floor of the United States Senate. "I believe in white supremacy and as long as I am in the Senate, I expect to vote for it. We have fought to subjugate the Negro in the South. It was costly; it was bitter; but how sweet the victory." With Republican help, Southern Democrats defeated all efforts to bring the bill to a vote. In the end, the filibuster could not be stopped. The bill was withdrawn.

Despite the defeat, there were victories. The NAACP emerged with its reputation enhanced. The fight had gathered national support and brought thousands of new members into the civil rights movement. The number of lynchings dropped to a low of two by 1939.

The Southern states began to pass local anti-lynching laws, although no one was immediately prosecuted. And Southern whites themselves joined the fight.

Jesse Daniel Ames, a white Texan and an activist, had long worked for interracial cooperation if not integration. For Ames, lynching was an insult to white women as well as an outrage on black men. She debunked the myth fostered by Southern white males that lynching was necessary to protect white women. White women did not need protection from black men, because relatively few black men raped white women.

In the early 1930s, Ames formed an organization of Southern white women to campaign against lynching. Called the Association of Southern Women for the Prevention of Lynching (ASWPL), the organization's mission was to get community leaders and law enforcement officials to sign pledges that they would do everything they could to prevent lynchings of prisoners in their communities. The pledge read in part, "We declare lynching an indefensible crime, destructive of all principles of government, hostile to every ideal of religion and humanity, degrading and debasing to every person involved. We pledge ourselves to create a new public opinion in the South which will not condone for any reason whatever acts of the mob or lynchers."

The women recruited local churches, social clubs, politicians, and law enforcement officials to sign pledges condemning lynching. They held lectures, published anti-lynching pamphlets, and talked at colleges and fraternal organizations. One woman wrote, "I got me as many officers of the law as I could to sign it. I felt they are the ones to enforce this pledge. They said . . . that they would do their part." Women made it clear to local officials that they had the vote and would use it accordingly. One ASWPL mailing to its members reminded them of their voting power: "If it is an election year, have you talked with your candidates for sheriff? Have you asked each candidate what he will do to prevent lynchings if elected? The voters will decide for or against elections this year."

When a suspect for a crime was taken into custody, the local ASWPL might send a telegram requesting the local sheriff to take whatever steps were necessary to prevent mob violence. The organization encouraged local people to call them if they heard rumors that a lynching might take place. One report read,

> On Friday, Mr. Glen Rainey heard someone boast that there would be a "dead nigger" at Decatur because he had raped a woman. Mr. Rainey came to the office and made a report. Mrs. Tilly called the sheriff Jake Hall. As he was not in she talked with Mrs. Hall who assured her there would be no killing. Mrs. Tilly then got in touch with the Methodist women in Decatur. These in turn called other people and asked them to also call the sheriff, the mayor, the chief of police and the county police. Early in the afternoon, the prisoner was removed from the Dekalb county jail for safe-keeping.

ASWPL women often ran into resistance. Jesse Daniel Ames reported, "Women went into communities where there had been a lynching. Many of the people were surly, belligerent. Women were by no means safe. They knew of the constant dangers and didn't forget to pray. Many were threatened. I know women who wouldn't tell their husbands the threat because they feared their families would make them quit work." She herself received letters condemning her. One anonymous letter came from Florida after the lynching of Claude Neal: "If you are that much of a Negro lover, you better go to the North where you can mingle with them. I am a free born Southerner and am glad to say I wish that they would have some more lynchings, just as they did this one."

Holland's, a Southern magazine, described the conditions under which some women worked: "These dauntless women have gone, times without number, to peace officers in charge of prisoners who might become victims of lynchings and pleaded for preventative action. They have gone into situations so tense few men would intrude. They have faced threats of all kinds from truculent individuals and even organizations in the South. They have been ridiculed. They have been ordered by municipal officials not to speak. They have gone into community after community, where lynchings have occurred and patiently searched out the facts of the case for their records."

Ames was against lynching, but she was also against federal intervention in lynching. She felt that it was up to the states themselves—pressured by Southern women—to pass and enforce their own anti-lynching laws.

As the decade came to an end, civil rights was now becoming a national issue, and blacks had good reason to hope. Paul Robeson returned to the United States in 1939 after being away for four years. He could see that after a decade of struggle, most blacks still labored as menials, too many were still unemployed, most were segregated in the North, and white supremacy still reigned in the South. When asked about his impressions, Robeson replied, "Conditions are far from ideal. They are not so much changed in fact as they appear to be in the hopes of liberals and Negro leaders. Change is in the air and this is the best sign of all."

Change *was* in the air. A tremor was felt throughout the South from deep in the piney woods to the lush cotton fields of the Delta, from sleepy towns and hamlets to the slowly growing urban centers. Change was shaking the seemingly impregnable bastion of Jim Crow. Whites and blacks, Southerners and Northerners, politicians and clergymen, ordinary citizens and civil rights leaders were calling for an end to some of the worst aspects of segregation lynching, the poll tax, and the white primary. They advocated better schools and better jobs for blacks. If most Southerners dared not call for integration, it was clear that the country was headed in that direction. Only a few Southerners had the courage to say what had to happen—the dismantling of all forms of segregation.

The high point of the liberal attempt to reform the South came at the convocation of the Southern Conference for Human Welfare, held in Birmingham in 1938. Southern liberal politicians, black activists, government officials, college professors, radical and mainstream labor organizations, grass-roots organizers, newspaper editors, and clergymen gathered to discuss modernizing the South. They raised a number of major issues, from ending lynching and abolishing the poll tax to making plans for Southern economic development and interracial cooperation. Eleanor Roosevelt attended with the president's blessing. The first two sessions were integrated despite a Birmingham law forbidding such gatherings to take place. When the Birmingham police ordered the convention to segregate its seating, Mrs. Roosevelt placed her chair on the dividing line between the races as an act of defiance. Virginia Durr recalled the atmosphere of the convention. "Oh, it was a love feast. There must have been 1,500 or more people there from all over the South, black and white, labor union people and New Dealers. Southern meetings always include a lot of preaching and praying and hymn singing, and this was no exception. The whole meeting was just full of love and hope. The whole South was coming together to make a new day. It was the New Deal come South!"

In the summer of 1941, as war began in Europe, defense industries began to boom in the United States, producing weapons for America and her ally, Great Britain. Though jobs were plentiful for hundreds of thousands of whites, they were almost nonexistent for blacks. Only a few thousand were hired—and most of these were jobs as porters and janitors. In the aerospace industry alone, out of its 107,000 workers, only 300 blacks were employed. Over 50 percent of defense employers said they would not hire black workers no matter how skilled they were.

Black leaders called a meeting in Chicago to devise a plan to force industry to open up more jobs for blacks. As one suggestion was made after another, one exasperated woman stood up. "Mr. Chairman," she reportedly called out, "we ought to throw fifty thousand Negroes . . . bring them from all over the country, any way they can get there and throw them around the White House until we get some action."

A. Philip Randolph, head of the Brotherhood of Sleeping Car Porters, seized upon the suggestion. He called for a massive demonstration of blacks in the nation's capital on July 1. Several days later he announced the March on Washington. He said that ten thousand people would demonstrate for jobs and fair treatment. "The whole National Defense System reeks with race prejudice, hatred, discrimination. It is time to wake up Washington as it has never been shocked before. . . . We would rather die on our feet fighting for Negro rights than to live on our knees as halfmen, begging for a pittance."

The announcement electrified the black community. Grass-roots support for the march sprang up everywhere. Church congregations raised money to rent buses. Schoolchildren saved their allowances. Almost every black organization agreed to participate. Whites began to panic. When blacks were accused by the press of being unpatriotic, one black youth replied, "The army Jim Crows us. The Navy only lets us serve as mess men. The Red Cross refuses our blood. Employers and labor unions shut us out. Lynchings continue. We are disfranchised, jim-crowed, spat upon. What more can Hitler do than that?"

President Roosevelt feared that a race riot would break out if the march took place. He asked his wife and several white civil rights leaders to intervene. Randolph held fast. Unless the President acted, the march would take place on schedule. Mrs. Roosevelt told Randolph that she felt the march would harm the cause for which Randolph was fighting. He replied that it had already done some good, "for if you were not concerned, you wouldn't be here." As the deadline approached, the press predicted that more than one hundred thousand people would march on Washington. Asked by reporters where the marchers would eat and sleep, Randolph, aware that Washington was a highly segregated city, replied that they would frequent white hotels and restaurants. The very thought that blacks would march into their hotels and restaurants, sleep on their sheets, and eat off the same plates terrified whites.

Roosevelt finally agreed to meet with Randolph and NAACP head Walter White. He used

Although most black soldiers were used in work details, some saw combat and distinguished themselves in battle. They served in the infantry, tank corps, and air force.

his considerable personal charm to dissuade them from the march. They refused. He asked how many would march. They replied that one hundred thousand would, an inflated number, but it impressed the President. He asked what they wanted. They told him they wanted him to integrate the army and forbid discrimination in defense industries. Roosevelt compromised. He said he could not integrate the army, but he would ban racial discrimination in industry. He issued Executive Order Number 8802, establishing a Committee on Fair Employment Practices with the authority to investigate and end discrimination in defense industries, government, and unions. Randolph called off the march. The order had limited effect in the defense industry, but it set an important civil rights precedent. For the first time, blacks had demanded their rights from the federal government rather than asked for them. And they had gained a partial victory.

When America entered World War II, the drive for black civil rights stalled. The primary objective of the nation was to win the war, just as a decade earlier it had been to end the Depression. Black leaders and celebrities pledged their full support for the war effort, including militants A. Philip Randolph and W.E.B. Du Bois, writers Langston Hughes and Richard Wright, world heavyweight champion Joe Louis, actress Hattie McDaniel, and singer Josh

White. The Communist Party, the strongest advocate for black rights and employment in the 1930s, now focused on Hitler as he invaded Russia and threatened the center of world communism. Although the *Pittsburgh Courier* launched a "Double V" campaign—victory over fascism in Europe and Jim Crow at home—in reality there was no systematic fight against Jim Crow during the war. Grievances were rarely harped on. Organizations considered militant received little support from the black community. Occasional demonstrations organized for civil rights were poorly attended. Contributions slowed to a trickle. The NAACP took a conservative course and increased its membership. There were race riots in the South caused by whites, and lynchings began to rise again. Thirteen men were lynched in 1940–1941, including two black teenagers, Charles Lang and Ernest Green, who were supposedly kidding around with a young white girl they were friendly with. A white passerby in a car interpreted the horseplay as an attempted assault and a mob hanged them from a bridge.

Many black soldiers suffered from racial discrimination. Jim Crow was practiced in Northern bases as well as Southern. Men and women in the army ate at segregated tables, slept in segregated barracks, and rode in segregated buses. Thousands wrote letters of racial protest to federal officials. Private Charles Wilson asked for an executive order "whereby Negro soldiers would be integrated . . . as fighting men, instead of . . . as housekeepers." Major Samuel Ransom, after pointing out how blacks were called "niggers" by whites regardless of their rank and were separated in barracks and mess halls, reported that the men felt that "they just might as well die in the guardhouse as in this slave camp." A soldier who signed himself as "a disgusted negro trooper" wrote, "This place is a living hell and we feel that we can't tolerate these conditions much longer." Others reported how they were beaten or their comrades were killed. Private Latrophe Jenkins wrote, "If this war is won by America who's going to help us win ours?"

Black women who joined the Women's Army Corps were also discriminated against. They were segregated from whites in many camps, and certain hotels and restaurants in non-Southern cities were declared off limits. Occasionally they suffered from police brutality. Four WACs who had been trained as orderlies were told by their white commanding officer, "I don't want any black WACS as medical technicians around this hospital. I want them to scrub and do dirty work." The WACs went on strike; they were court-martialed and sentenced to a year of hard labor. The case was reviewed, the verdict overturned, the nurses restored, and their commanding officer reprimanded.

Black soldiers sometimes fought and won their own battles. When a group of black soldiers who were carrying out a maneuver in rural Louisiana tried to buy some ice cream at a country store, the door was locked on them and a "gun totin' cracker" stood ready at the back door. The men returned to the carrier and pulled back a canvas to reveal a 50-mm machine gun.

The team that operated the gun pulled a belt of ammunition out of its box and slapped it into place, and the triggerman swung the gun around to cover the doorway of the ice cream parlor. "The only sound was of the activities of the men, no words . . . I stepped back into the carrier, picked up my rifle. All of our clips being slapped into place at the same time sounded like a cannon going off. None of us had any illusions as to what would happen when that fifty caliber opened up on the ice cream shack. It would cut it and everybody inside in half. We knew every white regiment and division in the state, plus the police at every level would be called down on our heads. Without a word we had decided to make our stand. Fortunately for all concerned, the crackers inside realized that this was for real, these were not 'niggers' playing soldier, these were black men who planned to kill and die for that right."

The door was unlocked and the men were served.

Yet despite the surge of racism, many blacks still hoped that by following a pattern of racial uplift, legal redress of grievances in the courts, and cooperation with the "better class" of whites, they would eventually achieve their goals. They pointed out that jobs were opening up, especially in the federal government. Many argued that persuasion, reason, and good behavior would eventually overcome race prejudice. They appealed to the conciliatory philosophy of Booker T. Washington, rather than directly confronting Jim Crow and the color line. They hoped that things would get better after the war. The question still remained: Who would risk making them better? To try could be lethal. When Elbert Williams, head of the NAACP in Brownsville, Tennessee, tried to organize a voter registration drive, he was lynched.

Yet there were countercurrents. In Winston-Salem, black workers, who were racially segregated in the factory, spontaneously went on strike in the 1940s to protest working conditions. They joined the CIO and forced the company to recognize them.

In Columbia, South Carolina, blacks organized a campaign to register to vote. At that time the registration books were kept in places of white-owned business. When a group of blacks wanting to register entered, the books suddenly disappeared from sight. When whites entered to register, the books mysteriously appeared again.

In one ward, blacks were standing outside a candy store where a white woman registrar had denied that she had the books, although they had seen whites registering. George Elmore, a light-skinned black man, entered the store for a Coke. Mistaking him for white, she encouraged him to register. As he did so she said to him, "Them damn niggers out there tried to get their names in our books but I didn't let them." When Elmore finished, the registrar checked the book to make sure he had signed in properly. When she saw that his address was in the black section of town, she screamed, "You're a damned nigger!" Elmore replied, "Yes ma'm." "Well," she said, defeated, "tell them other niggers they can come in here an' enroll if they want to." Elmore's name was later stricken from the books, but he challenged it in court and won.

Osceola McKaine, an NAACP organizer in Columbia, noted, "We are living in the midst perhaps of the greatest revolution within human experience. No nation will be as it was before peace comes." The war's end brought new jobs into the region and gave a vital boost of energy to a dying agricultural economy. Jim Crow had, in part, been sustained by the fact that most of the South was rural. Black and white relations were often defined by the cotton economy of landlord and tenant farmers. The war hastened the death of this relationship and brought a new consciousness in the minds of many blacks and some whites that things could no longer remain the same. Tens of thousands joined the NAACP to prepare for this change.

Hundreds of thousands of Southern blacks left the South for jobs in the North or joined the army. Most of the black soldiers in the army served in segregated units. The marines and the air force refused to take blacks into their service until later in the war. Most black soldiers were used in noncombat military jobs.

More than a million black civilians left the South as agriculture continued to decline and machines replaced human labor. For many black Southerners, the war enabled them to discover new experiences in large Northern cities. One of the biggest changes had to do with white women. James Nix, a veteran, remembered the taboos on white women imposed on him as a child. "We was on a bus and a little white girl got on with a long, pretty ponytail. And I told my father 'that girl has some pretty hair.' And my father told me to shut up. And when he got home, he gave me some hell. 'Don't you know stuff life like that will get you killed . . . get you hung!?'" Roscoe Pickett recalled that his mother used to warn him about white girls. "She told me over and over again, when you go to town with your daddy, don't you be looking at no white girls. And it never dawned on me to ask her why." When Pickett was stationed in Chicago by the army during the war, he was startled to discover that white girls thought nothing of sitting next to him on a bus. He also discovered that when he went to a movie, he could sit wherever he wanted in the theater. In Mississippi, he could sit only in the colored section of the balcony. These experiences helped him realize an important fact about himself—that he didn't have to accept the way of life that the white South wanted to impose on him. "I knew then that I wasn't going to go back on the farm. I knew that I was going to go to college somewhere. That's the thing that changed my life. I knew that a black man could do things other than mess around plowing with an ox, messing around cutting cross ties. That's the thing that changed me."

For James Jones, who served in the 761st Tank Battalion and saw action in Europe, it was the French who made a profound difference in his life. "The French had a certain kind of openness and warmth that they exhibited towards minorities that was just unexplainable. You wouldn't know you were black when you were in their company." One soldier recalled that when he was invited to dinner at the home of an English family, they put a pillow on his seat. Later the wife explained the pillow was put there so he wouldn't have to sit on his tail. "Whites," she said, "had told us that you had this tail and you were monkeys."

Relationships between black and white soldiers were mixed. Some white outfits were openly hostile toward black soldiers. The hostility would sometimes break into violence, and white soldiers would attack, beat, and even kill blacks. Some black and white soldiers formed friendships when serving together—especially men who fought together on the front lines. When they returned home, the color line once again reappeared.

One source of irritation to black soldiers was the way German prisoners of war were treated in the South. Despite the fact that the Germans incarcerated in the South had fought against America, and may have even killed American soldiers, they were allowed to take bus trips downtown and sit with other whites in the front of the bus, eat in restaurants, and enjoy other public facilities, all of which were denied to blacks.

The war changed many black attitudes about Jim Crow. Luella Newsome, who served as a

As the war came to an end, whites were determined to maintain segregation no matter what the cost. Returning soldiers once more returned to the back of the bus when they reached the South.

WAC, said, "It had to change, because we're not going to have it this way anymore." Many came back with a militant attitude ready to fight. Many black soldiers realized that Jim Crow was not inevitable, and the South didn't have to be that way. "We thought it was the way it was supposed to be," one soldier remarked. "We was dumb to the facts and didn't know." But when black soldiers were treated as human beings by other whites in different countries, "it opened up my eyes to the racial problems." Reverend Hosea Williams remembered how his attitude had changed, "I realized that hell, if I got to fight and we got to fight and die for America, why should we be treated like slaves in America? If we've got to fight and die for America just like the white boys, why can't we enjoy the same rights as white boys?"

In 1944, the United States Supreme Court, in a decision that would have profound repercussions in the postwar years, ruled in *Smith* v. *Allright* that the all-white primary—which had been the most effective tool for barring blacks from political participation in the South—was illegal. When the state of South Carolina refused to abide by the Court's decision, John McCray, publisher of the *Columbia Lighthouse and Informer,* along with Osceola McKaine, Modjeska Simkins, and Reverend James Hinton, organized the South Carolina Progressive Democratic Party (PDP) as an alternative to the regular Democratic Party. The quartet had been fighting for black rights throughout the 1930s and 1940s, organizing NAACP chapters, speaking and writing on behalf of black voting rights and equal pay for teachers. The PDP sent a delegation to the 1944 Democratic convention to challenge the seating of the regular delegation. The challenge was unsuccessful, but the PDP ran its own candidate, Osceola McKaine, for the U.S. Senate, the first black man to run for a statewide office since Reconstruction. Over the next five years, largely due to the PDP's statewide organizing efforts, the number of registered black voters in South Carolina increased from three thousand five hundred to fifty thousand.

As the war ended, Charles Houston, whose health was failing, was pleased. The court was headed in the direction he had anticipated, the NAACP was growing in number, civil rights was now a national issue, and black voter registration was starting to climb. Even though he was no longer working for the NAACP, Houston's strategy had transformed the legal culture within this country. But he knew that there was still a long way to go before the walls of Jim Crow would come tumbling down. The admonition he had issued a few years earlier still held true: "So far so good," but the fight had just begun. "Maybe the next generation will be able to take time out to rest, but we have too far to go and too much work to do. Shout if you want but don't shout too soon."

By the end of World War II, the legal walls of segregation were about to come tumbling down. The all-white primary had been struck down by the United States Supreme Court, to be followed in 1946 by segregation in interstate busing.

Chapter 9

The Breakthrough, 1945–1954

Boom times came to America. Americans had survived the Great Depression and a world war, and now they were rewarded with an abundance of consumer goods: Baggies and television sets, prefabricated homes and refrigerators, air-conditioning and automobiles.

In the postwar years, America was heading for a showdown over race relations. The minstrel stereotypes of black performers like Butterfly McQueen, Amos and Andy, and Step-and-Fetchit were fading out, while black heroes like Jackie Robinson, Sidney Poitier, and Ralph Bunche faded in. Blacks and progressive whites were assaulting Jim Crow at every opportunity. The United States Supreme Court was breaking down the barriers. By 1946, It had ordered several graduate schools to integrate their student body and declared the all-white primary and segregation on interstate buses unconstitutional. Some Southern liberals—many of whom were journalists—wanted both races to enjoy equal benefits but remain separated. They had not yet seen that equality was impossible as long as one race was segregated.

Despite the liberal trends, the old reactionary South still reigned supreme. If the South was no longer a land that time forgot, it was still a land rooted in the past. When it came to educating its children, providing a living wage for most of its people, offering decent housing, healthy diets, and reasonable medical care, the eleven states that had formed the Confederacy were still at the end of the line behind the thirty-seven other states. Collectively the Southern states spent half as much as non-Southern states educating white children and even less for their black children. One out of four Southern children of both races stopped school by the fifth grade. The South had the fewest doctors per capita and the highest death rate of mothers and babies at birth. Of the thirty-six million people living in the region, one quarter of whom were black, one out of three earned less than $250 a year. Most adults did not vote. In Virginia, less than 15 percent of the eligible voters went to the polls. For Southern farmers, mules still outnumbered tractors, thirteen to one. The lords of the South—the old-time politicians and "big mules" of industry—planned to keep the South just the way it was. It preferred the region to be poor (except for themselves and their cronies), undemocratic, and as separate from the North as possible. Most of all, they were determined to keep race rela-

Clinton Adams was ten years old when he witnessed a quadruple murder committed in Walton County, Georgia, in 1946. Threatened with death, he kept quiet about what he had seen until the 1990s.

tions frozen. White supremacy remained the foundation upon which the South had constructed its edifice, and any violation could end in death.

When blacks came home after the war, whites were prepared to "put them back in their place." Henry Murphy said that when he returned and called his father in Mississippi, his father warned him not to come home with his uniform on. "He said that the police was beating black soldiers and searching them. If they had a picture of a white woman in his wallet, they'd kill him." Murphy returned home dressed as a sharecropper in overalls and a jumper. Dabney Hammer, who came back to Mississippi wearing medals, encountered a white man in his hometown of Clarksdale. "Oweee, look at them spangles on your chest. Glad you back. Let me tell you one thing don't you forget . . . you're still a nigger." The homecoming of Reverend Hosea Williams, who was later to become Martin Luther King's right-hand man, was more traumatic:

And we got to Americus, Georgia, the hometown of ex-president Jimmy Carter. And I had to change buses there. Blacks could not go in the bus station. There was no place in the station for blacks. And if you wanted to purchase anything from the snack bar, it was a window, and you would peck on that window and this lady would open this window and sell you if she wanted to. And I tried to get her to give me a glass of water. She would never give me, she just ignored me. I looked through that window up at the front there, and there was a water fountain. And I didn't go in but I tried to lean inside and get me a cup of water, and those white people beat me till I was unconscious. They thought I was dead. Now, I had all these medals on. That's one thing you'd thought they might would have respected. And they beat me until they thought I was dead, and called a black undertaker who picked me up and found I had a pulse and still breathing, and carried me there to a hospital there in Thomasville, Georgia. And I laid there crying eight weeks wishing Adolf Hitler had won the war.

In Birmingham, Alabama, the police department, under the command of Eugene "Bull" Conner, unleashed its own private war against black veterans. Policemen were reported to have killed as many as five ex-soldiers in six weeks. In South Carolina, a policeman rammed the butt of his club into the eyes of Isaac Woodard, blinding him, because he had got into a shouting match with a bus driver. In Tennessee, black veterans and police had a shootout in which several police were wounded and two blacks were shot to death while in police custody. In Georgia, Maceo Snipes was shot to death for voting, and eight convicts were shot to death by the warden, who claimed they were trying to escape. John Jones was blowtorched in Louisiana because he had refused to part with a war souvenir and had criticized whites for cheating his grandfather.

One of the worst episodes of racial violence in Georgia occurred in Walton County. It began when a fight broke out between Roger Malcolm, a black farmer, and his white land-lord, Barney Hester. Some said Hester was trying to break up a fight between Malcolm and his wife. Others said that he had shown a sexual interest in her. Whatever the cause, Malcolm stabbed Hester and seriously wounded him. Malcolm was arrested and Hester hospitalized. By stabbing a white man in rural Georgia, Malcolm had broken one of the most inviolable racial taboos. Rumors that a lynching was imminent raced around the county.

George Dorsey, a returned veteran and Dorothy Malcolm's brother, asked his landlord, Loy Harrison, to intervene on behalf of his brother-in-law. Harrison, a cotton planter and bootlegger, could have been a poster boy for a Southern redneck. He was over six feet tall and weighed 250 pounds, with a large gut and a scar running down the side of his face. He resented the fact that Dorsey had shown a good deal of independence since his return home from the army. Ten-year-old Clinton Adams, a white sharecropper's son whose family also

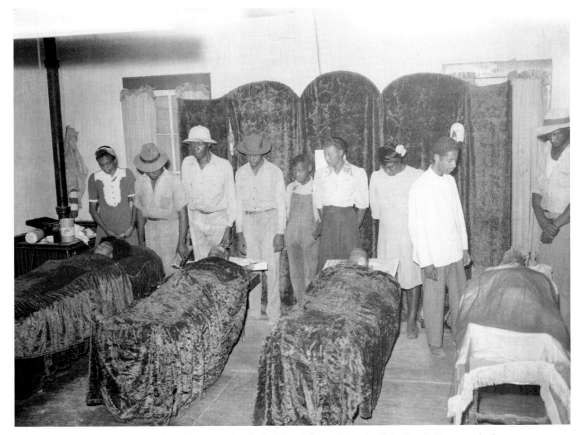

Four men and women were murdered because they had violated the racial code of the South. Roger Malcolm, one of the victims, had wounded a white man in a fight. Malcolm's wife, sister, and brother-in-law tried to help him avoid being lynched and were also killed.

worked for Harrison, was fond of his neighbor Dorsey. Dorsey had helped his family many times doing chores around the house when his father was sick.

Adams remembered Dorsey's return from the war and how his attitude had changed. "George came home from the army in 1945 and I met him down the road down there and walked him all the way home. And he was telling me about being in the army. He was real proud of that. And he had some medals on. He felt he was as good as any white man and if you was black in this county, you didn't cross a white man."

Dorsey asked Harrison if he would save his brother-in-law from a lynching by bailing him out of jail and putting him to work on his property until the trial. He knew that if Malcolm stayed on Harrison's land, nobody would bother him. Harrison first refused, then unexpectedly changed his mind. On July 25, Harrison, along with Dorsey, his common-law wife May Murray, and Dorothy Malcolm, bailed Malcolm out of jail. Inexplicably, the paperwork took all afternoon and bail was extremely low. As sundown approached, Harrison loaded the two couples into his car and headed toward his farm. Instead of using the main road, Harrison turned off onto a dirt back road that led past Dorsey's farm to Moore Ford's Bridge, which spanned the Apalachee River, and eventually to Harrison's farm.

Clinton Adams and a friend were playing by the river next to the bridge. They were curious when they saw Harrison's car go by, for cars seldom used that road. When Harrison reached the bridge, he found the road blocked by a car. Another car suddenly pulled up behind Harrison's. About fifteen or twenty men with guns came out of the woods and pulled the two men out of the car and tied them up. Dorothy Malcolm recognized one of the men, Harrison later claimed, and called out to him. "Please don't kill them," she said. The others immediately dragged the two pleading women out of the car and tied them up alongside the men.

Meanwhile, Clinton Adams and his friend, hearing the shouts and screams, ran over to the scene and lay down in the grass to watch.

And we seen it was Klan 'cause we knew some of them. And we said they're going to whoop [whip] them. Well, that's what the Klan was doing, whoop people, you know. And it didn't matter if you was black or white, if they had a notion to whip your butt, you were going to get one. And they pushed and shoved them and knocked them around. And all at once, these four guys, they just come up there and pull guns—and bang. And everything went into slow motion for me. And they started shooting people, standing up over them, shooting down on them. People was shooting in the trees, every which way. I was shaking so bad. And when they left, everything went silent. And I stood up, and when I stood up it was like right there. And George, I knew him because he was my good buddy. And you could see the smoke and air bubbling out. And their faces was just a mess, I mean literally shot to pieces.

The massacre at Moore's Ford Bridge caused a national cry of outrage. The governor of Georgia posted a ten-thousand-dollar reward for information about the killers. Journalists and ministers in Georgia condemned the killings. President Truman ordered the FBI to investigate the case. The local sheriff investigated the crime but found no suspects. The Georgia Bureau of Investigation, the state attorney general, and other law enforcement agencies also investigated. But no one would testify, least of all young Adams who, at first, was willing to tell what he had seen—until the local sheriff visited his family's farm. "Two or three days later the sheriff was asking momma questions and I was just sitting on the porch. I told them right quick who done it. Big-mouth me. And he said, 'Come here boy.' So I went over to him. 'I want to tell you something.' He said, 'I can put some of these people in jail but I can't put all of them. And if they found out you know what you know, it could come back on you, your momma, your sister, or your brother.' And he said the best thing you can ever do is never mention this again."

Adams kept quiet. So did the rest of the county. Lamar Howard, a black teenager, was severely beaten because white mob members knew he had seen some of them gather at a local icehouse where he worked, and suspected he had talked to the police. Louis Hutchison, one of the FBI agents assigned to the case, stated, "We received no help from the sheriff's department." Many local whites seemed unconcerned about the killings and more interested in finding souvenirs. One resident walked over to the crime scene, spotted a tooth from one of the victims, picked it up, and gave it to his girlfriend to wear on her charm bracelet.

The chief suspect in the killings was Loy Harrison. Harrison claimed that a member of the mob held him at gunpoint and he was helpless to do anything about what happened. He said he did not recognize any members of the mob. The FBI did not believe his story but was unable to break it.

Clinton Adams eventually left the state. Some years later, when he was an adult, he returned for a visit and spoke to Harrison about the killings. "I asked Mr. Loy. I said, 'Why did you and them people kill George and Doris?' He said, 'Well, before George went into the army he was a pretty good nigger, but after he got out he thought he was as good as any white man.'"

Not all Southern officials condoned violence. Georgia's governor, Ellis Arnell, offered a major reward for information leading to the arrest of the killers. Arnell and his assistant attorney general, Daniel Duke, prosecuted the Klan. Stetson Kennedy, a labor journalist who infiltrated the Klan and a neo-Nazi group, the Columbians, was able to gather evidence to convict several members. In the overwhelming majority of murder cases, no one was ever arrested. No suspects identified. No one prosecuted and no one convicted. The killers all had the same name as far as most grand juries were concerned: "death by parties unknown." A few courageous Southern attorneys managed to get an occasional indictment, but no jury would ever convict the killers, no matter how strong the evidence against them.

In spite of—and sometimes because of—the reign of terror, blacks relentlessly moved forward. In 1946, they mobilized to take advantage of *Smith* v. *Allright,* the Supreme Court decision that struck down the white primary. Voter registration drives were organized in every Southern state. In South Carolina, the NAACP began to register black voters. In Alabama, black veterans staged a march in support of black voting rights. In Mississippi, Medgar and Charles Evers decided that they would vote in the state election of 1946. They wanted to cast their ballots against Senator Theodore Bilbo, one of the most racist demagogues to hold office in Mississippi. One writer described him as "short—jug eared, pot bellied—a 'runt' by his own description," who reveled in racial spleen. Bilbo was running for reelection and there seemed little chance of defeating him. Yet thousands of blacks, many of them veterans like the Evers brothers, wanted to cast their protest vote against him. As Charles Evers recalled,

We had five of us and we went to vote that day. All those whites I had known all my life. I couldn't believe it. I just looked at them. They had the room blocked off. They had guns, shotguns and rifles. And I walked up to them and I said, "Get out of the way," just like that. And Medgar said, "No Charlie." I said "I'm going to register." And a little old white lady, I'll never forget that, came out and said, "Charles, not now. Your day will come." I said, "No, ma'am, I want to register. I want to vote today." And old Andy May said, "If you'll vote you'll be a dead nigger." I said, "Well, kill me now, then, you SOB." And she said, "No, Charles. Please. Not now." And Medgar was right behind me. He said, "Come on, Charlie, let's get out of here. We'll come back." He grabbed me by the arm. "You know what Dad said. Look a peckerwood in the eye and he can't do a thing." And you could hear a rat piss on cotton. And we just backed out and went on down the street.

In 1946, two years after the United States Supreme Court declared the all-white primary illegal, blacks began to register to vote. In Atlanta, Georgia, the black vote won the election for a white moderate Congresswoman over her conservative opponent.

Eugene Talmadge, the Georgia demagogue running for governor in 1946, promised that blacks would not vote in the Georgia primary. But African Americans continued to register despite Talmadge's opposition.

Bilbo was reelected, and many blacks who tried to vote were beaten. After the election, Mississippi whites were shocked when hundreds of black veterans who had been denied their right to vote challenged the results in court and at a special Senate committee hearing. The Republican-controlled Senate, which considered Bilbo a disgrace, voted not to seat him. The reason had more to do with politics than morality. Bilbo was alleged to have accepted kickbacks from contractors he helped win bids, and the Republicans were fed up with him. In order to avoid a standoff with Southern Democrats, the Republicans agreed to compromise. Bilbo, who needed an operation, would temporarily yield his seat. The issue would be resolved after the operation. Bilbo never returned. The man who had vituperated blacks all his political life died of throat and mouth cancer.

Blacks flexed their political muscle all over the South. In Atlanta, John Wesley Dobbs, head of the black Masons in Georgia, took the lead. For decades, Dobbs had preached his gospel of success as "the Buck, the Book, and the Ballot." "When ten thousand Negroes get registered," he said, "the signal light of opportunity will automatically change from red to green." In 1946, the light changed.

In 1947, Harry Truman became the first President of the United States to address the National Association for the Advancement of Colored People. He did so on the steps of the Lincoln Memorial.

The Masons and other organizations began to register black voters throughout Georgia. In Atlanta, Grace Hamilton of the All-Citizens Registration Committee helped women voters to register with the aid of teachers' groups. Mary McLeod Bethune encouraged them: "We women will ring doorbells, make house-to-house canvasses, work with the ministers and the churches, the good times clubs and the civics groups, the labor unions and the professional organizations of both races and all creeds."

In Atlanta, a close political contest had developed between the liberal and conservative congressional candidates in a special primary election. The liberal candidate, Helen Douglas Mankin, needed the black vote to win but couldn't openly court it because of the backlash it might trigger in the white community. On the night before the election, after the last edition of the evening newspaper had been published, the word went out to the black community: "Vote for the woman!" The next day, as the votes were counted, Mankin was slightly trailing her opponent. But the black wards were counted last. When their votes came in, Mankin was declared the winner.

There were other signs of progress. Black policemen and firemen were slowly being hired; a few black politicians were elected. Despite the fact that some 750,000 blacks were now voting in the South, compared to 50,000 in 1932 (a jump from 1 percent of the voting-age population to 15 percent), victories over the old guard were still few and far between. In Georgia, race-baiting Eugene Talmadge—whom Hosea Williams characterized as "the political Adolf Hitler of Georgia"—won the primary for governor. His campaign slogan was to keep blacks from voting in the primary. For the most part, die-hard segregationists continued to rule.

As the Cold War with the Soviet Union intensified, and the nation was becoming increasingly anti-Communist and intolerant, Harry Truman astonished everyone by suddenly turning his attention to civil rights. Truman had been outraged at the murder of dozens of black veterans. Although he once held strong racial biases—he had used the word *nigger* freely in his speech—he decided to make civil rights a national issue in 1947. He authorized a fifteen-man committee on civil rights to recommend new legislation to protect people from discrimination. On the steps of the Lincoln Memorial, he became the first President of the United States to address the NAACP. He promised that the federal government would act now to end discrimination, violence, and race prejudice in American life. Shortly afterward, his panel issued its report, confirming that segregation, lynching, and discrimination at the polls had to be put to an end.

In the election year of 1948, Truman continued to push for civil rights. While he felt that it was the right thing to do, he also was aware that he had to win the black vote in order to be elected. He was also being pressured by Henry Wallace, who was running for President on the Progressive ticket and had made civil rights a major issue of the campaign.

Although most political analysts predicted a Republican landslide, Truman believed that the election would depend on a handful of cities in the North. The balance of power would be held by the black vote. Senator Hubert Humphrey, who was deeply committed to civil rights, had successfully maneuvered the Democratic Party to support a strong civil rights plank—much stronger than Truman wanted—in its platform. Southerners charged that the civil rights program was Communist inspired. Strom Thurmond, governor of South Carolina, and a group of Southern delegates stormed out of the Democratic convention when the civil rights platform passed and formed their own States' Rights party based on segregation. A reporter asked Thurmond why he abandoned the Democrats when Truman wasn't doing anything different from Franklin Roosevelt. Thurmond replied, "Yes—but Truman really means it."

After the convention, Truman continued on course. He ordered the army integrated, a move brought about, in part, by the intense pressure of civil rights leader A. Philip Randolph. Randolph threatened to organize a boycott of the armed services by blacks if Truman failed to act. Truman's order mandated nondiscrimination in federal employment and equality of treatment and opportunity in the armed services. Truman's civil rights stance won him the black vote in 1948 and, with it, the presidential election.

Truman's victory overwhelmed Thurmond and the States' Rights Party. Not only did Thurmond lose seven out of the eleven Southern states, but Truman gathered many more white votes than Thurmond in the South. Southern blacks and liberals hoped that the President's victory would be a death blow to white supremacy and that liberal reform would move forward. But the forces of reaction quickly regrouped. The Congress that Truman faced in 1948 was dominated by reactionaries of both parties, all of whom were opposed to federal civil rights legislation. Taking advantage of the Cold War and the anti-Communist hysteria sweeping the country, the Southern old guard launched a vicious propaganda campaign linking black civil rights with communism. Anyone who was for the former was obviously a member of the latter.

The resistance of Southern politicians to change resonated throughout the South, especially in school districts where blacks were fighting for better education for their children. When Reverend Joseph De Laine and James Gibson asked R. W. Elliot, the chairman of the Clarendon County, South Carolina, school board, if the board would pay for a bus for black children—there were thirty buses for white children and none for blacks—Elliot unsurprisingly replied, "We ain't got no money for buses for your nigger children." The answer was what De Laine had expected—even hoped for—even though he knew it might cost him his life.

Clarendon County was a cotton county of about four thousand farms, 85 percent of which were owned by whites. Most blacks earned less than one thousand dollars a year and had a fourth-grade education. Blacks who violated the code of white supremacy immediately felt the pressure. They could lose their jobs, homes, and possibly their lives.

Schools for black children consisted of dilapidated shacks, underpaid teachers, overcrowded classes, and lack of supplies. Clarendon spent $179 for each white child and $43 for each black child. In some areas, pupils had to walk ten or more miles to get to school each day.

De Laine and his wife were both teachers and had grown up in the county. He was also a minister, like his father before him. Inwardly seething at the injustice that surrounded him, De Laine remained outwardly compliant. One day he attended a summer session at Allen University in Columbia, South Carolina, where Reverend James Hinton of the NAACP gave a lecture. De Laine's life was never the same afterward.

Reverend Hinton was one of a coalition of freedom fighters in Columbia that included Modjeska Simkins, Osceola McKaine, and James McCray—all members of the NAACP. After the war, they had been instrumental in organizing voter registration drives in South Carolina that shook up the white establishment. Black schools in the state were atrocious, Hinton said. The conditions needed to be challenged in the courts. A good place to start was with the inequality of transportation. Not only had the school district failed to provide a bus, but when the parents bought their own bus, the school board even refused to pay for gas.

De Laine met with Thurgood Marshall, the chief legal strategist for the NAACP, for advice. Marshall told him that to bring a suit he needed at least twenty names on the petition to go to court. In Clarendon County, it was a formidable task. Almost every black man was beholden to whites. And there was always the Klan.

De Laine's first task was to get rid of a corrupt principal the whites had appointed to run one of the black schools. He had stolen money, bullied his teachers, and cheated his students. De Laine gathered the local people together and told them that in order to get the white school board to move, they had to jointly sign a petition. They were willing to do it, but they wanted De Laine to lead them. He declined. Twice more they insisted and finally he accepted, but on one condition: The fight they were about to begin had to be carried all the way to the state education board if necessary and, if that failed, then into the courts. They agreed. Two days later, De Laine was fired, as he had expected.

The state education board put pressure on the local board to resolve the matter. The board reluctantly complied. The principal was fired. The white superintendent then offered the job to De Laine—in return for which he would call off the protest. De Laine refused. The superintendent appointed his wife as acting principal. De Laine still refused to yield. Eight months later, he got the twenty names Marshall had requested. Since the names were listed in alphabetical order, the case was identified by the first name on the petition; it became known as *Briggs* v *Elliot.* After Briggs signed, he was asked by his boss at the gas station where he worked if he knew what he was doing. Briggs replied that he was doing it for his children. The day after Christmas, he was fired. Shortly afterward, his wife was fired from her job as a chambermaid and his credit was cut off at the bank.

De Laine continued his fight. He was sent death threats by the Klan, his wife and nieces were fired from school, a twenty-thousand-dollar lawsuit was filed against him by the crooked principal. The situation become so intolerable that De Laine's denomination transferred him to another church away from the community. De Laine was gone, but the case now had a life of its own.

As the Briggs case began its slow-motion journey through the courts, another sleeping giant was waking in Farmville, Virgina. This giant was a sixteen-year-old girl by the name of Barbara Johns.

Farmville was located in Prince Edward County, the tobacco-growing region of south-central Virginia. Farmville's population was under five thousand in 1950. Both Robert E. Lee and U. S. Grant had stopped at Farmville during the Civil War, a few days apart.

Farmville was not the virulent Deep South of Mississippi but the seemingly benign Upper South of Virginia. Kennell Jackson, a black resident, did not think of the town as a "racially oppressive place." Farmville, he said, was "not only a good community and a supportive community for blacks, but an ambitious community." If the Klan was around, few people knew and nobody advertised it. Most farmers, black and white, were small, independent landholders. Black and white relationships were cordial. But blacks still drank from the colored water fountain, used the colored public bathroom, did not try to eat at the white drugstore or restaurant, and sat in the "roost" of the movie theater. Hodges Brown, a high school student, said that he was once told that the reason blacks had to sit upstairs was that in case of a fire, the whites downstairs would be able to get out first. John Stokes remembered that the first time he became aware of segregation was when he was seven or eight years old. "I was down there at J. J. Newberry's and started to the water fountain and momma said, 'no you can't go there.' And I said, 'why?' And momma said, 'that's because it's for whites only.' And I knew then that we were living in a world that had differences due to color." Reverend Samuel Williams experienced the separation at an early age. "You are there and we are here. We worked for you and that is all. We don't worship together. We don't play together. This is a white school over here. This is a black school over there with lesser facilities. You go your way as white people and we go our way as black people."

Traditionally, Farmville—like the rest of Virginia—had not been enthusiastic about education for any of its children. A high school for white children was not built until the 1920s. Farmville's whites did not see a need for black education. What would they do with it? Most would do only menial work they could learn on the job. One white resident later explained, "If the Negroes wanted a library or swimming pool, we'd help them get it. But they're not interested. They want pool rooms and dance halls. They're more interested in drinking and carousing than in reading and swimming. We have a saying around here. 'Be a Negro on Saturday night and you'll never want to be a white man again.'"

Farmville's black parents wanted a high school for their children, but they ran into white resistance. They had to put a great deal of pressure on the white school board even to get it to expand their elementary school to the eleventh grade. In 1939, the board, with federal money, finally capitulated to black demands and built the Robert Russa Moton high school, after a black Virginian who had succeeded Booker T. Washington at Tuskegee.

The high school accommodated 180 pupils. On opening day, 165 students registered. The following year, 219. By 1951, the school population was 477 and still climbing. Hodges Brown recalled classes being held on the stage of the auditorium and even on a school bus. Many of the supplies that the students received were hand-me-downs from the white school. Writing scribbled in books by the previous users was erased.

The parents of Moton children had formed a PTA and brought pressure on the board to build a new and better high school for black students. John Lancaster and Reverend Leslie Francis Griffin were two of the members of the PTA. Griffin was a sophisticated, well-educated minister who had studied the works of two outstanding theologians, Paul Tillich and Reinhold Niebuhr. Born and raised in Farmville, he had returned home after serving in a tank corps under General George Patton during World War II. Griffin took over the First Baptist Church after his father died. He believed that Christianity demanded social action, and he felt that his mission was to inspire his congregation to question the way things were in

Farmville. As part of his program, he recruited the required fifty people needed to form a chapter of the NAACP.

Edna Allen loved to hear his sermons: "He was bright. He was articulate. He was well read. He had an agenda. His sermons were totally different. You usually left his church a little disturbed. He made me want to read and find out more things." Reverend Griffin felt that most black people in Farmville were docile. The conservative black leaders whom whites consulted when they wanted to know anything about the black community were cut in the mold of Booker T. Washington. They believed that by staying on the good side of whites, never protesting or causing trouble, they could ask favors of whites and in that way make some progress. Griffin wanted to shake up this way of thinking, but he knew that he had his work cut out for him. Too many blacks were dependent on whites for their livelihood.

Griffin and Lancaster, along with other PTA members, attended the school meetings over a period of several years, urging them to build a new high school for black students. The board was willing in principle but extremely slow in practice. A new school would require floating a bond issue, which Farmville's white residents would have to support. Most voters would be reluctant to support it, as they did not believe blacks needed much of an education.

Lancaster knew that the board was deliberately dragging its feet. "1944, 45, 46, 47, 48, we were going through this process. We even went so far as to go to the board with a three-point plan. And I remember very specifically one board member looked at it and said if we build a school like that, every Tom, Dick, and Harry will be going to school. And that was the first time it dawned on me that there wasn't any intention for us to go to school."

But if the physical plant of the school was poor, the teaching staff was excellent. Kennell Jackson maintains that Moton "was a great engine of achievement and ambition on the part of the students . . . and the teachers. They were surpassing the limitations that the school system had imposed on us and were doing a great job of educating the people." John Watson recalled, "I didn't need an integrated student body to get a good education. Our teachers were on us all the time to do our best. It wasn't about sitting beside a given person. It was about a quality education and we could no longer get a quality education in this building."

The school board offered an interim compromise. Until they could raise the money to build a new school, they would put up temporary buildings to relieve the overcrowding. The board built shacks made of wood with tarpaper roofs. Students called them "chicken coops." Edna Allen recalled how the shacks compared to the white school. "They had an atrium in the center of the school where you could walk out of the cafeteria and kind of sit in a garden and eat. Damn we didn't even have a cafeteria. The building was beautiful. And I couldn't believe that this was what they had for a building and I'm sitting in those shacks with an umbrella up on rainy days so the ink wouldn't run on my paper."

Carl Allen recalled the potbelly stove used to heat the rooms. The students who sat by it in the winter would get red hot while those by the door turned blue with cold. They had to keep their coats on in class. Sometimes, the gym teacher would hold boxing matches in the shacks. "You were in trouble if you got too near those stoves."

For Farmville blacks, the shacks were another example of white contempt. And none felt it more keenly than Barbara Rose Johns.

Barbara Johns was sixteen years old when she organized the students at the Robert Russa Moton High School in Farmville, Virginia, to go on strike to protest their inferior school facilities. The strike led to a lawsuit that became one of the five cases the United States Supreme Court reviewed when it overturned segregation.

Although she was born in New York City in 1935, where her family had migrated to find work, Barbara Johns's family was rooted in Prince Edward County. Her parents and grandparents had been born there. During World War II, Barbara Johns lived on a tobacco farm with her maternal grandmother, Mary Croner. Barbara's younger sister, Joan Johns Cobbs, says that Croner was "the backbone of the family. Kept us all in line and kept us together."

Barbara Johns helped care for and pick tobacco in her free time and worked in the country store owned by her uncle, Vernon Johns, who was also a strong influence on her life. Vernon Johns was a minister and a legend in Prince Edward County and elsewhere in the South. Well educated, a dynamic speaker, a believer in the church as an agent of change, he sought to shake up his congregations by exhorting and chastising them for their complacency and docility. He would also stand up to whites. Joan Johns Cobbs remembers how Uncle Vernon would constantly test them. "He was the type of person who always questioned us about history or some current affair. So a lot of times we'd try and avoid him because we didn't know if we knew the answer to some of his questions. I mean he felt that we should know our history. And if we couldn't give an answer he'd say, you should know this because it's part of your history. He was constantly challenging our minds."

Barbara Johns's grandmothers were both strong women who were not afraid of whites. Joan Johns Cobbs remembers that Barbara was of the same mold. "She used to get angry that white customers would come into the store and call her family relatives by their first name or use "uncle" or "auntie" when addressing them. She was especially upset about everyone calling my mother and father Violet and Robert, and we had to address them as mister or missus. And so she asked a white man one day why did he call our mother by her first name? And he called my father 'uncle Robert.' And she said, 'He's not your uncle, so why do you call him uncle Robert?' She would often say things like that to white people."

Barbara Johns keenly felt the difference between her school and the white school. "I remember thinking how unfair it was," she once said. "I kept thinking about it all the way home. I thought about it a lot while I was in bed and I was still thinking about it the next day."

Other students were also aware of the difference between the two schools. Hodges Brown envied the white school's baseball team. "I used to go over to their ballgames. You couldn't go inside, you had to stand at the fence, you know, and look through. They had beautiful uniforms, big band. . . . And that's the kind of thing I always wanted you know if I were to go to high school. But it wasn't that way. Those things happened down South." Carl Allen remembered the hand-me-down football uniforms they received. And John Watson recalled the used textbooks. What infuriated one student was the movies they showed the students.

Every movie we saw in this auditorium had all white actors and actresses. You might see a black actor playing a subservient role. But the one film that they had that featured an all black cast with only one white actor was a film they had on personal hygiene. And it was about the pitfalls of gonorrhea and syphilis. And all the people who had gonorrhea and syphilis were blacks. The only white person in that film was the doctor. And in my head, all the white kids that would see that film and then look at me, they would see the worst that society had to offer. Because how do you know that this young man here doesn't have syphilis. Because we saw it in the movie and when you see it in a movie, it's true.

Barbara Johns decided to act. She called a meeting on a football field with five students she could trust. John Stokes was one. "Barbara came up with the idea. She said, 'we'll go on strike.' I was churning inside because I knew that we were skating on thin ice. We were really playing with something that we didn't know had that much power. We were scared at the time. But we knew we had to pull it off."

The major obstacle was the presence of the principal M. Boyd Jones. "Jones was a strong man," John Watson recalled. "We knew that if he was on campus, there was not going to be a strike."

Watson and the others formulated a plan to get Jones off campus on the day of the meeting. "We pretended we were businessmen calling to tell him that his students were downtown making disturbances and would he please come down and take care of it. As I think back on it, I don't think we fooled him. I think he just played along."

Barbara's sister was in class when an announcement was made to go to the assembly, something that seemed perfectly normal. When she arrived in the auditorium, she was astonished to see that the students had asked the teachers to leave. They all complied, although some were reluctant. "Barbara came in and walked onto the stage. And I remember saying to myself 'What is going on? Why is she up there?' And she started to talk and tell us how very bad conditions were in the school and how she needed everyone's cooperation. And that in order to effect change, we had to go out on strike. And I remember sitting in my seat and sort of cowering down because she was talking so forcefully and without any fear. And I remember the first reaction I had was fear. I thought 'Oh my goodness what's going to happen to us now?' Later she chastised me for my fear. I was crying at one point, because I was afraid that our family would be torn apart in some fashion. But she said, nothing's going to happen."

One student was electrified by her speech. "She put into words what I had been feeling, words I didn't know how to say, perhaps afraid to say them because of the repercussions. But she put it all into words and it was so simple—that we have a right to these things. We have a right to decent books. We have a right to good teachers. We have a right to have a school equal to the white kids. She didn't talk about integration. She talked about equality."

Some students were scared. "A lot of people were scared," Stokes remembered. "Some of Barbara's closest friends were scared to death for her. They said why did you do that. She said, we have to make a change and I mean right now. You know Barbara was very dynamic when she wasn't quiet. And then you'd look over there and you see this docile person and you would say, she isn't anything like that. Oh yes she was. And that is why she made such a good leader. We could not have selected a better leader."

The students made signs and marched into town. They met with T. J. McIlwaine, superintendent of schools, who believed that the strike was not the students' idea but that they were being manipulated by adults. He ordered them to return to their classes. John Stokes was at the meeting. "He said, 'You are upstarts. And you need to go back to school before all your parents are in jail.' And that's what frightened us when he said our parents were going to jail. And when a member of my family said, 'How big is the Farmville jail?' from that point on there was no stopping us." The students escalated the conflict. They asked the NAACP to help them.

The NAACP in Virginia, led by attorneys Oliver Hill and Spottiswood Robinson, had launched dozens of legal assaults on the Virginia schools in the courts. Their strategy had been to force the state to make black schools equal to white schools. If schools had to be separate, then according to *Plessy,* Hill said that they "damned well" better be equal. Hill and Robinson won a major victory when the courts authorized that black teachers had to receive the same pay as white teachers. They had other victories, such as requiring school districts to provide equal transportation. Even a few country districts were willing to provide equal schools. Many school districts balked at fulfilling the court's mandates, even though board members were personally fined by the courts for dragging their feet. The NAACP was being worn down by having to bring hundreds, maybe even thousands of cases to force each school district to provide equal facilities. When school boards complained they didn't have the money to upgrade the black schools, Hill suggested an easier solution: integrate them. The cost would be minimal. One enraged school board member threatened, "The first little black son of a bitch that comes down the road to set foot in that school, I'll take my shotgun and blow his brains out." But despite the threats, Thurgood Marshall was resolved the time had come for David to take on Goliath. No more piecemeal attacks on segregation. It was time to throw out the whole system.

The NAACP attorneys met with the parents and students at the First Baptist Church in Farmville to ask them whether they would support a lawsuit for integrating the schools. The striking students were in favor, but the question was whether their parents would support them. When a former principal, J. B. Pervall, rose to criticize that step, Barbara Johns stood and shouted out, "Don't let Mr. Charlie, Mr. Tommy, or Mr. Pervall stop you from backing us. We are depending upon you." Reverend Griffin seconded her remarks. "Anyone who would not back these children after they stepped out on a limb is not a man. Anyone who will not fight against racial prejudice is not a man." The parents cheered. They would back their children. John Stokes never forgot that moment.

> That night at the Baptist Church was one that I shall remember as long as I live. I mean it was just like watching Jackie Robinson in Ebbets field. It was the most beautiful sight I've ever seen. And they [the parents] came in there and they were truly behind us. Really and truly behind us. The NAACP was astounded to find that people who had been dormant and quiet for so long quiescent for so long were ready to back their children. And he [Griffin] said, if you are really ready to back them, then you have to sign this petition. And that's how we found out we could separate the wheat from the chaff. Because some of the blacks didn't sign. My mother and father signed.

The case entered the court as *Davis* v. *County School Board of Prince Edward County.* Whites believed that Reverend Griffin, John Lancaster, and M. Boyd Jones were somehow behind the strike and that they and the NAACP had manipulated the children. They retaliated, and black families suffered. Kennell Jackson's mother and aunt were fired from their teaching jobs. His father lost his business. "It was like the town had been hit by a neutron bomb," Jackson said. "Everything was standing but nothing was going on. The whole economic, educational infrastructure was sort of vacuumed out of the town. For all intents and purposes, black Farmville died during this time." Whites stopped buying vegetables from John Stokes's family. Some stopped speaking to them. Edna Allen's parents lost their jobs. Some parents received anonymous threatening phone calls, and Barbara Johns was threatened with death and sent to live with her uncle Vernon in Alabama. Most students were concerned that their actions might cause M. Boyd Jones to lose his job. Stokes said that he had told him in front of his parents, "You all have to do what you have to do. I'll find a job. I'll find a job. Because this is bigger than any of us." He was fired.

Like streams flowing into a river, the Farmville case merged with the Briggs case from South Carolina and three other cases and flowed past the federal district courts—where the suit was rejected—to the United States Supreme Court. In 1954, the Court, in a unanimous decision, achieved with great effort by Chief Justice Earl Warren, ruled that segregation in the field of education was inherently unequal. John Stokes was overjoyed: "When I heard of the historic decision I said, thank God. Thank God. At last someone has listened to us. And those were my very words. Someone has listened to us. Hopefully we shall see a change."

In 1954, the United States Supreme Court acknowledged the seventy-year fight of African Americans to have Jim Crow declared unconstitutional. The Court ruled that segregation in education is inherently unequal. This opened the door to overturning legal segregation in other areas of public life.

In 1954, eighty-nine years after the end of the Civil War, the death knell of legal Jim Crow tolled. The United States Supreme Court ruled segregation in education unconstitutional, destroying the legal rationale for Jim Crow. In some ways, America was already on the road to integration by the 1950s. Black and white athletes played together on the same professional teams. White and black teenagers danced to the same music. Blacks became more visible in public life. National television and radio programs were reaching Southern audiences, communicating new ideas and the changing times. Many hoped that after the initial shock of the *Brown* decision, the South would accept reality and adapt itself accordingly.

But many Southern whites were filled with passionate intensity to preserve segregation. In 1956, 101 congressmen from the South issued a Southern Manifesto that rejected the Court's decision and pledged "to use all lawful means to bring about a reversal of this decision." Southern school districts began to devise strategies that would circumvent the Court's decision. In some areas, parents were allowed to send their children to whatever school they wanted, even if it was out of their community. Few black parents wanted to risk sending their children to an all-white school where they would be harassed and possibly beaten. District courts with judges often sympathetic to segregation granted extensive delays.

President Dwight D. Eisenhower waffled on the issue. He refused to provide the leadership so badly needed at that time. Many believed that he was opposed to the decision and regretted the fact that he had appointed Earl Warren as chief justice of the Court. He acknowledged that the Court decision was now the law of the land, but at the same time he admitted that it would be hard, perhaps impossible, to change people's thinking in the matter. When federal court orders to integrate the University of Alabama and a high school in Mansfield, Texas, were ignored Eisenhower did nothing. In 1957, as some citizens of Arkansas were trying to work out a means to integrate the schools as ordered by a federal court, Governor Orval Faubus ordered the Arkansas national guard to block black students from entering. A reluctant Eisenhower was finally forced to send paratroopers into the community to restore order and integrate the schools. His moral weakness encouraged further white resistance. Antisegregationist White Citizen's Councils, its members middle-class whites, sprang up all over the South. The Ku Klux Klan jumped into action. Blacks who supported integrating the schools were fired, lost their financial credit and bank loans, and sometimes were beaten and murdered. For a brief moment, it seemed that the South would successfully resist integration. But the walls of the fortress of segregation had been irrevocably breached, and through them would pour the armies of the civil rights movement.

Black people once again would make their own history. In February 1960, four black college students from North Carolina Agricultural and Technical College entered a Woolworth's in Greensboro, sat at the white-only lunch counter, ordered coffee, and were refused service. An hour later they left, but they returned the next day. On Thursday, white students from the University of North Carolina's women's college sat with them. The act of defiance caught the imagination of black and white students throughout the country. By the end of the year, some fifty thousand students had staged sit-ins throughout the South, and the civil rights movement was launched.

White Southerners suddenly found themselves trapped between the hammer and the anvil. As civil rights activists, led by Dr. Martin Luther King, Jr., and student leaders shook the foundations of segregation with protests, demonstrations, and sit-ins, the federal government hammered them with civil rights laws and court decisions. Whites sometimes responded with violence, murder, and beatings, but despite their resistance, the victory had been secured. Black and white students gradually went to school with each other. Blacks sat downstairs in movie theaters, ate at once segregated lunch counters, shopped in stores previously closed to them, and worked at jobs that had been denied them.

But if the battle was won, the war against racial prejudice continued. By the 1970s, a counterreaction began to set in as Northern as well as Southern whites resisted black gains. Conservative Supreme Court justices began to circumscribe black rights. Parents sent their children to all-white private schools as public schools became increasingly black. The Republican Party in the South became identified as the champion of white interests and gained political power in almost every Southern state.

All of this would not have been surprising to Ned Cobb, the Alabama sharecropper who recounted his life to two Harvard graduate students in the 1970s. Cobb had been born in the 1880s and had lived through the worst years of Jim Crow between 1890 and 1970. He had stood up against the system in 1931 when he supported a union drive to organize black farmworkers and went to prison for thirteen years as a result. By the end of his life in 1972, he had lived long enough to watch with joy as the school bus passed his house every morning carrying black and white children to the same school. But he knew that the great victory he had helped bring about was far from won.

How many people is it today that it needs and it required to carry out this movement? . . . It's taken time, and it will take more time before it's finished. Who's to do it. It's the best people in the United States to do it, in defense of the uneducated, the unknowledged ones that's livin' here in this country. They're goin' to win! They're goin' to win! But it's going to take a great effort. It won't come easy . . . it's going to take thousands and millions of words, thousands and millions of steps to complete this business. I'd love to know that the black race has finally shed the veil from their eyes and the shackles from their feet.

The veil has been lifted, but the shackles remain. Though Jim Crow is no longer codified in the laws, and the racial climate has decidedly improved, white supremacy is still a vital part of the American psyche. Racial violence toward blacks, though no longer rampant, explodes periodically. Schools have slipped back into a pattern of segregation. The doors of business, once closed to blacks, are only barely open. Race prejudice still has its appeal to millions of Americans. Civil rights activists charge that the United States Supreme Court once again supports the opponents of racial equality and justice.

To continue the battle against racial prejudice in the future requires strengths borrowed from the past. Those who struggle today can draw inspiration from the men and women who stood up and said no in the time of Jim Crow.

BIBLIOGRAPHY

Anderson, James. *The Education of Blacks in the South, 1860–1935.* Chapel Hill: University of North Carolina Press, 1988.

Andrews, Sidney. *The South Since the War.* New York: Arno Press, 1969.

Apthker, Herbert. *A Documentary History of the Negro People in the United States, 1910–1932, Vol. 3.* New York: Carol Publishing Group, 1933.

Ayers, Edward. *The Promise of the New South: Life After Reconstruction.* New York: Oxford University Press, 1992.

Baker, Ray Stannard. *Following the Color Line: American Negro Citizenship in the Progressive Era.* New York: Harper & Row, 1964.

Barnett, Ida Wells. *On Lynching: (Southern Horror: A Red Record: Mob Rule in New Orleans).* New York: Arno Press, 1969.

Bauerlein, Mark. *Negrophobia, A Race Riot in Atlanta, 1906.* San Francisco: Encounter Books, 2001.

Bechet, Sidney. *Treat It Gentle: An Autobiography.* New York: De Capo Press, 1978.

Bethel, Elizabeth Rauh. *Promiseland.* Philadelphia: Temple University Press, 1981.

Broughton, Virgina W. *Twenty Years Experience as a Missionary:* Chicago: The Pony Press, 1907.

Brundage, Fitzhugh W. *Lynching in the New South: Georgia and Virginia, 1880–1930.* Urbana: University of Illinois Press, 1993.

Cobb, James C., and Michael V. Namorato, eds. *The New Deal and the South.* Jackson: University Press of Mississippi, 1984.

Cortner, Richard C. *A Mob Intent on Death, the NAACP and the Arkansas Riot Cases.* Middletown: Wesleyan University Press, 1988.

Daniel, Pete. *The Shadow of Slavery: Peonage in the South, 1901–1969.* Urbana: University of Illinois Press, 1972.

Davis, Elizabeth. *Lifting as They Climb: The National Association of Colored Women.* Washington, D.C.: National Association of Colored Women, 1933.

Dittmer, John. *Black Georgia in the Progressive Era, 1900–1920.* Urbana: University of Illinois Press, 1977.

Du Bois, W.E.B. *The Autobiography of W.E.B. Du Bois.* New York: International Publishers, 1958.

———. *The Souls of Black Folk.* New York: Avon, 1965.

Duster, Alfreda. *Crusade for Justice: The Autobiography of Ida B. Wells.* Chicago: University of Chicago Press, 1970.

Edmonds, Helen. *The Negro and Fusion Politics in North Carolina, 1894–1901.* Chapel Hill: University of North Carolina Press, 1955.

Egerton, John. *Speak Now Against the Day.* Chapel Hill: University of North Carolina Press, 1995.

Engs, Robert Francis. *Educating the Disfranchised and the Disinherited: Samuel Chapman Armstrong and Hampton Institute 1839–1893.* Knoxville: University of Tennessee Press, 1999.

Foner, Eric. *Reconstruction: America's Unfinished Revolution 1863–1877.* New York: Harper & Row, 1988.

Foner, Philip. *Organized Labor and the Black Worker.* New York: International Publishers, 1974.

Fredrickson, George M. *The Black Image in the White Mind.* New York: Harper & Row, 1971.

Friedman, Lawrence. *The White Savage: Racial Fantasies in the Post-Bellum South.* Englewood Cliffs, NJ: Prentice Hall, 1970.

Gaines, Kevin. *Uplifting the Race: Black Leadership, Politics and Culture in the Twentieth Century.* Chapel Hill: University of North Carolina Press, 1996.

Gaither, Gerald. *Blacks and the Populist Revolt: Ballots and Bigotry in the New South.* Tuscaloosa: University of Alabama Press, 1975.

Gatewood, Willard. *Black Americans and the White Man's Burden, 1898–1903.* Urbana: University of Illinois Press, 1975.

———. *"Smoke Yankees" and the Struggle for Empire: Letters from Negro Soldiers, 1898–1902.* Urbana: University of Illinois Press, 1971.

Giddings, Paul. *Where and When I Enter: The Impact of Black Women on Race and Sex in America.* New York: William Morrow, 1984.

Gilmore, Glenda. *Gender and Jim Crow: Women and the Politics of White Supremacy in North Carolina, 1896–1920.* Chapel Hill: University of North Carolina Press, 1996.

Gossett, Thomas. *Race: The History of an Idea in America.* New York: Schocken Books, 1965.

Greenwood, Janet. *Bittersweet Legacy: The Black and White Better Classes in Charlotte, 1850–1910.* Chapel Hill: University of North Carolina Press, 1994.

Hair, William Ivy. *Bourbonism and Agrarian Protest: Louisiana Politics, 1877–1900.* Baton Rouge: Louisiana State University Press, 1969.

————. *Carnival of Fury: Robert Charles and the New Orleans Race Riot of 1900.* Baton Rouge: Louisiana State University Press, 1976.

Harlan, Louis. *Booker T. Washington, the Making of a Black Leader.* New York: Oxford University Press, 1972.

————. *Booker T. Washington, the Wizard of Tuskegee, 1901–1915.* New York: Oxford University Press, 1983.

Harlan, Louis R., et al., eds. *The Booker T. Washington Papers.* 14 vols. Urbana: University of Illinois Press, 1972–1989.

Hayden, Henry. *The Story of the Wilmington Rebellion* (booklet). Wilmington, NC, 1936.

Haynes, Robert V. *A Night of Violence, The Houston Riot of 1917.* Baton Rouge: Louisiana State University Press, 1976.

Hermann, Janet Sharp. *The Pursuit of a Dream.* Jackson: University Press of Mississippi, 1999.

Higginbotham, Evelyn Brooks. *Righteous Discontent: The Women's Movement in the Black Baptist Church, 1880–1920.* Cambridge: Harvard University Press, 1993.

Holmes, William. *The White Chief: James Kimble Vardaman.* Baton Rouge: Louisiana State University Press, 1970.

Holtzclaw, William Henry. *The Black Man's Burden.* New York: Neale Publishers, 1915.

Howard, O. O. *Autobiography of Oliver Otis Howard, Major General, United States Army.* New York: Baker and Taylor, 1907.

Hunter, Tera. "Household Laborers and Work in the Making: Afro-American Women and Work in the Urban South, 1861–1920." Manuscript.

Jones, Jacqueline. *Labor of Love, Labor of Sorrow: Black Women, Work and Family from Slavery to the Present.* New York: Basic Books, 1985.

Kelley, Robin. *Hammer and Hoe: Alabama Communists During the Great Depression.* Chapel Hill: University of North Carolina Press, 1990.

————. *Race Rebels: Culture, Politics and the Black Working Class.* New York: Free Press, 1994.

Key, V. O., Jr. *Southern Politics in State and Nation.* Knoxville: University of Tennessee Press, 1996.

Kirk, Allen, J. "A Statement of Facts Concerning the Bloody Riot in Wilmington, North Carolina, Thursday, November 10, 1898." Durham, NC: Duke University Library.

Kirwan, Albert. *Revolt of the Rednecks: Mississippi Politics, 1876–1925.* New York: Harper & Row, 1951.

Kluger, Richard. *Simple Justice.* New York: Vintage Books, 1977.

Kousser, J. Morgan. *The Shaping of Southern Politics: Suffrage Restriction and the Establishment of the One-Party South 1880–1910.* New Haven: Yale University Press, 1973.

Lawson, Steven F. *Black Ballots, Voting Rights in the South, 1944–1969.* New York: Columbia University Press, 1976.

Levine, Lawrence. *Black Culture and Black Consciousness: Afro American Folk Thought from Slavery to Freedom.* New York: Oxford University Press, 1977.

————. *The Unpredictable Past.* New York: Oxford University Press, 1993.

Lewis, David Levering. *W.E.B. Du Bois: The Biography of a Race, 1865–1919.* New York: Holt, 1993.

————. *W.E.B. Du Bois: The Fight for Equality and the American Century, 1919–1963.* New York: Holt, 2000.

Lincoln, Eric. *The Black Church in the African American Experience.* Durham: Duke University Press, 1991.

Litwack, Leon. *Been in the Storm So Long: The Aftermath of Slavery.* New York: Alfred A. Knopf, 1979.

————. *Trouble in Mind: Black Southerners in the Age of Jim Crow.* New York: Alfred A. Knopf, 1998.

Logan, Rayford. *The Betrayal of the Negro: From Rutherford B. Hayes to Woodrow Wilson.* New York: Collier, 1965.

Lomax, Alan. *Mister Jelly Roll.* New York: Pantheon, 1965.

Mays, Benjamin. *Born to Rebel: An Autobiography.* Athens: University of Georgia Press, 1971.

McMillen, Neil. *Dark Journey: Black Mississippians in the Age of Jim Crow.* Urbana: University of Illinois Press, 1990.

Meier, August. *Negro Thought in America 1880–1915: Racial Ideologies in the Age of Booker T. Washington.* Ann Arbor: University of Michigan Press, 1966.

Oshinsky, David. *Worse Than Slavery: Parchment and the Ordeal of Jim Crow Justice.* New York: Free Press, 1996.

Painter, Nell Irvin. *Exodusters: Black Migration to Kansas after Reconstruction.* New York: W. W. Norton, 1976.

Pickens, William. *Bursting Bonds.* Boston: Jordan and More, 1923.

Proctor, Henry Hugh. *Between Black and White: Autobiographical Sketches.* Boston: Pilgrim Press, 1925.

Rabinowitz, Howard. *Race Relations in the Urban South, 1865–1890.* New York: Oxford University Press, 1978.

Raper, Arthur. *The Tragedy of Lynching.* New York: Negro Press, 1969.

Reddick J. L. "The Negro and the Populist Movement in Georgia." Master's thesis, Atlanta University, 1937.

Redding, Saunders. *Lonesome Road.* New York: Doubleday, 1958.

Redkey, Edwin. *Black Exodus: Black Nationalist and Back-to-Africa Movements, 1890–1910.* New Haven: Yale University Press, 1969.

Reid, Whitelaw. *After the War, A Southern Tour.* New York: Harper & Row, 1965.

Rosengarten, Theodore. *All God's Dangers: The Life of Nate Shaw.* New York: Alfred A. Knopf, 1975.

Rouse, Jacqueline Anne. *Lugenia Burns Hope, Black Southern Reformer*. Athens: University of Georgia Press, 1989.

Shapiro, Herbert. *White Violence and Black Response from Reconstruction to Montgomery*. Amherst: University of Massachusetts Press, 1988.

Simkins, Francis Butler. *Pitchfork Ben Tillman*. Baton Rouge: Louisiana State University Press, 1944.

Sitkoff, Harvard. *A New Deal For Blacks*. New York: Oxford University Press, 1978.

Smith, Robert. *They Closed Their Schools, Prince Edward County, Virginia, 1951–1964*. Farmville: Martha E. Forrester Council of Women, 1996.

Stampp, Kenneth M. *The Era of Reconstruction, 1865–1877*. New York: Alfred A. Knopf, 1965.

Sterling, Dorothy, ed. *We Are Your Sisters*. New York: W. W. Norton, 1984.

Sullivan, Patricia. *Days of Hope, Race and Democracy in the New Deal Era*. Chapel Hill: University of North Carolina Press, 1996.

Thorne, Jack. *Hanover, or, The Persecution of the Lowly: A Story of the Wilmington Massacre*. New York: Arno Press, 1969.

Tindall, George. *The Emergence of the New South, 1913–1945*. Baton Rouge: Louisiana State University Press, 1967.

Trelease, Allen W. *White Terror: The Ku Klux Klan Conspiracy and Southern Reconstruction*. New York: Harper & Row, 1971.

Trowbridge, J. T. *The Desolate South 1865–1866: A Picture of the Battlefields and of the Devastated Confederacy*. New York: Duell, Sloane and Pearce, 1956.

Wadelington, Charles and Richard F. Knapp. *Charlotte Hawkins Brown and Palmer Memorial Institute*. Chapel Hill: University of North Carolina Press, 1999.

Washington, Booker T. *The Negro in Business*. New York: Johnson Reprint Co., 1970.

———. "A Town Owned by Negroes." *World's Work* 18, no. 3 (July 1907).

———. *Up from Slavery*. New York: Avon, 1965.

Washington, Booker T., and W.E.B. Du Bois. *The Negro in the South*. New York: Citadel, 1970.

Wells-Barnett, Ida. *On Lynchings: Southern Horrors, A Red Record, Mob Rule in New Orleans*. New York: Arno Press, 1969.

———. *Southern Horrors and Other Writings*. Boston: Bedford Books, 1997.

White, C. C. *No Quittin' Sense*. Austin: University of Texas Press, 1969.

White, Walter. *A Man Called White*. Athens: University of Georgia Press, 1995.

Williamson, Joel. *The Crucible of Race: Black-White Relationships in the American South Since Emancipation*. New York: Oxford University Press, 1984.

————. *Rage for Order.* New York: Oxford University Press, 1986.

Woodward, C. Vann. *Origins of the New South, 1877–1913.* Baton Rouge: Louisiana State University Press, 1987.

————. *The Strange Career of Jim Crow.* New York: Oxford University Press, 1974.

————. *Tom Watson: Agrarian Rebel.* New York: Oxford University Press, 1937.

LIST OF CREDITS

Harvard Theater Collection, Houghton Library: frontispiece

Duke University, Rare Book, Manuscripts and Special Collections Library: xii

Valentine Richmond History Center: xvi, 50

New-York Historical Society: 1, 4, 10

Library of Congress: 6, 9, 12, 14, 20, 21, 22, 24, 28, 31, 38, 42, 45, 46, 47, 55, 65, 68, 74, 82, 85, 104, 108, 110, 125, 126, 149, 150

Collection of Joan W. and Thomas H. Gandy: 18, 26, 52-53, 62, 89

Kansas State Historical Society: 33

Photographs and Prints Division, Schomburg Center for Research and Black Culture, New York Public Library: 44, 129, 158, 162

From the Collection of the Florida State Archives: 49

Syracuse University Library, Department of Special Collections: 56

North Carolina Room, Durham County Library: 59

University of Chicago Library, Special Collections Research Center: 64

Xavier University Archives and Special Collections: 69, 106

H. W. Parlee, Erik Overbey Collection, University of South Alabama Archives: 78

Cape Fear Museum: 81

North Carolina Collection, University of North Carolina Libraries at Chapel Hill: 83, 91

North Carolina Office of History and Archives: 84

North Carolina Department of Cultural Resources, Office of Archives and History: 87

Hogan Jazz Archive, Tulane University: 92

New Orleans Public Library: 97

Holsinger Studio Collection, Albert H. Small Special Collections Library, University of Virginia: 104

Special Collections and Archives, W.E.B. Du Bois Library, University of Massachusetts at Amherst: 103, 115

Atlanta History Center: 112

Yale Collection of Literature, Beinecke Rare Book and Manuscript Library: 113

Fort Sam Houston Museum: 118

National Archives: 120

Doris Ulmann Photographic Collection, University Archives, University of Oregon Library: 126 (PH.3499), 135 (PH.5301)

Morgan County Archives: 137

Private Collection, Ted and Dale Rosengarten: 140

Museum of Natural History: 144

Denver Public Library: 146

Bettmann/Corbis: 154, 167, 182

Washington, D.C., Public Library: 164

Courtesy of Clinton Adams: 166

Special Collections Department, Georgia State University: 170

Hargrett Rare Book and Manuscript Library/University of Georgia: 171

Harry S. Truman Library: 172

Courtesy of Joan Johns Cobb: 178

INDEX